FOR RICHER, FOR POORER

FOR RICHER, FOR POORER

The New U.S.-Japan Relationship

Ellen L. Frost

Council on Foreign Relations

COUNCIL ON FOREIGN RELATIONS BOOKS

The Council on Foreign Relations, Inc., is a nonprofit and nonpartisan organization devoted to promoting improved understanding of international affairs through the free exchange of ideas. The Council does not take any position on questions of foreign policy and has no affiliation with, and receives no funding from, the United States government.

From time to time, books and monographs written by members of the Council's research staff or visiting fellows, or commissioned by the Council, or written by an independent author with critical review contributed by a Council study or working group are published with the designation "Council on Foreign Relations Book." Any book or monograph bearing that designation is, in the judgment of the Committee on Studies of the Council's board of directors, a responsible treatment of a significant international topic worthy of presentation to the public. All statements of fact and expressions of opinion contained in Council books are, however, the sole responsibility of the author.

Library of Congress Cataloging-in-Publication Data

Frost, Ellen L.
    For richer, for poorer.

    Bibliography: p.
    Includes index
    1. United States—Relations—Japan.   2. Japan—
Relations—United States.   I. Title.
E183.8.J3F73   1987   303.4'8273'052   87-9150
ISBN 0-87609-025-0
ISBN 0-87609-024-2 (pbk.)

To my mother
Mildred K. Frost

Contents

Preface

In 1987 the United States unilaterally imposed prohibitive tariffs on certain highly visible imports from Japan. The action was the first of such magnitude in the entire postwar U.S.-Japan relationship. Shortly thereafter, investigators uncovered a major export control violation: a Japanese company had covertly sold high-precision milling machines to the Soviet Union. Japanese moves to punish the company in question and to tighten existing law eased but did not dispel American outrage over the damage inflicted on national security. Observers on both sides of the Pacific wondered whether these episodes—coming after nearly two years of sporadic "Japan-bashing" in the U.S. Congress—signaled a more pervasive deterioration of the U.S.-Japan partnership.

The underlying source of these tensions, it seems to me, is the rapid shift in the relative wealth of Japan and the United States. In relation to each other, Japan has gotten richer and the United States has gotten poorer. Adjusting to this transition alone would strain any partnership, let alone one that seeks to transcend differences in race, language, and culture, memories of World War II, and the world's biggest body of cold water.

While countless thousands of Americans and Japanese have overcome the barriers of language and culture and built new partnerships in the process, countless others have not. Many Americans and Japanese today confess to feeling uncomfortable or even hostile in each other's presence. Unlike the generally benign encounters of the early postwar period, their relationships rarely include the funny, the irrational, or the touching. Suspicion breeds counter-suspicion, so that dark predictions are frequently fulfilled and "horror stories" reaffirmed.

Nevertheless, managing the U.S.-Japan partnership is not only important but inescapable, for the two countries are so closely intertwined that "divorce" is virtually impossible. Americans and Japanese need to understand their differences and—equally important—their similarities. The door to dialogue is heavy but not locked; pushing it further open is the overarching purpose of this book. My aim is to analyze the emotional and political core of the U.S.-Japan relationship, and to help its participants see themselves and each other in clearer perspective. For that purpose, I have tried to be reflective, practical, and even provocative rather than definitive and scholarly. While I have tried to weave the insights of experts and scholars into my description of the basic tissue of Japanese-American relations, I set out to write this book not for the specialists, but for the many people who are caught up in the consequences of this momentous alliance yet remain relatively ignorant of its basic ingredients.

I see these people everywhere I look. My work on U.S.-Japan relations has brought me into daily contact with Americans in business, politics, government, and other professions who have no detailed knowledge of Japan. These are educated and aware people who may be relatively familiar with Europe, but they are encountering Japan "up close" for virtually the first time in their career. In Japan, on the other hand, I have encountered people who know a great many details about the United States but who have great difficulty understanding characteristically American points of view.

In writing this book, I have tried to work through some very basic questions in my mind. As Japanese and Americans face each other and the world, what makes them think and feel the way they do? Given their substantial common interests, why don't they get along better (some would say even better) than they do? Must they continue to talk past each other, or can they learn to "fight within the family"? While preserving their differences, can they, together, identify their common priorities and make better use of their complementary resources in pursuing them?

Questions as complex as these preclude easy generalizations. The first caveat is that there is obviously no absolute, stable platform from which to view a culture, let alone two. Instead, we tend to look for what we think is important, using a set of prisms and priorities that varies with culture, personality, and time. I am a member of the civil rights generation, born during the period when the United States and Japan were at war but too young to remember it. Ten years in the U.S. Government—the U.S. Senate, the Treasury Department, and the Pentagon—and six in the Washington office of a large private company have turned me into a kind of foreign-policy "practitioner" seeking tangible solutions to current U.S.-

Japan conflicts, but my academic training leads me to search for long-term patterns and explanations as well.

Another difficulty in writing about U.S.-Japan relations is that there is neither an "eternal America" nor an "eternal Japan"; each is continually changing, and influencing the speed and direction of change in the other. Even as I try to supply the reader with a snapshot of characteristic differences, the societies that produced them are generating new images of themselves and each other.

Generalizations about people are similarly hazardous. America and Japan are complex, pluralistic societies, each containing elements of the unique and elements of the universal. The differences between generations are frequently greater than the differences between nationalities. I have used the phrases "the Japanese" and "the Americans" merely as shorthand references to dominant patterns and values that influence— but do not monopolize—a majority of business and government leaders.

Finally, there is something artificial about fishing out two countries from the entire sea of global politics, even two as important and interrelated as Japan and the United States. One cannot discuss U.S.-Japan relations without mentioning China and the two Koreas, the Soviet Union, and Western Europe, all of whom have a vital stake in the U.S.-Japan relationship and whose decisions both shape and reflect its evolution. Wherever possible, I have tried to remind the reader of the regional and global context, which sometimes overwhelms purely bilateral perspectives, but I have been unable to do justice to its full complexity.

From start to finish, this book was guided by a group of dedicated professionals assembled under the auspices of the Council on Foreign Relations: James Auer, Samuel R. Berger, Timothy J. Curran, Gerald L. Curtis, I. M. Destler, Richard A. Freytag, Yoichi Funabashi, Carl J. Green, Richard Heimlich, Robert Immerman, Merit E. Janow, Marius B. Jansen, Kenneth I. Juster, Fuji Kamiya, Paul H. Kreisberg, David W. MacEachron, Richard W. Petree, William Piez, Richard J. Samuels, Isaac Shapiro, George Stalk, Yoshindo Takahashi, Robert Uriu, Craig M. Watson, Charles Weiss, Jr., and Michael K. Young. Of these, Richard Samuels was particularly heroic, commenting on several versions of the draft in their entirety. The chairman of the group, Professor Gerald Curtis of Columbia University, added relevance and discipline to my entire thought process. From the West Coast, Robert Scalapino served as reader, critic, and teacher. Alan D. Romberg, Senior Fellow at the Council and project director for this book, provided both painstaking assistance with the draft and unwavering encouragement. My editor, May Wu, remained gracious despite my careless penmanship and generally trying behavior. I marvel at her ability to spot repetition, inconsistency, and fuzzy thinking.

In Japan, a number of friends and colleagues went out of their way to help me. Organized and led by Hisashi Owada of the Foreign Ministry, a group that included Koji Watanabe, Makoto Watanabe, Yukio Satoh, and Ryozo Kato gave up precious free time to review the manuscript and emerged with a detailed and extraordinarily useful critique. Professor Masashi Nishihara of the National Defense Academy added substance and perspective to every chapter. Professor Seizaburo Sato of Tokyo University suggested many relevant points. Tatsuo Arima, currently Japan's Consul General in San Francisco, caught several errors. Takeshi Isayama of MITI arranged a series of meetings and interviews that broadened my contacts and contributed immeasurably to my knowledge of the issues. Tadashi Yamamoto of the Japan Center for International Exchange opened many doors to me, sponsoring a memorable trip in 1984.

In Washington, Junko Ohshima of the Ministry of Labor, then a student at the Wharton School of Economics, spent most of the summer of 1985 doing research on the U.S. and Japanese economies, assembling material that contributed substantially to Chapters 2 and 3. Professor Catherine Kelleher of the University of Maryland read the draft and commented thoughtfully on several key security issues. Fumiko Mori Halloran set high standards of writing and thinking, adding fresh perspectives on Japanese society and culture and offering intriguing tidbits of information otherwise unavailable to me. All of these people influenced this book in quite different ways, but they cannot be blamed for my own limitations and eccentricities.

Throughout the whole process I enjoyed unflagging support from my supervisors and colleagues at Westinghouse Electric Corporation. Francis P. Cotter, F. Leo Wright, and James S. Moore blessed the project and gave me precious time to work on it. Marita Klimkos patiently taught me the mysteries of the word processor; on more than one occasion she saved a long chapter from digital destruction. Much of the mechanical burden of producing the book, however, fell on Dianne Streat. To meet my numerous deadlines, she moved mountains of paper between the printer, the copying machine, and the mail system, taking personal pride in the book in a way that raised my own morale.

I owe thanks above all to Thomas J. Murrin, President of the Energy and

Advanced Technology Group at Westinghouse. More than anyone else, he encouraged me to learn about Japan and listened patiently to everything I had to say on the subject. I drew heavily on his generosity, vision, and personal leadership.

There ought to be a monument erected to the families of people who write books. For over a year and a half I wandered around the house distracted and preoccupied by the enormity of what I had undertaken. My husband, Bill Pedersen, and our children, Mark and Claire, looked on with pride and sympathy. Together with our longtime babysitter and pillar of the family, Gracie Graves, they kept the household running and cheerfully welcomed me back to normal family life when the ordeal was over at last.

Washington, D.C.   Ellen L. Frost
August 1987

All Japanese names in this book are given
in the Western order—given name first,
followed by the family name

One

Beyond "Bashing"

There is so much that Japan and America can do together; there is much that they cannot do apart. Their combined resources are the envy of the world. Failure to use them constructively would be at best a wasted opportunity and at worst a disaster.

With a combined population of 360 million people, a mere 7 percent of the world's total, they produce more than 30 percent of the world's economic output. As the largest sources of investment capital and the most dynamic training ground for those who will invent tomorrow's technology, they have the potential to alter the future of the world.

The combined weight of the United States and Japan brings common problems and challenges as well as common blessings. Together they consume about one-third of the world's raw materials, accounting for about half of the Western world's oil bill. They both face the challenge of sudden economic dislocations, whether from oil shocks or from the competitive exports of newly industrializing countries. They both confront debt, despotism, social upheaval, and human misery in much of the Third World. They have a common stake in continued stability on the Korean peninsula and in Southeast Asia, as well as in political moderation and economic modernization in China. Their respective defense policies are oriented in large part to the growth of Soviet military power.

These international challenges alone do not distinguish the U.S.-Japan relationship from all others. What is different and remarkable is the intensity and magnitude of interdependence, combined with the depth of shared values and interests at home and abroad: a strong commitment to democracy, market-oriented economic growth, and peace.

These common values and achievements are so basic that they are frequently ignored. Yet in the years immediately following World War II, the entire Asian region was economically weak and politically shaky; Japan's success in these domains is a solid monument to what the Western alliance stands for. The fate of the U.S.-Japan alliance is therefore not just a bilateral problem, exotic and faraway; it is, or should be, of compelling interest to leaders all over the world.

For the United States, Japan is the most stable and reliable ally in Asia, a quiet but constructive foreign-policy partner, a major link in America's global defense network, the largest overseas market, an important participant in high-technology cooperation, a key player in global financial flows, the largest direct foreign investor, a source of high-quality consumer goods, and the home of a rich and sophisticated culture. For Japan, the United States is the leader of the Free World, the pivot of its security, the largest overseas market, an attractive magnet for investment, a key source of food and raw materials, a pacesetter in research and development, a fertile field for higher education, and a major influence on popular culture. The two countries have become so closely intertwined that forced separation would be wrenching and probably impossible. They are are in it for good, so to speak, thrown together for richer and for poorer.

Ironically, the very features common to both societies—the dynamism of industrial competition, a challenging global environment, and the relentless scrutiny of a free press—greatly complicate the task of alliance management, for they intensify and publicize the pressures associated with the most vexing problem plaguing the relationship in the 1980s: the virtual explosion of trade and budget deficits in America, combined with record trade surpluses and high savings in Japan.

One symptom of these pressures is recurrent "Japan-bashing" in Washington—virulent, emotional criticism of Japan as a whole, without distinguishing among its components.[1] Such outbursts tend to receive more attention than the substance of the problem that they are intended to address. Moreover, they put progressive Japanese on the defensive and lend credence to those least trustful of America.

In these new circumstances, forward-looking efforts to ease the tensions now plaguing the alliance are more essential than ever. Unless the forces of economic change are anticipated and widely understood, conventional diplomacy may not be enough to prevent a vicious circle of mutual recrimination and resentment, leading to a severe contraction of bilateral relations.

"So what?" American critics might ask. "They need us more than we need them, right?" The few—very few—Japanese who reason thus conclude: Japan can tighten its belt, but America is "soft," right? A handful of business leaders on each side have bragged publicly that there is nothing their country really needs from the other.

Ultimately, this reasoning leads to a doomsday scenario. For if a U.S.-Japan trade war should escalate to the point where the relationship really breaks down, the entire non-Communist world would suffer. Prices of consumer goods, both domestic and imported, would rise. Trade balances would probably not improve significantly, because the strained finances of other countries would not permit the purchase of more imports and because all countries would probably erect new and discriminatory barriers against trade and capital flows. Financial markets would swing wildly or collapse. Governments and private buyers would vie to lock up supplies of energy and raw materials, bidding up world prices in the process. As the United States retreated behind the walls of Fortress America, Japan would lurch back into pessimism, insularity, and defensive nationalism—just as it was beginning to feel more comfortable with the outside world. Aided by Mikhail Gorbachev's new and more positive diplomacy in Asia, the Soviet Union would surely try to exploit this new climate.

The Postwar Record

It seems necessary to call attention to both the opportunity and the potential disaster because U.S.-Japan relations appear to have taken a turn for the worse in the last few years. The question is whether the alliance is undergoing temporary difficulties related to short-term trade tensions or whether it is entering a new and dangerous historical phase.

If the history of postwar U.S.-Japan relations were the only guide, one would conclude that the chance of disaster is so remote as to be non-existent. On balance, the postwar relationship, like the proverbial glass, has been at least half full, if not overflowing.

Considering what it might have been, the American Occupation proved to be, on balance, a surprisingly positive experience for both the victor and the vanquished. American leaders encouraged the economic recovery of their former enemy, correctly perceiving that an economically sturdy Japan would be a strategic plus. Of course, they had no way of knowing that Japan would become an economic superpower, challenging the United States. They merely wanted to foster a level of economic activity that would discourage the Communist movement and relieve America's financial burden.

Changes in Japanese society fostered or initiated by American authorities ranged from land reform to women's suffrage to the reorganization of the educational system. Many if not most of these reforms proved to be unexpectedly durable despite their alien origin. Attempts to reject them on nationalistic grounds have generally failed.

In foreign policy, Japan supported—and indeed benefited from—America's Korean War effort. Subsequent agitation against the U.S.-Japan Security Treaty, antinuclear demonstrations, and student riots jolted but did not snap the security framework. The return of Okinawa, a pressing political-military goal for postwar Japanese, was accomplished slowly but nonetheless successfully.

In the Nixon era, the partnership sagged but did not founder. Neither Richard Nixon nor Henry Kissinger had any particular sympathy for Japan, finding Tokyo unresponsive on trade problems and lacking in the strategic political-military mind-set for which Kissinger is famous. The Vietnam War created special problems, but at least in some Japanese circles America's efforts in that unhappy arena were—and continue to be—appreciated. More damaging were the two "Nixon shocks": the inconvertibility of the dollar and the associated 10 percent surcharge on imports imposed in 1971, and the sudden development of U.S. relations with the People's Republic of China. A short-lived but psychologically upsetting U.S. soybean embargo followed in 1973.

The Carter Administration, with its emphasis on trilateralism, Third World development, and international cooperation, was in some ways an improvement. One constructive effort aimed at upgrading trade disputes, so to speak, by addressing their underlying macroeconomic and structural causes. By asking both Japan and West Germany to serve as "locomotives" to reflate the world economy, the United States recognized Japan as a major economic player and a more active partner.

On the security front, however, the record of the Carter Administration is mixed. In 1977, apparently without consulting Tokyo, the incoming administration announced its intention to withdraw U.S. troops from South Korea despite their strategic significance to Japan. To Tokyo's relief, the decision was subsequently revoked. Meanwhile, Washington was reluctant to permit Japan to reprocess nuclear fuel, despite the latter's acceptance of internationally approved safeguards and obvious support for the goals of Carter's nonproliferation policy. This stance not only propelled Japan to seek greater self-sufficiency in the nuclear fuel cycle, but also raised doubts about the reliability of America's commitments. Despite these two sour notes, Tokyo generally went along with other American foreign-policy initiatives. Following the Soviet invasion of Afghanistan in 1979, for example, Japan cooperated with U.S. efforts to impose multilateral sanctions.

Since 1980, diplomatic relations have remained on a generally positive and even keel, with the celebrated "Ron-Yasu" friendship between President Ronald Reagan and Prime Minister Yasuhiro Nakasone adding a personal and cordial touch. Washington's security commitments have remained firm, and persuasive presentations on Capitol Hill have dampened (but not eliminated) charges that Japan is taking a "free ride" at U.S. expense. The disagreement over nuclear fuel has been eased and de-escalated. In foreign policy, Japan cooperated fully with the United States on sanctions imposed in the wake of the disturbances in Poland, the deployment of intermediate-range nuclear forces in Europe, intelligence-sharing in the aftermath of the shooting down of a Korean Air Lines passenger plane by the Soviet Union, and efforts to secure the release of American hostages in Lebanon.

On the economic front, the Reagan Administration's behavior throughout its first term was substantially similar to that of its predecessors. As the trade deficit mounted, however, the White House initiated a series of trade-relief cases and negotiated several new bilateral trade-limiting agreements. In 1986, the U.S. Government asked Japan and three other countries to impose "voluntary" restraints on their exports of machine tools. A more contentious example of the new stance on trade was the semiconductor arrangement concluded in that year. In early 1987, Washington accused Japan of violating this agreement and imposed 100 percent tariffs on Japanese electronic products worth some $300 million. But the administration seemed unwilling to escalate what became known as the "chip war," and continued to emphasize its basic friendship with Japan. Indeed, some of the tariffs were lifted only a few months later.

On the financial and macroeconomic front, the dialogues between Treasury Secretary James A. Baker and Finance Minister Kiichi Miyazawa were unusually close—even as the dollar tumbled and as waves of "bashing" periodically broke over their heads. Some observers even began to speak of a "G-2," or "Group of Two"—as opposed to a more normal "G-5" or "G-7."[2] In Western Europe, fears were expressed that this "G-2" was making economic decisions of global significance, excluding the Europeans from the process.

Throughout the postwar period, cultural and not-so-cultural contacts and friendships have multiplied. The first McDonald's restaurant in Japan opened in 1971; today, there are well over four hundred. Words such as "Kabuki" and "Toyota" were almost unknown in America in the 1950s; now suburban department stores feature fashions by Hanae Mori, and sushi is as commonplace as quiche.

New Challenges

Even if the record of the past forty years is largely positive, the present and the future give some cause for alarm. The alliance must now adjust to two new and different challenges: the rapid shift in the relative wealth of the two partners, and the economic shockwaves rocking the world around them.

Barely a generation ago, Japan accounted for less than 2 percent of the world economy, while the United States accounted for about 35 percent. By 1980, Japan's share of the world economy had ballooned to about 10 percent—equal to West Germany's and Great Britain's combined. In the meantime, America's share had dropped to about 20 percent.

An evolution of this magnitude would be enough to strain any alliance. But the change has taken place in a global economy reeling from unprecedented levels of Third World debt, massive capital flows, and soaring and crashing energy prices. With several hundred billion dollars changing hands in major currency markets every day, the sheer wave of money has now reached breathtaking levels.

A major cause of economic dislocation, however, is not global as such. It is rather the juxtaposition of trends *within* the United States and Japan: America's swollen consumption, fed by a high propensity to import and low domestic savings; and Japan's strong propensity to export, low propensity to import, and extremely high savings rate. Because the two economies are so closely intertwined, each country's momentum has deeply affected the other's.

In the 1980s, while America chalked up record trade and budget deficits, Japan accumulated record trade surpluses and brought its budget deficit under control. By the mid-1980s, Japan accounted for roughly one-third of the U.S. trade deficit, and financed roughly one-third of the U.S. budget deficit. One consequence was the steep rise in the value of the yen in 1985–86. By 1987, the yen was 55–60 percent higher in relation to the dollar than at the beginning of 1985. It was then Japan's turn to pay a high price: sluggish growth and record unemployment.

Although many if not most of the pressures generated by such massive economic swings are domestic and economic, the strains associated with them tend to express themselves bilaterally and politically in the form of trade conflicts. Typically, intense pressure from Washington is met with stalling and resentment in Tokyo, and ends with last-minute compromises in a highly politicized context. The opening of Japan's telecommunications market, the negotiation of bilateral agreements on semiconductors and machine tools, and the participation of American construction companies in the multitrillion-yen Kansai International Airport project are only some of the major conflicts handled in this fashion.

A number of factors add special pungency to these mini-dramas, complicating the adjustment to new realities.

Outdated Self-images. In both countries, adjustment to new economic realities is thwarted and retarded by the outdated self-images and long-standing domestic behavior of ordinary citizens who have not fully grasped the consequences of their country's altered position in the global economy. Most Japanese do not seem to feel as wealthy as the rest of the world thinks they are. And most Americans, long accustomed to being "number one," tend to be more complacent about their economic system than the trends would justify.

Policy Paralysis. These out-of-date perceptions hamper the reorientation of domestic behavior and make it difficult to obtain a consensus on what aspects of that behavior need to be changed first. Japanese consumers are confused by the uneven effect of the yen/dollar realignment—to the point where the government finds it difficult to put together a convincing policy package. Most Japanese recognize that their economy needs restructuring so as to promote more economic activity at home, but they cannot agree on how to do it. Almost everyone in the United States agrees that the U.S. budget deficit must be cut, but there is no agreement about where the cuts should fall. Thus, massive and crosscutting economic shifts paralyze policymaking in both countries.

Europe versus Japan. Until the 1970s, America was fighting most of its major trade skirmishes with Western Europe; the grandfather of the "chip war" was the "chicken war" with the European Economic Community. Today, the primary locus of the perceived threat to American economic interests has shifted to Japan. In 1986–87, even a major trade battle with the European Community failed to arouse the sense of threat that Japan evoked—at least in some U.S. circles. Similarly, most Japanese tend to downgrade the threat from Western Europe, even though manufactured exports from Western Europe to Japan appear to be rising much faster than those from the United States.

Proliferation of Actors and Messages. Another factor complicating the management of the relationship is the proliferation of influential foreign-policy actors and interests in both countries over the past decade. Ministries and departments whose responsibilities used to be almost ex-

clusively domestic now participate routinely in international negotiations. Japanese parliamentarians and members of the U.S. Congress frequently cross the Pacific, playing an independent role in the continuing
dialogue. Trade associations—ranging from the Japan Automobile Manufacturers Association to the American Rice Millers Association—act behind the scenes, together with their consultants and lawyers. Companies, unions, local politicians, and other domestic interest groups also
absorb the time and energy of senior government officials. The press requires daily attention. All of these actors claim a share of the formulation
and implementation of policies governing U.S.-Japan relations, challenging those who have traditionally managed foreign policy and leaving
them little time to cope with anything but today's crisis.

While the proliferation of actors has added explosive potential to the
political fuse, the revolutions in transportation, information, and communications technology have shortened it. Anger and resentment are
beamed or airborne across the Pacific in minutes or hours instead of days.
Protectionist and otherwise negative comments intended for domestic
audiences are translated and printed overnight for foreign readers. In the
context of massive swings in the global economy, the very intensity of
U.S.-Japan economic interaction may transcend the ability of the alliance
to manage the resulting tensions.[3]

New Leaders.   Until recently, leaders in both countries came from a
generation that had personal memories of the war and its aftermath. They
lived through the transition from bitter conflict to surprisingly close cooperation. Although it is difficult to prove, younger leaders on both sides
appear to lack a certain historical perspective, and their contacts appear to
be more business-oriented and less personally meaningful than those experienced by the older generation.

"We" versus "They".   While many Americans and Japanese enjoy
excellent personal relations, some think of relations between the two
countries in terms of mutually exclusive and opposing national camps. In
private, more than one U.S. executive is explicit on the subject: "They"
are out to get "us," so it is "us" versus "them." Some of their Japanese
counterparts are similarly hostile and defensive.

To listen to some Americans, one would think that every Japanese goes
to bed at night praying for the opportunity to take a job away from an
American worker. Recollecting the bitterness of defeat in World War II,
he pursues this goal with the patience of the forty-seven *ronin*[4] and with

the backing of a fanatic samurai-style military-industrial complex dedicated to world domination.[5]

These same Americans tend to doubt that today's Japan is substantially different from the nation that fought the war. They see a single-minded national purpose and unrelenting economic expansionism, coated with soothing words designed to keep foreigners at bay. They say that Tokyo's trade behavior exemplifies a combination of narrow self-interest and resistance to genuinely free competition. They note that each "market-opening package" has been long on intention and short on implementation. They chafe at Japanese unwillingness to establish a timetable for the specific changes repeatedly sought by American business and government leaders, and believe that Tokyo will make tangible concessions only when pushed or even hammered. Recalling prior trouble-shooting U.S. missions that went away empty-handed,[6] they are profoundly skeptical about near-term prospects. Asked to assess Japan's sincerity in carrying out market-opening measures, one American trade lobbyist replied sarcastically, "The Japanese will be laughing all the way to the bank."

This "we versus they" mentality often masks the search for a scapegoat. Even the casual bookstore browser, surveying shelf after shelf of books on Japanese and American business, comes away with the impression that "we" are tottering and "they" are bursting with vigor. The message of these books is that America's supposedly tired and declining industries, or its lagging education system, or whatever needs a massive injection of Japanese know-how. To do nothing is to invite Japanese domination. America is portrayed as well-meaning but naive, the vulnerable guarantor of the Free World's security and trade, a "helpless giant" whom foreigners take advantage of routinely.

Closely associated with this set of beliefs is a lingering "number one" mentality which makes it difficult for Americans to make room for others at the top. America—a nation of winners—seems to have lost ground, and a little too suddenly at that. In 1983, the President's Commission on Industrial Competitiveness put it quite thoughtfully: while "some slippage" of our postwar dominance is inevitable and desirable, "we should be concerned about how rapidly the U.S. lead has diminished."[7] As early as 1980, a Congressional report on U.S.-Japan trade warned that America was beginning to resemble a developing country, losing manufacturing jobs and becoming an exporter of raw materials. It cited "devastating" evidence that, apart from the export of aircraft, the United States had already become a "developing nation" with respect to Japan. The report continued, "We are Japan's plantation, haulers of wood and growers of crops, in exchange for high technology, value-added products."[8]

Some Americans see Japan as the prime beneficiary of the relative decline in America's economic power and prestige; some see it as the cause. But all of them associate Japan with negative numbers—the cavernous trade deficit, rising external debt, and trade-related unemployment in certain manufacturing sectors—even as U.S. dependence on Japanese technology and investment is growing.

To listen to some Japanese—or rather, to read their minds, for they are unlikely to speak so bluntly to their American "guests"—Europe is dead and America is dying. With the possible exception of the nuclear umbrella, Japan no longer needs the United States. Even the huge U.S. market, attractive as it is, is not indispensable; in any case, Americans are too dependent on Japanese products to close it. In manufacturing and services, the "Japanese way" is clearly superior to "American decadence" or the "American disease." Americans deserve to lose because they don't try hard enough, because their average educational level is appallingly low, and because their spiritual backbone has grown soft. Rather than solve the problems they have created for themselves, Americans lash out at foreign scapegoats.

Some Japanese wonder whether American politics will permit adjustment to new competitive realities. They ask: Are Americans simply bad losers? How is it that so many members of Congress seem to believe that theirs is a free market economy when "Buy America" restrictions, "voluntary" trade restraints, complex labor laws, tax preferences, military priorities, environmental controls, and budget deficits continue to distort the flow of resources and undermine American competitiveness?

Urged by Americans to be more frank, Japanese leaders occasionally give vent to themes that many people in Washington don't really want to hear. Stung by the "bashing" that broke out in Congress in 1985, some Japanese responded in print, describing Americans as "coddled into complacency," "shooting themselves in the foot," and "putting people out of work in their pursuit of the almighty bottom line." A common theme is that if Americans don't mend their ways, they may even drag others down with them. One Japanese commentator, formerly employed as a productivity/quality expert at a major company, put it in these words:

If the United States continues to call its opponents unfair to justify its self-inflicted deindustrialization, the collapse of its manufacturing industry will continue unabated, and this may lead to the breakup of the free-world community.[9]

Other Japanese have obliquely challenged America's faith in the market mechanism and criticized the absence of a forward-looking industrial policy. They find the emphasis that U.S. trade negotiators place on agriculture inappropriate in light of America's industrial problems. Commenting on the typical list of trade complaints that U.S. officials bring to Tokyo, a Japanese politician remarked, "Washington's negotiating priorities are those of a developing country." To be sure, agriculture has become a high-technology industry in America. Yet only in recent years has trade in certain high-technology manufacturing sectors, such as telecommunications, joined the list of major U.S. priorities. The negotiating menu is still largely edible.

Japan's Economic Planning Agency (EPA) blandly attributed recent trade friction to "the lack of smooth progress in industrial coordination in advanced countries receiving Japanese exports"[10]—that is, the inability of other countries to behave like Japan. In other words, Japan's behavior is perfectly legitimate, and other governments—including America's— ought to adjust to it by scaling down their noncompetitive industries. After all, the Japanese Government has done just that; it has helped to promote the steady shrinkage of a number of industries, including shipbuilding, cement, and aluminum. By contrast, the abrupt and large-scale layoffs that scarred many U.S. industrial sectors in the 1970s and early 1980s strike most Japanese as callous and socially irresponsible. One official at the Ministry of International Trade and Industry (MITI) stated frankly that, in adjusting to the yen/dollar realignment, Japan would try to avoid repeating the U.S. experience, which the Japanese associate with unemployment, crime, and social decay.

This is not to say that Japanese perceptions of America are mainly negative. Quite the contrary. Many Japanese envy such features of the U.S. economy as its vigorous venture capital market—a product of that very faith in the market mechanism which they question—and strong research capability. Some admire what they perceive as the direct, no-nonsense efficiency of motivated Americans on the job, and tend to associate Americans with such qualities as humor, openness, and kindness to strangers.

All the same, there are distinct signs that the Japanese are getting tired of being "bashed." A popular book published in 1987 bears the title *The Bad One is America, Not Japan*. Many Japanese, believing that Americans are picking only on them, overlook or minimize the history of U.S.-European trade conflict. Privately or otherwise, they wonder whether racism is at work. Despite extensive knowledge of facts about America, many Japanese do not always grasp the true diversity of American opinion, let alone the pluralism of American politics. As a result, they tend to believe that each new volley represents a single "American" point of view.

Certain attitudes are even reminiscent of the 1930s, when Japanese leaders believed that Americans were "self-indulgent and flabby, with no stomach for war."[11] Not a few of today's leaders, seeing Americans wallowing in self-induced industrial stagnation and extravagant spending habits, are displaying a new arrogance, which Americans sometimes interpret as the "true" Japanese personality finally coming out.

Another similarity with the 1930s is that Japanese leaders are beginning to feel cornered by the United States. Many seem to believe that American pressure leaves Tokyo little choice but to go along with what Washington wants. There is a danger that this sense of humiliation, already dramatized by some elements of the Japanese press, will fuel the flames of racial-national arrogance and hostility to Western values—leading eventually, some fear, to authoritarianism at home and conflict abroad.[12]

In short, an ominous combination of attitudes has appeared. America's lingering complacency, residual "number one" mentality, and new sense of vulnerability are the mirror image of Japan's lingering sense of vulnerability and new arrogance. These attitudes give rise to disputes that soak up precious time—time that could be devoted to defining and pursuing the goals that the two countries could achieve together. They are also dangerous.

One after the other, commissions and experts on U.S.-Japan relations have stressed that the two societies can no longer disengage very easily, even if they wanted to. The report of the President's Commission on Industrial Competitiveness, for example, stated, "Quite simply, no longer is there a truly domestic U.S. economy."[13] The United States-Japan Advisory Commission, composed of distinguished business, labor, and former government leaders, reported in 1984: "No two countries possess the essential ingredients of a vital bilateral partnership—economic, political, and security ties—in greater degree than the United States and

Japan."[14] A vice-president at Mitsui went as far as to say that Japan and the United States are not just trading with each other, "they have become part of each other."[15]

Even in the domain of defense, where the scope of collaboration is smaller, similar conclusions abound. A special panel of the Defense Science Board, a prestigious group of businessmen who advise the Pentagon on science and technology issues, concluded, "In the long run, at least, there is no such thing as 'cutting off' Japan."[16] The Japanese Government, for its part, has moved from cautiously affirming the U.S.-Japan "alliance" during Prime Minister Masayoshi Ohira's term in the late 1970s to declaring in the Nakasone era that Japan and the United States share a "common destiny" (*unmei kyōdōtai*).

Why, then, aren't Tokyo and Washington getting along even better than they do now? One set of answers lies in the role of trade in the American political system.

The Politics of Trade

It is not surprising that the U.S.-Japan trade balance—or rather, imbalance—has acquired such visibility in Washington, for it is there that national statistics of any kind wield the most political influence and reach the largest political audience. And trade statistics have swollen to enormous proportions.

The overall U.S. trade deficit in 1986 amounted to some $170 billion, of which almost $59 billion—up from about $50 billion in 1985 and $37 billion in 1984—accrued from trade with Japan. Also in 1986, the ratio of U.S. imports from Japan to U.S. exports to Japan was about 3:1. Since 1980, in fact, U.S. imports from Japan have grown more than six times faster than U.S. exports to Japan.

With a few important exceptions, however (e.g., machine tools and automobiles), U.S. negotiators are more concerned with securing access to Japan's domestic market than with limiting Japanese exports to the United States. One obvious reason is the sheer size of that market—over 120 million people, and a GNP roughly equal to the GNP of France and of West Germany combined. Another is the sheer logic of competition in today's world, which forces a company to be competitive in all three major markets at once—North America, Western Europe, and Japan.

Apart from the mounting trade deficit itself, what finally drove the Reagan Administration to trade relief was that the Japanese tactic of offering market-opening "packages" had begun to backfire by the mid-1980s. When originally conceived in the late 1970s, the package approach seemed brilliantly designed to suit the taste of a people captivated by kits and how-to-do-it devices. By the seventh such package, however, American patience had worn thin. Each new collection of import-liberalizing measures announced by the Japanese Government seemed to confirm the alleged barrenness of concessions offered in the last one. It seemed more meaningful to pursue specific bilateral agreements featuring firm quantitative targets, such as market share and price.

Special political circumstances also help to explain why trade became a particularly virulent issue in the mid-1980s. When the growing gap between imports and exports was front-page news in 1985, the Democrats, virtually leaderless and in gloomy disarray, believed that they had found a ready-made weapon against the White House. Trade was seen as a convenient and visible teaching aid, a handy means of bringing home to the voters an economic message otherwise too complex for the average person to understand. Unlike the Republicans, the Democrats felt free to criticize the Reagan Administration not only for the trade deficit, but also for the inflated dollar prior to 1985 and the high level of debt.

Mindful of the 1986 and 1988 elections, fearful of economic contraction but unable to attack their own extraordinarily popular leader, Republicans were able to seize on trade without undue criticism of the rest of the President's economic program. Focusing the blame on foreigners enabled Republican candidates to sidestep what C. Fred Bergsten has called the Reagan Administration's "studied neglect" of the trade problem prior to 1985.[17] During the 1986 election campaign, trade was perhaps the single issue on which Republican candidates distanced themselves the most from the White House.[18]

Most political leaders have become aware that larger macroeconomic factors contribute heavily to America's trade problems. Yet when it comes to remedies for these problems, there is a disproportionate concentration of attention on trade relief, as opposed to other forms of assistance to U.S. industry based on other kinds of analysis. Even when the issue is not the need for relief as such, some people favor the idea of using import restrictions to "punish" Japan for the import-resistant nature of its domestic market—regardless of the effect on prices and the quality of goods available to American consumers.

The average voter does not seem to share these sentiments. Surveys suggest that the general public holds a more favorable view of the U.S.-

Japan relationship than some of the politicians. Despite the criticisms voiced in Congress, Japanese respondents to a poll conducted jointly by Gallup and the *Yomiuri Shimbun* in 1986 continued to rank America first among "especially trustworthy" countries, while American respondents ranked Japan fifth in the same category, up from fourteenth in 1970 and eighth in 1985.[19] (Other polls have ranked Japan as high as third in overall popularity.) Even in the thorny field of trade, the public appears to take a more tolerant view than some politicians. There is no evidence that protectionist sentiment contributed much to the Democrats' success in the 1986 elections. Indeed, except in certain communities adversely affected by imports, trade played a very small role as an election issue.[20] Similarly, Walter Mondale's brief fling with protectionism during the 1984 presidential campaign was viewed by many observers as a political mistake. Even during the height of the "chip war" in 1987, Americans generally said they admired Japan.[21] On the whole, Americans seem more inclined to blame their problems on the erosion of American values—the work ethic, a commitment to excellence, a spirit of cooperation—than on foreigners.

Beyond short-term politics are several broader and deeper influences that explain Washington's preoccupation with trade as the central issue in U.S.-Japan relations. Some are characteristic of all industrial societies, while others are uniquely American.

In the former category is the very nature of political representation. Policymakers in Washington tend to hear from people with problems, not people who are satisfied. Pressured by business and labor lobbyists, and faced with a relatively passive executive branch throughout most of the 1980s, many members of Congress have felt compelled to focus on the job losses associated with import competition—or with lost export opportunities—rather than on investment or technology transfer, where relationships tend to be less strained. Similarly, those recounting success stories in the field of trade tend to be less active in Washington than those recounting horror stories.Sources of outside funding and political support, notably some—but not all—labor unions, may also be disproportionately protectionist-minded.

Once an issue reaches the floor of the Congress, arguments against Japan-targeted protectionism made in the name of "national security"— e.g., the strategic value of a strong Japanese-American alliance in the western Pacific—do not get very far. Unless they serve on the armed services or foreign relations committees, most members of Congress devote little time to defense issues other than base closings, local defense contractors, and the defense budgét. In any event, they become suspicious when the executive branch invokes national security. When that happens, they complain that trade is being "politicized"—that is, subjected to broader diplomatic considerations that transcend the merits of the import relief at issue and inevitably soften the final decision. A major trade bill passed by the House of Representatives in 1986, for example, would have shifted authority to make final decisions on trade relief from the President to the U.S. Trade Representative, whose outlook is supposedly more hard-headed. In final form, new trade legislation will make it easier to secure import relief, but how it is implemented will depend ultimately on the President.

Among the uniquely American ingredients of trade politics is, paradoxically, a widespread indifference to trade in general, and to exports in particular. What the Japanese would call America's "continental mentality" permitted the trade deficit to balloon in the first place. The culprit is neither laziness nor narrow-mindedness, but simply America's huge domestic market. As recently as the 1960s, the United States exported on average only 4.4 percent of its GNP. Although that percentage almost doubled by 1980, some industry leaders still treat exports as an afterthought or as a way of disposing of excess stock. With some powerful exceptions, the "export or die" mentality so prevalent in most other countries is largely missing in America.

Americans express their indifference to exports in several ways. Perhaps the most typical is their tendency to view the outside world primarily in moralistic terms—or to forget about it altogether. Another is their apparent conviction that other countries "need" American exports more than vice versa. Polls indicate that Americans see exports—especially high-technology exports—as a kind of favor to other countries. They assume that other countries will not retaliate even if the United States adopts across-the-board protectionism.

This perspective helps to explain the appeal of embargoes as a form of "punishment" when another government commits a transgression. The notion that Americans have a right to export and that restraints are a necessary evil is vaguely unpopular except in business circles. Various U.S. Government studies have called for the removal of disincentives to exports, especially targeted controls imposed for foreign-policy reasons, but they are watery and negative.

Lukewarm support for exports is mirrored by overall indifference to the level of imports, Japanese and otherwise. That most Americans do not object to the large volume of imports as such has its advantages for U.S.-Japan relations. On the other hand, most Americans do not feel particularly threatened by proposed restrictions on imports either. In other words, free trade is a bit like gun control: those who support it tend to be politically inactive, whereas those who oppose it do so with energy and passion. When the majority is indifferent, there are few rewards for members of Congress who publicly oppose a vociferous lobby. That many of them do is much to their credit.

Yet another "American" reason why U.S.-Japan disputes are funneled somewhat disproportionately toward trade restrictions is the nature of American law and regulation. Compared to other potential remedies, trade laws are more concrete and well-defined. Virtually no other available instrument has the same visible impact in the short run. Laws applicable to competitiveness, innovation, or industrial restructuring— in short, whatever it takes to compete—are tangential or nonexistent. Congressional leaders tried to address this problem by including education, research, and other priorities in the text of the trade bill passed by the House of Representatives in 1986, but trade provisions clearly have the most "bite."

Finally, armies of lawyers are quick to translate grievances stemming from the meshing of two complex economies into the relatively simple language of import relief. In Washington alone, the number of lawyers jumped from an estimated 32,000 in 1980 to 44,000 in 1986.[22] Although most of them are not engaged in trade law, there seems to be some basis to the Japanese perception that Washington lawyers are quick to invoke the threat of litigation at the outset rather than to approach a decision-making process by defining and building on a general framework of agreement. The problem, as *Asahi Shimbun* editor Yukio Matsuyama sees it, is not just the number of lawyers but the widespread legalistic frame of mind in America that promotes a self-centered, win-lose approach, regardless of the merits of the client.[23]

Perspectives on "Fairness"

Given these attitudes toward trade, what do Americans mean when they say the Japanese are "unfair"? This is by no means an academic question. "The definition of unfairness has become a central trade policy problem," wrote C. Michael Aho and Jonathan D. Aronson in their candid analysis of the next round of trade negotiations.[24] There is no clear definition of "fairness" even within the United States, let alone in the international community.[25]

Fairness has always loomed large in American history, even in periods of relative prosperity. Contrary to the perception of many Japanese, Americans have also called their European allies "unfair" in the context of sharing the defense burden and trade surpluses.[26] In fact, to take swings at foreigners seems to be a historical pastime. Rudyard Kipling noted that Americans engaged in England-bashing in the 1890s; forty years later, a bumptious mayor of Chicago even threatened to punch the King of England in the nose.

Today, Americans term "unfair" such practices as dumping, subsidies, infringement of intellectual property rights, and violations of U.S. rights under international agreements. Fairness is also at issue in such fields as patents ("stealing"), technology transfer ("copying"), government procurement ("chosen instruments"), and foreign aid ("tied exports").

Metaphors and analogies to illustrate what Americans mean by "fairness" and "unfairness" are often drawn from sports. A "fair" competition is one that takes place on a "level playing field," with one set of clearly defined rules for both sides. "Fairness" in the context of the marketplace means that everyone can compete on the basis of price, quality, service, and the like.

Restrictions on market access, real or imagined, are obvious deviations from the ideal of a level playing field. So are dumping, subsidies, cartels, and other forms of price-fixing and collusion. These practices amount to cheating; denying the evidence only makes things worse.

Americans also characterize as "unfair" a competition in which the competitors are not perceived to be of the same size. Larger players are said to have an unfair advantage, especially when they have the active support of their governments. Americans tend to side with the "little guys," even when they are as hefty as, say, Texas Instruments or Motorola. Some Japanese have pointed out that, unlike Western-style wrestling, sumo—Japanese-style wrestling—routinely pits smaller wrestlers against larger ones. No one calls this "unfair"; indeed, the smaller competitors frequently win.

Yet another aspect of what Americans consider "unfair" is the apparent secrecy of Japanese decision makers, who manipulate rules and regulations or try to hide their very existence from foreigners. The term of art is "lack of transparency." MITI's quiet and informal "administrative guidance" is the most frequently cited example.[27] While the American record on "transparency" is far from perfect, Americans see their own system as being more open.

It would be one thing if America's industrial woes stemmed solely from the natural evolution of comparative advantage. But critics charge that intervention by the Japanese Government—and many others—has made this evolution occur at a rate that not only is unfair, but also defies traditional economic analysis. Conventional theory may divide countries into two categories, "market economies" and "centrally planned economies," but many so-called market economies are, in fact, highly directed when it comes to trade and investment, practicing some form of "targeting" or selective export-oriented assistance. Government-created market distortions include home-market protection, tax policies, antitrust exemptions, assistance for technology development, preferential domestic and export financing, investment controls, and government ownership.[28] In the postwar period, Japan has adopted many if not all of these "unfair" practices. The goal of the Japanese Government is to ensure that the invisible hand of the marketplace is guided in the right national direction. Although such measures are not necessarily illegal, they are viewed as "unfair" because U.S. firms, while no longer handicapped by the strong dollar of the early 1980s, continue to face not only their foreign commercial competitors, but foreign governments as well.

To make matters worse, the Japanese are "unfair" in another sense: they do not seem to be pulling their own weight in the world. Some Americans accuse Japan of enjoying a "free ride" in defense, profiteering while Americans protect them. Others criticize Japan for not shouldering its fair share of the burden in terms of aid to Third World development. Underlying these arguments about "fairness" is the perception that Japan is taking advantage of American generosity.[29]

Paradoxically, by casting its arguments in terms of "fairness," the United States may be weakening a stronger force—the perception in Japan that world opinion has mounted to the point where change must occur, regardless of the merits. Sustained group pressure by itself is frequently enough to change Japanese behavior, at least at the margins (see Chapter 4). As matters stand, however, Americans have in effect taught Japanese how to argue back in the same terms.

One counterargument often made by the Japanese is that Americans started out talking about rules, but are now switching to results. Many Americans assume that if they don't keep winning, the whole system must be "unfair."[30] "What disconcerts [us] most is not so much their logic as their naive sanctimoniousness," wrote one Japanese commentator. "They believe their position is a universal truth."[31] Japanese political leader Kiichi Miyazawa told an American audience that rules and regulations are born of socioeconomic conditions and cultural traditions, and that to call them "unfair" simply fuels cultural prejudice.[32] An anonymous group of officials from a Japanese economic ministry fought back more forcefully:

> Can we say Americans always play fair? Or are the Americans going to play prosecutor and judge in determining whether one particular trading practice is unfair by using a yardstick of equity they set up? To non-Americans, this is nothing but unfair.[33]

Few Japanese have gone so far as to say publicly that Americans are unfair. Privately, however, some wonder how Americans can preach to others about fairness in light of the U.S. Government's internment of 120,000 Japanese-Americans during World War II, not to mention its treatment of blacks and native Americans.

Finally, thoughtful people in both countries note that Americans may be "unfair" to themselves, at least when it comes to the global market. America's unilateral export restraints, legal prohibitions against "foreign corrupt practices," and antitrust policy may reflect distinctively American values, but they are arguably self-imposed obstacles to U.S. competitiveness abroad.

The underlying question in the "fairness" debate is: To what extent does fairness consist of universally applicable norms and values, and to what extent is it the product of a unique culture and history?

To a great extent, laws, policies, and associated regulations are national in origin and application, reflecting the goals of their respective societies. Hence, what is "fair" in a society that emphasizes justice through law may not impress a society that emphasizes harmony. The value assigned to fairness itself may vary, depending on prevailing norms. American insistence on equal employment opportunity, for example, may seem out of place in a society where individual achievement is supposed to take a back seat to seniority and group loyalty.

These differences have become an issue in the "fairness" debate between the United States and Japan because the two societies assess their legitimacy from very different perspectives. The Japanese, isolated and introverted for several centuries, still cling to a sense of uniqueness.

Americans, by contrast, tend to believe that what is right for them is automatically good for the rest of the world.

Indeed, the Founding Fathers cast their experiment in self-government in terms of a universal mission. Images of a "shining city on a hill," eyed with hope by a waiting world, recur frequently in American rhetoric. Americans pursue their interests abroad with a kind of naive universalism, often expressed in moralistic terms. Describing the activities of nineteenth-century Americans in East Asia, diplomatic historian James Thomson called them "sentimental imperialists."[34] Many Japanese policymakers see the imperialism rather than the sentiment.

While the Japanese resent American pressure exerted in the name of universal fairness, their own self-righteousness sometimes goes to the other extreme. They tend to exaggerate the culturally specific aspects of fairness and deny its universal elements.

Not everything is relative, however. Consider an example of "fairness" drawn from a family context. If a Japanese parent with two children brings home a present for only one child, the other child would complain about favoritism (*eko-hiki*) or use the word "dirty" (*kitanai*). An American child in the same situation would no doubt do the same.

Japanese society is governed today by certain universal forms of justice. Civil rights and individual liberty may have been adopted or imposed as a reaction to militarism, but due process is now firmly grounded in Japanese thought and history. Readers' letters to Japanese newspapers frequently complain about bureaucrats who exercise arbitrary authority or incidents in which the strong exploited the weak. They may use the words "bad" or "shameful" rather than "unfair," but an American would instantly recognize the emotion and its sources.

The concept of fair competition is not totally absent in Japanese business circles either. Japan has a Fair Trade Commission patterned on America's Federal Trade Commission. But while the commission has repeatedly criticized MITI-sponsored cartels, its power to enforce "fair trade" is notoriously weak. As deregulation proceeds and MITI's role diminishes, companies and consumers alike may find it in their interest to reinforce the commission's original mandate or to develop noninstitutional means of promoting the same idea.

One approach to "fairness" that might avoid the charge of "cultural imperialism" is for Americans to urge the Japanese to enforce their own laws, period. This approach to resolving trade friction is quite different from the notion of "reciprocity." The "reciprocity" school of thought, which has given rise to some major bills in the U.S. Congress, holds that American companies in Japan should be treated in exactly the same way as Japanese companies are treated in the United States.

Superficially, the notion of reciprocity simply radiates fairness. A closer look, however, reveals some flaws. It is questionable whether the United States, with its numerous restrictions imposed in the name of national security and its "Buy America" barriers at the federal and state level, should serve as a model for Japan. If "reciprocity" were to prevail, Japan would be justified in restricting U.S. imports in the name of "Buy Japan" and Japanese national security. The example is, of course, absurd, but it illustrates the difficulties of imposing American rules on a very different society.

A more practical and arguably more "fair" approach would be to ensure that Japanese and American companies receive similar treatment *in Japan,* just as they—in theory—receive similar treatment in America. This goal, known as "national treatment," has a long and respectable history in trade negotiations, and continues to be the principal rationale for a series of market-opening initiatives. To seek "national treatment" for U.S. companies in Japan may prove to be the most constructive approach in the long run—especially if the Japanese perceive it to be in their own interest and not simply another concession to foreigners.

The Lag Effect

Even if political leaders succeed in ironing out the issue of fairness, a certain level of tension in U.S.-Japan relations will persist. Feelings run high, transcending day-to-day politics; they are not simply contrived by lawyers or political strategists. Something more fundamental is at work, something historical and institutional, something even deeper than the intellectual tradition of fairness.

Broadly speaking, the world is shrinking faster than the ability to manage U.S.-Japan conflict is growing. Beyond the short-term politics of trade, beyond differences in the concept of fairness, a kind of "lag effect" is in evidence. The rapid economic surges spilling over into U.S.-Japan tensions have greatly outpaced corresponding changes in domestic institutions, attitudes, and styles of communication.

Not only goods and services are crossing borders in record dimensions, but also people, technology, ideas, entertainment, culture, and even fads. Although domestic developments in one country can have a profound impact on domestic developments in the other, most people still think primarily in domestic or national terms.

Japanese scholar-diplomat Hisashi Owada puts this point in historical terms. He observes that while economic activities have become truly transnational, "the international legal order has remained basically unchanged since it was first established in 1648 in the Treaty of Westphalia." The characteristic of that order, notes Owada, is to compartmentalize competence to deal with those activities in the sovereign economic states.[35]

From the perspective of national security, this is still a world of nation-states. The very concept of defense is heavily territorial in nature. Attempts to pool or otherwise maximize defense-related resources within military alliances are correspondingly difficult, as the history of NATO amply illustrates. In a war one naturally hopes to be as self-sufficient as possible. A healthy economy lends vital support to the defense industrial base. Moreover, national economic strength is an asset in the global competition with the Soviet Union and its allies.

For these reasons alone, national trade statistics must be taken seriously. At the same time, the world needs equally visible global, regional, and subnational statistics that convey the crosscutting benefits of trade to individuals, groups, and sectors within each nation.

Unless the clash of these historical trends—national and transnational—is properly understood and managed, it will intensify the "we versus they" mentality and further encourage backward-looking economic nationalism in both Japan and the United States. If, as it appears, cherished and culturally distinctive values on both sides threaten fundamental national interests—in this case the U.S.-Japan alliance—they will have to be redefined or downplayed in favor of a more universal mind-set.

At stake is the ability of the two countries to improve economic conditions at home and abroad, cope with the problems of industrial and postindustrial society, preserve and enhance democracy, cooperate in foreign policy, and maintain mutual security. Instead of threatening and cornering each other, Japan and the United States need to understand their differences, discover their similarities, improve their communication, and bring their substantial resources to bear in solving the problems at hand. These are the themes explored in the rest of this book.

Two

Images of Wealth and Poverty

s Japan a rich or a poor country? On balance, poor, say many middle-aged and older Japanese, including a number of high-ranking business and government leaders. They remain painfully aware of their country's dependence on imported food and raw materials, its high prices, cramped housing, and frequently inadequate plumbing and sewage. Rich, say most policy-minded Americans—and many younger Japanese. They read of a country with a $100 billion trade surplus, the highest life expectancy and the lowest infant mortality in the world, and a per capita GNP of some $17,000.

When the same question arises about America, a corresponding contrast in perceptions emerges. Seen through a telescope, America appears enormously wealthy by Japanese standards. Seen from up close, America seems plagued with deficits and industrial unemployment whose onset is associated with Japan's new wealth. Which image is more accurate?

The question matters because fundamental perceptions and self-images of wealth and poverty lie behind many if not most economic disputes. If resource-poor Japan is still seen as fragile and vulnerable, then the United States should protect and forgive in the manner of an older brother. If, on the contrary, Japan is seen as waxing fat and wealthy while Americans suffer poverty and unemployment, then the Japanese are spoiled and arguably "unfair."

This chapter pursues the theme that both in Japan and America, adjustments to new economic realities are retarded by lingering self-images and outdated behavior. It begins by examining each country's self-image and tries to show how the values associated with them have given rise to significant structural differences between the two economies. These differences, in turn, prolong the "we versus they" mentality and fuel the "fairness" debate.

"Japan is Poor"

Although the standard of living in Japan is dramatically higher than it was thirty years ago, many Japanese see only part of their country's new wealth. They are perplexed by foreign criticism of their economic be-havior because they do not feel all that affluent.[1] In particular, middle-aged and older Japanese still tend to assume almost automatically that Japan lags behind the wealthy and powerful West—and that the key to catching up lies in learning.

There are powerful historical reasons for this "catch-up" mentality. Only a century ago, Japanese leaders watched as China crumbled under the pressure of Western imperialism. Instead of clinging to Confucianism as China's rulers did, Japan's Meiji-era reformers sought national power not only in military strength and industrial technology, but also in the guiding ideas behind them. Their quest for self-strengthening led them to embrace with enthusiasm—if not always with consistency—both the teachings and the material achievements of the West.

Commodore Perry's "black ships," fearsome as they were, offered Japan its first opportunity to learn directly from foreigners after its retreat into isolation in the early seventeenth century. Groups of Japanese soon climbed all over them, taking detailed notes. Barely six years after Amer-ican gunboats forced the historic opening of the country upon a reluctant Shogunate, an all-Japanese team had learned to sail them across the ocean.[2]

Western ideas came under similar scrutiny. Study teams were dis-patched to America and to Europe to study constitutions, tax laws, local government, and other features of the modern state system. The sense of urgency was acute; a Japanese student at Rutgers who literally studied to death became a hero to his Meiji-era colleagues and their successors. Within a few decades, Japan had built up a rigorous educational system, a modern industrial base, and one of the world's most formidable military arsenals.

By the 1930s, Japan in many ways resembled a Western industrial state, with a strong capital-goods sector and a substantial armaments industry. Yet daily life remained largely unchanged, and material conditions were austere. World War II reduced that austerity to desperation. In the grim months after Japan surrendered in 1945, Tokyo was littered with home-less people dressed in tattered rags, huddled empty-eyed and silent around fires in the empty streets. One eyewitness wrote, "They looked like things, not men."[3]

Small wonder that economic recovery was almost an obsession in the first decade and a half after the war. Thanks in large part to the catch-up mentality, postwar reconstruction proceeded rapidly. Custodians of America's high-technology factories and laboratories were struck by the thoroughness of Japanese "study tours" and by the ability of the Japanese to imitate and improve upon American discoveries. Frequently, Japanese engineers were the only ones to grasp and take advantage of a relatively obscure engineering breakthrough occurring somewhere in the world.[4]

Even when the so-called Japanese miracle began to take off in the early 1960s, industrial production was only a third of what it would be in 1975. Fully half of Japan's economic strength burst on the world only after 1966.

The Japanese preoccupation with catching up persists to this day: Students pore over textbooks noteworthy for their "bland taste and encyclopedic quality";[5] the study of mathematics has become an "ongoing national campaign";[6] university entrance examinations are laced with questions about Western history so detailed that even a well-prepared American history major would probably fail; MITI directors still consider it their job to collect up-to-date information on technology developed in Western Europe and North America and distribute it to Japanese firms.

Old Poverty

Japan's new wealth has not erased its old poverty in the physical sense. Some of the basic facts contributing to its so-called small-nation mentality have not changed.

To begin with, Japan's land area—some two-thirds of which is unsuitable for cultivation—is only three-tenths of one percent of the global landmass. Its population, however, is fully half that of the United States. It is as if half of America's population lived in Montana.

Into greater Tokyo, Osaka, and Nagoya—a mere 6 percent of the total acreage—are squeezed some 42 percent of Japan's 121 million people. The area lying within 50 kilometers of Tokyo alone is home to roughly 25 million people; greater Osaka holds another 15 million. When Japanese tell foreigners what a crowded country they live in, they are thinking primarily of the greater Tokyo complex.

Postwar migration greatly intensified this urban crush. Between 1950 and 1975, the proportion of urban residents to the total population doubled, rising to approximately 76 percent. The physical infrastructure has still not caught up: urban housing is notoriously cramped; the average office space—75 square feet per person—is about one-third the U.S. average. According to a Ministry of Housing report, the highest percentage of "substandard" housing is found in Tokyo and Osaka.[7] On a sunny day in Tokyo, laundry drying outdoors is a common sight—not only because bedding is traditionally aired, but also because there may be no room for a dryer in a tiny apartment.

Nationwide, although almost all Japanese homes have adequate tap water, only a little more than a third are serviced by municipal sewage systems; the rest depend on local truck collection. In Britain and the United States, sewage systems service roughly 97 percent and 72 percent, respectively, of all homes. Only about two-thirds of Japanese homes have flush toilets, compared to over 90 percent of homes in the United States, Britain, and West Germany. Little land is set aside for public parks: less than 3 percent in Tokyo, compared to almost 20 percent in Washington and Paris and 14 percent in London. Paved roads, sidewalks, and other infrastructure are also typically below Western averages.

Partly for such reasons, many Japanese just do not feel as rich as the macroeconomic statistics might suggest or as the rest of the world sees them. Asked to describe favorable aspects of present-day Japanese society, most of the respondents to a nationwide poll chose adjectives such as "peaceful" and "stable"; only about 10 percent selected "affluent."[8]

To be sure, money is flowing around, but it tends to wash into banks and companies and wash out again—frequently abroad, or else into mammoth expense accounts. Tokyo's night life floats on expense accounts; no one could afford it otherwise. Whereas a small but comfortable room in a respectable provincial hotel may cost only $40, a few drinks in a Ginza bar can easily total $300. Farm families are doing well because of policies favoring agriculture, but the general urban population is hardly awash with cash. Indeed, overall growth rates for household consumption have remained sluggish.[9] A poll of 6,000 households in 1985 revealed that some two-thirds had economized on living expenses and were planning to do so again in the following year.[10]

One reason for Japan's relatively frozen standard of living is that wage-earner income has remained stagnant. Disposable income has not risen for over a decade.[11] Meanwhile, the basic cost of living remains extremely high. The ratio of expenditures on food to total consumer spending has fallen in recent years, but is still close to 30 percent. Since much of Japan's food is imported, one would have expected a drop in consumer prices following the substantial revaluation of the yen in 1985–86. Yet, padded by subsidies and absorbed by Japan's stubbornly inefficient distribution system, the prices of most imported food items dropped only slightly or stayed the same.

The repayment of housing loans takes another 14 percent or so of nationwide disposable income. Housing costs in urban areas are especially steep; in Tokyo they are astronomical. In 1986 alone, land prices in central Tokyo rose by 76 percent, pushing the prices of building sites as high as 150 million yen per 3.3 square meters—close to $1 million at prevailing exchange rates. A condominium apartment in Tokyo might cost $10 million.

Energy prices are another component of the high cost of living. Although world oil prices fell by over 50 percent in 1985–86—the first drop of such magnitude since 1973—Japan's electricity rates fell only marginally. The price of energy from other sources has also remained relatively constant.

Education costs figure heavily in household budgets, as worried parents steer their children into intensive and expensive after-school tutoring programs (*juku*). Tutorial fees increased ninefold between 1970 and 1983, and are still on the rise.

All in all, Japanese consumers still feel somewhat pinched in their day-to-day life. Although an overwhelming majority of Japanese define themselves as "middle class," the image of the middle class in Japan does not convey as much material comfort as it does in the West. "Japan is supposed to have all this money," remarks LDP Diet member Motoo Shiina, "but my constituents don't see it."

Another hallmark of old poverty is continuing dependence on imports. Dependence is not synonymous with either poverty or vulnerability, but in Japan the distinction is sometimes blurred.

Food is a major concern. Virtually all of the soybeans and about two-thirds of the grain consumed in Japan are grown abroad. America benefits enormously from this dependence, finding a ready market for almost 20 percent of its agricultural exports—about $6 billion in 1986. By comparison, annual sales to its next two largest customers—the Soviet Union and the Netherlands—average $2 billion each.

While the threat of hunger may be largely lost on younger Japanese, it has not entirely disappeared from the minds of those old enough to re-member the grim years of the 1940s. In a poll conducted in 1984, more than half of the respondents aged 50 and over agreed with the view that Japan should produce its own food, even if imported food is cheaper.[12]

This lingering sense of vulnerability shows up again with respect to energy and raw materials. As Tokyo likes to remind the world, almost 100 percent of Japan's oil—accounting for about three-fifths of the country's total energy needs—is imported. Dependency on imported aluminum, nickel, iron ore, tin, and copper exceeds 95 percent.

Dependence on imported food and raw materials might not seem so threatening if supply lines were not so long and uncertain. In terms of food security and import dependence, Japan is roughly comparable to Switzerland. Yet everything must come by sea, and usually over a long distance. About a third of Japan's exports and imports pass through the Strait of Malacca. Some 70 percent of its oil imports must pass through not only the Strait of Malacca, but also the Strait of Hormuz.[13] Tankers over 200,000 tons must detour through the Lombok Strait, controlled unilater-ally by Indonesia. Uncertainty has increased since the 1970s, when many nations extended their fishing rights to a distance of two hundred miles.

To reduce its dependence, Japan has pursued such policies as diversifi-cation of sources, overseas resource development, stockpiling, domestic substitution, the maintenance of a strong merchant fleet, and a variety of export and development projects. These policies have a strategic charac-ter comparable to national-security doctrines in the United States.

From time to time, Americans have taken or threatened to take uni-lateral actions that reinforce Japan's residual sense of vulnerability. Exam-ples include President Nixon's soybean embargo of 1973 and a private-sector trade complaint filed against Japan's protected rice market in 1986. By raising the specter of food shortages, such measures have the unin-tended effect of forcing Japanese leaders to appease one of the least effi-cient groups in the economy—small farmers.

To Japanese planners, a strategy emphasizing self-sufficiency in rice production, raw or unfinished imports, and manufactured exports was merely common sense. Lacking adequate food, energy, and raw mate-rials, the Japanese had no choice but to rely on their manufacturing skills to pay the import bill. Over time, however, other nations—not just the United States—began to take offense at this strategy, to the point where Japan's failure to absorb its perceived share of manufactured exports from the developing world has become a major political issue.

A common complaint heard in the 1980s is that whereas the United States absorbs more than 60 percent of the manufactured exports of non-OPEC developing countries, Japan accounts for only about 7 percent. In fact, the gap is actually wider than it was a decade ago. The governments of many developing countries are voicing their grievances with increasing forcefulness. In some Congressional circles, it is *this* imbalance—not the imbalance in U.S.-Japan bilateral trade—that is seen as really "unfair." Yet change is slow in coming, partly because of Japanese doubts about the quality and reliability of such imports, and partly because of Japan's long-standing preference for self-sufficiency in ordinary manufactured goods.

Even those Japanese who concede that their country's wealth is real fear that it may not last, or at least think that it should never be taken for granted. Believing that they are at the mercy of "black ships" and foreign "shocks," earthquakes, fires, and typhoons, the Japanese are characteristically pessimistic. A world in which most food and raw materials must be imported is an inherently unsafe place. The only way to hold fast to new wealth and to avoid slipping back into poverty is to work hard. It is like riding a bicycle: if you stop pedaling, you fall off.

Numerous surveys have shown that the Japanese take greater pride in their industriousness than in their wealth. Perhaps Japanese culture is not predisposed to value wealth as highly as other cultures. But a more likely explanation is that the perspectives and values of the majority of Japanese are still shaped by a sense of poverty that corresponds less and less to reality.

Some Japanese who are conscious of this incongruity are pessimistic for other reasons. They jump to the conclusion that the old poverty-driven patterns of sacrifice and export-led growth have largely exhausted their usefulness. They point to Japan's rapidly aging society, the increasing competitiveness of the newly industrializing countries (especially South Korea), and the possibility that Japanese culture and education inhibit the innovative spirit needed for success in the twenty-first century. From now on, they reason, Japan will stagnate relative to the rest of the industrialized world.

Other Japanese, more optimistic and perhaps more realistic, cite Japan's ability to adapt to changing circumstances and predict that it will continue to do well in the world despite sluggish domestic growth—just as it did following the 1973 oil shock. Indeed, even though Japan's growth rate in the 1970s was significantly below what it was in the double-digit boom years of the 1960s, it averaged 8.7 percent. Economic analysts assume the growth rate will be lower still in the next decade, on the order of 2 percent or so. Yet even these lower growth estimates presume a continuation of world trade at more or less current levels—an assumption that could be invalidated by escalating trade tensions.

Actually, Japan is less dependent on trade than most West European countries, exporting roughly 20 percent of its GNP compared to their 40 percent. Still, there is no doubt that Japan's postwar prosperity to date has depended heavily on the opportunity to sell its products abroad and to buy food, oil, and other resources essential to its national life. One does not have to be particularly pessimistic to recognize that the political strains associated with import-linked unemployment pose a serious threat to the world trading system, and to Japan in particular.[14] And if trade collapses, so will much of Japan's new wealth.

"Japan is Rich"

Other commentators scoff at the idea that Japan should still be considered poor and vulnerable. They insist that Japan is a rich country and that it should behave like one, at home as well as abroad.

Since 1965, Japan's overall GNP has climbed to more than half of America's. Following the yen/dollar realignment of 1985–86, Japan's per capita GNP in dollar terms ($17,000) surpassed that of the United States ($16,000).

In 1985, the year America sank into debt for the first time since World War I, Japan became the world's biggest net creditor nation, recording net external credits of nearly $130 billion—an increase of almost 75 percent over the previous year. By 1987, its trade surplus had ballooned to an estimated $94 billion—inflated by cheaper dollars but comparable in significance to the record-breaking $61 billion of 1986. The amount of yen traded daily in the three largest currency markets in 1986 approached $65 billion, some $20 billion more than trading in the mark. As of 1987, central banks hold an estimated 10 percent of their reserves in yen, a percentage exceeded only by their holdings of dollars and German marks.

Japan's new wealth now washes around world financial markets like tidal waves. A new catchword, *zai-teku*, literally "financial technology," refers to multibillion-yen flows orchestrated by corporate computers. Japanese buyers now figure so prominently in U.S. Treasury bond offerings that traders expect yields will adjust to whatever rates the Japanese will accept. They pay record prices for real estate, not just in Japan, but also in Manhattan. Tokyo ranks as the world's third largest financial center after New York and London, and will become even more important as financial liberalization proceeds.

Many Japanese officials are complaining about the unfavorable consequences of the yen/dollar realignment for growth and employment, but there are few sympathizers to be found. For the late 1980s, the Economic Planning Agency is officially predicting annual growth of about 3.5 percent (although 2.0–2.5 percent might be more realistic). Three percent unemployment may be historically high for Japan, but it pales by comparison with the double-digit unemployment that has gripped parts of Western Europe and the 6–7 percent that stubbornly persists in the United States.

Even Japan's alleged vulnerability in energy supplies is far less pronounced than before, as a result of policies undertaken in the aftermath of the 1973 oil shock to shrink or export energy-intensive industries, promote conservation, seek energy suppliers outside the Middle East, accelerate research on alternative energy sources, and expand nuclear-power capacity. This is perhaps the prime example of Japan's famous consensus and adjustment process.

Vital statistics tend to support the "Japan is rich" thesis. Life expectancy in Japan is the highest in the world—roughly 80 years for women and 78 years for men, up from roughly 54 and 50, respectively, right after the war. The comparable statistic for the United States is 79 years for white females and 72 years for white males. Japan's infant mortality is the lowest in the world—5.5 infant deaths per 1,000 live births in 1985, compared with 7.0 in Sweden and an estimated 10.9 in the United States.[15]

Japan has more hospital beds per person than any other major industrial country except West Germany. Medical insurance was extended to the entire population in 1961. Social security as a proportion of national income is approaching U.S. levels and is expected to exceed them by the year 2000.[16]

Education statistics tell a similar story. Virtually every child receives a rigorous education. Test scores in math and science are the highest in the world. Functional illiteracy among adults, variously estimated at 13–17 percent in America, is virtually nonexistent in Japan.

Even housing statistics reflect considerable achievement. Some 62 percent of Japanese now own their houses or apartments—a very respectable figure by global standards. The average floor space of homes in Japan—except in the four or five biggest cities—is comparable to that in West Germany and larger than that in France. Moreover, construction as a percentage of GNP is higher in Japan than in either the United States or Europe, in part because the Japanese frequently prefer rebuilding to renovation, in part because new housing is rising at a rapid rate.

Inside the home, the use of electric appliances now surpasses that of the United States. Japan boasts more television sets per capita than any country in the world. In telephones, Americans still hold the lead, but the Japanese come next. More Japanese now travel abroad than Americans. (Some designer stores in Paris have even put up signs asking their Japanese customers to leave some of the merchandise for others.) Stores are packed with young people buying clothing and electronic gadgets in record numbers. Sportily dressed adolescents consume elaborate ice-cream dishes at expensive coffee shops. Contrary to Western stereotypes, Japan is a hive of consumerism.

All the same, the widespread American perception that Japanese consumers suffer at home while Japanese companies make a killing abroad is an irritant in U.S.-Japan relations. "What infuriates many people in Congress is the way Japanese continue to deprive consumers of a better life even though they have all this money," observed a former Congressional staff aide who was directly involved in trade legislation in 1986.

Americans are not entirely wrong of course. Japanese consumers still contend with unduly high prices and cramped housing. Yet in most surveys of what the Japanese Government calls the "national life," respondents express an overall sense of well-being. Moreover, according to periodic surveys conducted by Japan's Economic Planning Agency, satisfaction with the standard of living has been rising steadily, from 57 percent in 1978 to 64 percent in 1984.[17]

Even if swelling treasuries and capital surpluses should prove short-lived, Japan's other assets are more durable. In fact, Japan is wealthy precisely where it counts: people and know-how. Newspaper editor and columnist Masahiko Ishizuka has summed it up neatly:

> Today, more important than natural resources or raw materials and energy are technology and the manpower and systems that support it. Japan abounds in these new vital resources and viewed in this way, it can no longer be called resource-poor.[18]

Many of those who share Ishizuka's view believe that Japan will emerge from the economic downturn associated with the yen/dollar realignment leaner and more competitive than ever. In the wake of the last major yen appreciation, in 1977–78, Japan responded by saving more, cutting costs, improving quality, and promoting exports—"in short, by being Japanese."[19] This time around, companies have intensified their efforts to cut costs and promote efficiency. Even agriculture and services will not be able to remain inefficient forever.

"We will come out of this crisis stronger," declares Naohiro Amaya, architect of the MITI "visions" of prior years.[20] Reflecting the new arrogance that Americans find so troubling, some Japanese go as far as to assert that a historical process is at work: America's decadent, Roman-style decline makes way for a vigorous new world leader—Japan.[21]

"And America is Getting Poorer"

Corresponding to the "Japan is rich" thesis is the zero-sum conclusion that America is, if not poor, at least proportionately less rich than it could be—and in certain sectors actually poorer. This strikes some Americans as particularly unfair because America somehow deserves to remain "number one."

These perceptions raise two quite separate issues: whether the United States can accurately identify and cure its economic difficulties, and whether it can hold its own against Japanese competition in domestic and world markets. America's "Japan-bashers" sometimes confuse the two, blaming Japan for problems that lie far beyond Tokyo's reach. Conversely, those Japanese who now openly scoff at American competitiveness may be mistaking recent U.S. macroeconomic distortions for permanent Japanese "superiority."

Certain very real macroeconomic trends make it seem that America is indeed getting poorer: the decline of smokestack industries, overproduction and debt in the agricultural sector, a large appetite for imports, and a relative lack of interest in exports. These trends add up to some alarming statistics.

As the recession in the United States hit bottom in 1982, investment in basic industrial plant and facilities plummeted. Between 1948–52 and 1978–82, manufacturing employment as a share of all payroll employment dropped from 34 percent to 22 percent. Since 1980, the United States has lost more than two million manufacturing jobs, of which fewer than half are likely to return. The cost in human suffering has been incalculable—not to mention the social costs associated with unemployment, such as health and welfare payments and even crime.

Compared to the 1975–80 recovery, the recovery of the mid-1980s proved to be uneven, perhaps even illusory. Real economic growth was erratic. Unemployment, historically high for an economy in an early stage of an expansion, did not fall below 6 percent until 1987. Corporate profits were weak and investments sluggish. Consumer debt was higher than it was during the 1975–80 expansion. Although holding steady in absolute terms, exports dropped from 8.5 percent to 6 percent of GNP. Throughout the early 1980s, imports greatly outpaced exports. In the post-1982 recovery, they grew three times as fast (in real terms) as GNP. By 1986, net debts owed to foreigners exceeded $200 billion.

The picture seemed gloomy even in sectors normally considered strong. In May 1986, for example, despite the cheaper dollar, U.S. farm trade ran its first monthly deficit in twenty-seven years. The agricultural sector was in such dire straits that Congress authorized subsidized exports to the Soviet Union—despite loud cries from America's major grain-exporting allies, particularly Australia. Meanwhile, experts warned that trade deficits averaging even $100 billion could push cumulative U.S. foreign-held debt past $1 trillion by 1990 and close to $2 trillion in less than a decade. These indicators seemed to overshadow the good news: low inflation, falling interest rates, a buoyant stock market, and an apparently high level of consumer confidence.

In retrospect, a combination of events swelled America's budget and trade deficits, greatly damaging American competitiveness and accelerating the export of manufacturing jobs. The budget problem consisted largely of runaway nondiscretionary entitlements (i.e., benefits mandated by existing law), a 92 percent increase in defense spending (from roughly $70 billion in the 1980 budget authorization to nearly $133 billion in 1985), and the Reagan Administration's refusal to support higher taxes. High interest rates and a demand for dollars kept the value of the dollar high: the yen/dollar rate went from 176:1 in 1978 to over 260:1 in the early 1980s.

During the recovery, the United States acted as a "locomotive" for the world economy, growing at a heady rate of 8 percent in 1983–84. What fueled this growth was not new productive wealth, but rather a marked propensity to import. In the language of economists, there is a threefold difference between America and Japan in the "income elasticity of imports." In other words, for every extra unit of income, America has a tendency to import three times as much as Japan.[22]

Contrary to what some Japanese like to believe, a large share of U.S. imports consists not of consumer goods, but of office or factory-automation equipment. While these imports are arguably a sign of health—signifying a certain degree of industrial revitalization and modernization in the U.S. economy—their short-run effect has been to worsen the bilateral trade deficit with Japan, which supplies almost half of such equipment.[23]

Trade disputes between the two countries are, of course, nothing new. As early as the 1960s, Japanese exports began to penetrate U.S. and Third World markets to the detriment of American firms. The very success of Tokyo's catch-up policy began to breed its own backlash. As was the case in Europe, Japan's refusal to stay shattered turned out to be less comforting in practice than in theory. Also in the 1960s, overt and disguised Japanese barriers to imports blocked many potential American sales and channeled foreign investment in directions designed to benefit Japan. Under MITI's "administrative guidance," some American companies operating in Japan were more or less bludgeoned into transferring technology to Japanese firms and limiting their domestic sales. IBM is perhaps the most well-known case in point.[24] America registered a trade deficit in non–R&D-intensive goods as early as 1968.

What is new is the degree of Japanese import penetration and the more or less permanent transformation of key industrial sectors in the United States. Automobiles and steel are but two examples of sectors that have been laid low and are unlikely ever to recapture their prior level of employment. To laid-off workers in Detroit and Pittsburgh, it is small comfort to know that the service sector is flourishing or that Japanese investments are creating jobs for Americans in other parts of the country.

These trends have put American supporters of free trade on the defensive. Whereas in the late 1970s the Automobile Importers' Association rallied (ultimately unsuccessfully) against the imposition of "voluntary" restraints on Japanese car exports, few would take such a position publicly in the mid-1980s. Bankers and businessmen tend to voice support for free trade, but they now do so with qualification. And no major group has objected publicly and specifically to the recent quasi-cartels in semiconductors and machine tools; indeed, the punitive tariffs imposed on certain Japanese electronic products in early 1987 were presented to the public as a defense of the so-called semiconductor arrangement. Far more common today is a kind of economic nationalism, punctuated by what one trade expert and former U.S. trade negotiator calls the "politics of blame."[25]

In the judgment of many Japanese, America has no cause to behave like a poor relation. Despite real problems in the manufacturing sector, by no stretch of the imagination is America getting poorer. They note that whereas Japan's wealth is partial and possibly ephemeral, America's is real. The United States is blessed with an enormous temperate-zone land-mass, abundant natural resources, rich farmland, a population of almost a quarter of a billion people, and the largest and strongest economy in the world. During their long train rides back to crowded houses or apart-ments, Japanese commuters read about all this wealth. They see on televi-sion images from an America that seems addicted to conspicuous con-sumption. On their visits to the United States, Japanese leaders fre-quently marvel at the amount of available space and, in particular, the size of American homes. One Diet member from a rather poor agricultural district in northern Japan said he found it difficult to reconcile the economic hardships supposedly afflicting Silicon Valley with the palatial homes of its top executives.

Images like these have convinced many Japanese that Americans fail to take full advantage of their assets and, in some cases, are frittering them away. Accusations of "unfairness" simply shift the blame for what America is doing to itself. One Japanese commentator wrote: "No sooner do valuable new technologies start to create jobs within the United States than the work is snatched away and shipped abroad." This particular "America-basher" went even further:

> There is a famous American expression about self-destructive be-havior. It has to do with shooting yourself in the foot. Well, U.S. busi-ness is taking dead aim at itself. . . . While a chorus of special interests in the United States calls Japan's trade practices "unfair," deindus-trialization spreads like cancer in America. There is an unfortunate resemblance to Nero fiddling while Rome burned.[26]

The impression that America is "deindustrializing" is central to the thesis that America is relatively poorer. In fact, U.S. manufacturing out-put has stayed relatively constant in the 1980s, both as a share of GNP (about 23–24 percent) and as a share of the total production of member countries in the Organization for Economic Cooperation and Develop-ment (OECD). Although growth in U.S. manufacturing output has been less rapid by comparison with Japan, it has outstripped that of most Euro-pean countries. A few large industries—notably steel and automobiles—have become partly "deindustrialized," but this should not be confused with overall deindustrialization.[27]

"But America Must Remain a Superpower"

Comparing wealth and poverty in Japan and America is especially difficult because the two countries have chosen to compete on a different footing. While Japan has defined its goals primarily in economic terms, the United States has done so in military terms in the context of superpower rivalry. At least until recently, U.S. leaders tended to take America's number-one economic position more or less for granted. At the highest levels of government, the priority has been—and to a great extent still is—"national security," a phrase virtually synonymous with "military" or "political-military" power. To the extent that Americans have a catch-up mentality, it is focused on military rivalry with the Soviet Union. Examples include reactions to the Sputnik "shock" of 1957, the alleged "missile gap" of the Kennedy era, and the "window of vulnerability" in the Reagan Administration.

Thoughtful Americans, however, have repeatedly warned that a healthy economy is an essential component of national security. Former Senator Stuart Symington was fond of saying that the three pillars of national security are defense, institutions, and the dollar. The President's Commission on Industrial Competitiveness stressed that economic competitiveness is "vital" to national security.[28] In 1984, a report by the Business Roundtable called policies to ensure a stable, growing, and competitive economy "central" to U.S. national defense and foreign policy, and deplored not only the absence of national consensus on this issue, but also a framework to promote such policies.[29]

The U.S. defense industry has joined those calling for a policy framework to strengthen the nation's industrial base. In 1986, a high-level defense-industry advisory committee recommended that general U.S. trade and economic policies and "even areas as diverse as research programs of civilian agencies and education policy" take into account industrial-base considerations. Yet as the committee observed, neither Congress nor the executive branch is organized effectively to formulate policy on this basis.[30] In sum, as Chrysler executive Lee Iacocca puts it, America has a military-industrial policy and an agricultural-industrial policy, but not an "industrial-industrial policy."[31]

As many Japanese see it, the United States is undermining its leadership of the Western alliance by its failure to offset galloping consumption with the creation of new productive wealth. Few—if any—American leaders seem to have thought through the implications of this erosion of economic leadership. America has no counterpart to MITI's "visions." No one with any authority in the executive branch is charged with identifying and communicating long-term trends and incorporating them into the policy-making process. Even to hint at the need for a long-term perspective smacks of national planning, a particular American bugaboo.

In the absence of such projections, Congress tends to overreact to short-term industrial dislocations, and hence to their most visible symptom— the trade deficit. But "trade" in the narrow sense of goods shipped across national borders is a subject that is increasingly artificial and limited.[32] Trade is now greatly overshadowed by many larger but less visible international transactions—flows of capital, technology, and people.

Structural Consequences

These various images of wealth and poverty have given rise to certain structural differences in the U.S. and Japanese economies—differences that are diminishing, but still significant enough to generate friction as the two economies interact. From a structural perspective, the current friction in U.S.-Japan economic relations can be described as a "grinding of gears." Adjusting these domestic "gears" is of crucial importance, because what Tokyo decides to do for essentially domestic reasons often has a significant spillover effect on the United States, and vice versa.

Over time, American interest in the Japanese economy has greatly intensified. Like light through a magnifying glass, scrutiny of Japan's domestic policies and their effect on trade has been focused and ignited through periodic concentration in the mass media. Experts offering various keys to Japan's success have led the American public on a dizzy chase through companies, ministries, laboratories, schools, and even the classics of swordsmanship.

From these surveys, some Americans go so far as to conclude that Japan's whole economy is "unfair": not only can Americans never compete with Japan on a "level playing field" in global markets, but Japan's domestic economy is structured in a way that is inherently unfair to foreigners. No matter how much U.S. companies invest in R&D, improve product quality, or lower their prices, Japanese companies are bound to win because the whole game is rigged.

Until perhaps the mid-1970s, American business and labor leaders pointed to cheap labor as an "unfair" advantage of Japanese firms, but they have long since stopped doing so. (The yen/dollar realignment of

1985–86 pushed average Japanese wages some 12 percent *higher* than American wages.) For a while, a leading explanation of Japanese success was the family-like treatment companies accorded their workers, and the company loyalty that developed as a consequence. This explanation coexisted with the image of "Japan, Inc.," with its suggestion that Japan's economic prowess stemmed from industrial policies formulated and carried out under the guidance of MITI, with the full cooperation of Japanese management and labor.

After the 1979 oil shock sent the yen tumbling, the overvalued dollar (overvalued, that is, in relation to the yen) was accused of undermining America's industrial competitiveness. When the yen/dollar realignment of 1985–86 failed to correct America's sluggish export performance, blame shifted to the currencies of America's other trade competitors, many of which fell along with the dollar. Blame also spread to American big business itself, which was said to be bloated by "corpocracy" and averse to risk.

A more sophisticated American critique has highlighted the "unfair" financial advantages enjoyed by Japanese manufacturers. The focus is not misdirected, for differences in the two financial systems—corresponding to the "rich/poor" values described earlier—have profoundly influenced the manufacturing environment in the two economies. Compared to the United States, Japan is noted for relatively cheap capital, relatively little concern for short-term profits, a relatively high level of corporate borrowing, and a deep pool of savings.

Cheap capital means that required rates of return on investment are lower for a Japanese firm than they are for an American firm. To be sure, the difference is not as great as some Americans assume. To borrow large amounts of money in Japan, corporations are required to deposit a compensatory balance and pay certain hidden fees. More important, Japan's low rate of inflation—one to two percent in recent years—means that the gap in real interest rates between the two countries is not as great as the spread in nominal percentage points suggests. Still, capital is clearly cheaper in Japan than in the United States. The effect has been beneficial to long-term Japanese investment—a goal consciously sought by the Japanese Government.

Another advantage sometimes labeled unfair by American competitors is the relative absence of pressure on Japanese companies to show short-term profits. Japanese firms are seen as free to pursue so-called predatory pricing because their stockholders take a long-term view of competitive success. Most major firms belong to clearly demarcated corporate families, tied together by interlocking ownership and centered around a major bank; their stockholders are often affiliated companies. This pattern is also said to permit a high level of borrowing relative to equity ownership, known as a high debt-to-equity ratio. In the United States, by contrast, both Wall Street and feisty individual stockholders are said to insist on quarterly profits.

Measuring profitability is not a simple matter, however. Hidden assets, subsidiary finance companies, leases, and bookkeeping treatment of corporate debentures are among the items that may or may not appear in direct "on-the-book" comparisons of Japanese and American firms. The same is true of low-interest housing loans to employees and greatly understated values of land and securities portfolios held by Japanese companies. In other words, the profits of Japanese firms may be greater than they seem on the books. Still, by standard U.S. measurements—whether percentage of sales or return on investment—Japanese executives do seem to attach less importance to short-term profit than their American counterparts. One major survey, for example, indicated that the number-one target of Japanese businessmen is larger market share. By contrast, American executives responding to the same survey ranked return on investment and increasing the price of shares as their first and second most important goals, respectively, ahead of market share.[33] Annual compensation differs as well: Japan's top executives get between $140,000 and $200,000, including benefits; in America, compensation for top executives ranges from $500,000 to well over $1 million.

The second advantage, a high debt-to-equity ratio, has been a necessary feature of Japan's postwar industrial development. With their assets shattered and property destroyed, companies initially had little choice. In some companies, however, a high debt-to-equity ratio came to signify an aggressive strategy rather than a sign of weakness. During the 1950s, for example, Honda's drive to unseat Tohatsu, then the leading producer of motorcycles, relied on a debt-to-equity ratio of 6:1, more than four times higher than that of its target. During the 1970s, when Japanese companies concentrated on massive export drives, the average debt-to-equity ratio was 2:1. In the United States, by contrast, it was 0.5:1. This picture is changing, however. Some companies, including the legendary Toyota and Matsushita, have virtually no debt. Overall, the gap between U.S. and Japanese companies has narrowed, with Japan's average debt-to-equity ratio falling to 1.6:1, and the U.S. ratio rising marginally to 0.6:1.

The difference, though noteworthy, is hardly "unfair." Nothing prevents American companies from pursuing more aggressive financial policies, unless it is their own finance departments—or the equivalent thereof—which tend to be more powerful than those in Japanese firms.[34]

The third advantage is a large river of savings that keeps replenishing that pool of cheap capital. Some Americans claim that this, too, is "unfair," as though the Japanese Government deliberately holds down consumption to squeeze cash from an unwilling population. Many Japanese commentators have also focused on savings, but they consider thrift a virtue to be rewarded. Indeed, a standard defense against American "bashing" is that the Japanese deserve to get ahead in the world because they save so much more than profligate Americans—a Japanese twist to the Horatio Alger story.

Like profitability, savings are hard to measure. By measuring net savings as a percentage of gross income, some studies conclude that the rate of savings in the United States is 3 percent or lower, while in Japan it is 15 percent or higher.[35] Others make the case that education and consumer durables (in particular, housing) should be treated as components of U.S. savings. By that measure, Japan's gross savings rate is only one-third higher than America's. And if the conventional definition of savings is stretched to include net *military* investment—an extremely high national priority—then the U.S. savings rate rises by almost 20 percent.[36] However wide the gap, economists agree that Japan's "income elasticity of savings" is distinctly higher. In other words, for every extra unit of income, a Japanese would save more of that increment than an American.

In earlier years Americans, too, put aside more of their personal earnings for a rainy day. Credit-card consumerism is a relatively recent phenomenon, mistrusted by many older Americans who never quite got over the Great Depression of the 1930s. For many Japanese, the critical event was the devastation of World War II some fifteen years later. One does not have to be either Confucian or Spartan to see that savings represent a lifeline to a secure future in an age of potential economic ruin.

The value placed on savings has given Japan a major structural asset, the postal savings system. Next to central banks, Japan's postal savings system is the world's largest financial institution, with estimated deposits of 100 trillion yen (more than $600 billion at 1987 exchange rates). This vast reservoir of money accounts for more than 30 percent of Japan's total private-sector savings.

Despite periodic complaints from commercial banks, the postal savings system normally offers higher interest rates. Moreover, interest on deposits of up to 3 million yen (roughly $20,000 at 150 yen to the dollar) is exempt from income tax. This feature has made postal savings very popular to date as a source of legal but tax-free income. From the government's point of view, the system has been very effective in raising capital to fund Japan's industrial development.

Cheap capital, less emphasis on short-term profits, a high debt-to-equity ratio, and a high savings rate are the strengths of the Japanese economy, propelling Japan from the ashes of history to the vanguard. But the economy has weaknesses as well. Like the strengths, they are linked to traditional values—some of which may hinder the economic innovation required for the future.

One of these weaknesses is a strong aversion to risk. Such caution may stem from Japan's image of itself as poor and vulnerable; many Japanese may still feel they simply cannot afford to fail. Another likely cause is a certain rigidity and regimentation in the economy—a residue of centuries of government regulation compounded by closed-group behavior.

One symptom of the aversion to risk is the feeble venture capital market. The number of firms specializing in venture capital has increased some sevenfold in the 1980s—from nine to sixty by one count—but funds from this source are still extremely limited. Some have suggested that joint research projects sponsored by MITI and other forms of government "signaling" associated with Japan's industrial policy can be thought of as a substitute for the kind of flourishing venture capital market that exists in the United States.

Poorly developed research ties between universities and corporations are another weak point in the Japanese economy. Scientists at prestigious public universities may engage in government-approved research projects, but individual research contracts with private firms are normally frowned on or prohibited. Finally, patterns of lifetime employment, though diminishing, still preclude a free-floating class of talented entrepreneur-managers. Few start-up firms are genuinely independent, and many fail for want of management and marketing skills.

In the short term, the Japanese Government can do little about these and other deep-seated weaknesses. In any event, Americans should keep them in mind when sifting through the "fairness" debate.

The hallmarks of the U.S. economy reflect concern for national-security goals, combined with a relatively laissez-faire and haphazard approach to

the economy as a whole. As a result, the United States pursues two different sets of policies—one focused and oriented toward military priorities,
the other unfocused and divorced from national-security concerns. At
times this combination has given rise to both real and apparent contradictions. Thus, while Washington rejects an explicit industrial policy and ex-
tols the virtues of the free market, it has in fact influenced the allocation of
resources and negotiated sector-specific import restraints. By 1984, according to one estimate, some 21 percent of American imports (by value)
were covered by import protection. Others have placed the percentage of
imports subject to restraints at 40 percent or more.[37] But Washington has
restricted trade and intervened in the economy in a piecemeal fashion,
and for reasons that have little to do with international economic competitiveness as such.

National security is perhaps the one area where America displays a
catch-up (or keep-up) mentality comparable to Japan's. Government intervention in the interest of national preparedness and defense mobiliza-
tion has been substantial. During the 1950s, for example, using support
programs authorized by the Defense Production Act of 1950, the U.S.
Government doubled aluminum capacity, quadrupled tungsten capacity,
boosted the nuclear industry, and basically created the titanium industry.
Even the 1956 law authorizing the expansion of the U.S. highway system,
which (combined with cheap gas) put millions of Americans on the road,
was called the National Defense Highways Act.

Also in the 1950s, the U.S. Air Force funded the development of certain
kinds of computer-controlled machine tools and integrated circuits. Aircraft originally developed for military use evolved into highly successful
commercial models: the Boeing 707 evolved from the B-47 and the B-52,
and the Boeing 747 evolved from the losing design in a military cargo
airplane design competition. Typically, a company receiving such funds
would share both the resulting production savings and the new know-
how with the sponsoring military service, which in turn would pass the
technology along to other defense contractors. The government's involvement has had long-term consequences; as of the mid-1980s, the
aerospace trade account is still strongly in the black, with annual exports
of close to $20 billion.

Funding for industrial development under the Defense Production Act
gradually withered away. But even in the 1980s, small amounts were
committed to various programs of technology modernization.

When the Reagan Administration managed to engage the Japanese

Government in a high-level dialogue on Japan's industrial policy, Tokyo pointed to such nonmarket practices as evidence of a hidden U.S. "industrial policy." Neither side pressed the point too hard, for both seemed to agree that the aim of U.S. defense-related industrial policies (such as they are) is not to boost America's international competitiveness, but to strengthen a manufacturing base that can sustain the defense of the Free World—including Japan.

Expressions of alarm over the state of the U.S. industrial base resound most forcefully when national security is perceived to be at stake. Characteristically, it was concern for national security that first drew significant Congressional and public attention to long-term industrial-base trends.

In 1980, a House Armed Services Committee report drew attention to imbalances, bottlenecks, low productivity, foreign dependence, and manpower shortages in the defense industrial sector.[38] The General Accounting Office (GAO), long aware of these problems, followed suit with a series of reports documenting the weakness of "industrial preparedness" in the event of a major conflict and concluding that "the industrial base is not capable of surging production rates to meet short-term emergency situations."[39] In 1986, a Defense Science Board panel expressed alarm about the consequences of heavy dependence on the Japanese (and others) for electronic components used in military systems.[40] The Board of Army Science and Technology is known to be concerned that the "brains" of many so-called smart weapons (e.g., the small Navy missile known as the Sparrow III) are, for the most part, manufactured abroad.

Such reports typically acknowledge that if foreign components are prohibited, costs would rise and performance would plummet, at least initially. Hence the solution has to lie in upgrading the U.S. industrial base. High-ranking Pentagon officials, however, are often unfamiliar with industrial problems. Nor do they have much influence on macroeconomic decisions affecting the overall performance of U.S. industries.[41] In Japan, by contrast, the relationship between defense spending and overall economic and industrial goals receives close attention. A key defense procurement job—that of Director General of the Equipment Bureau of the Japan Defense Agency—has invariably been held by a MITI official. A similar arrangement between the Pentagon and the Commerce Department is inconceivable.

When the issue is Japanese investment in U.S. industry, the "national security" mind-set sometimes excludes other American goals, generating mixed signals from Washington. Thus, a Japanese equity investment in a high-technology American firm may be welcomed for economic reasons, but grounded for reasons of national security if the firm in question has even a small defense contract entailing classified work. For similar reasons, a friendly takeover may be wholly or partially blocked if the U.S. target company is one of the few remaining suppliers of a particular product for the defense industry. Once cognizant Pentagon officials have had a chance to review the data, these contradictions can usually be resolved, but not without some initial indignation in Japanese business circles and the press.

National-security goals also bear heavily on America's research and development. Roughly half of America's R&D is funded by the U.S. Government, and of that amount fully half to two-thirds is defense-related. To be sure, a certain proportion of defense-related research—notably in aerospace and electronics—has commercial implications. In 1983, for example, the Defense Advanced Research Projects Agency (DARPA) launched the Strategic Computing Program, with projected expenditures of $600 million over five years. The program encompasses such commercially relevant fields as high-performance device technology, large-scale integrated circuits, computer architecture, and artificial intelligence applications. The Very High-Speed Integrated Circuit (VHSIC) Program also received large-scale funding.

The U.S. Government itself serves as a voracious customer, permitting the early introduction of economies of scale. In the 1960s, fully half of all semiconductors produced in the United States were purchased by NASA and the Pentagon. Nowadays, the Defense Department consumes significantly less (an estimated 7 percent or so in electronics), but leading-edge technology development still tends to be funded under the military budget. Meanwhile, in response to budget-cutting pressures of the mid-1980s, the Reagan Administration's requests for funds for nonmilitary research have been trimmed or held constant.

Whether defense-related research still benefits overall American competitiveness is debatable. Special design requirements, security regulations, and other aspects of military research seem to hinder rapid and efficient commercial application. The Strategic Defense Initiative (SDI), for example, has boosted R&D substantially, but some fear that excessive secrecy will stanch any significant spillover to the commercial sector.

Indeed, a question worth pursuing is why does the United States not seem to take sufficient commercial advantage of the billions of dollars spent on R&D in the name of national defense. In 1983, a seminal conference of business, government, and academic leaders called for policies to transfer technological breakthroughs achieved through military R&D programs to the commercial sector. A common theme of the conference papers was that military R&D expenditures "can encourage industrial development and should be considered an investment in America's economic security.[42] To date, this important message has not been picked up in Washington—even though it bears directly on the issue of U.S. competitiveness. A vast gap remains between industrial programs undertaken in the name of national security and policies justified in the name of economic vitality.

All things considered, then, who is rich and who is poor? In terms of economic realities, the answer seems to be that each country, relative to the other, is "richer" in some ways and "poorer" in others. Compared to the rest of the world, the United States is still rich and Japan has become so, but the gap between them has narrowed abruptly and unevenly. The key difference between them lies not so much in aggregate economic achievement, but in their lingering self-images and values.

If both Japan and America are partly "rich" and partly "poor," then reality is more complex than that suggested by the typical "fairness" debate. History has left different footprints on the two economies; it is foolish to waste time arguing over who is richer and who is more fair. It would be more sensible for the two countries to pool their resources—huge markets, flourishing R&D, complementary skills, and sheer energy—to make the common pie bigger.

To do so, each country must adjust certain time-honored attitudes and institutions that have become outdated and even counterproductive in the context of new economic realities. Both must adjust *politically* to a new—and mixed—economic self-image. Japan needs to modify its small-nation mentality, poverty-driven values and preoccupation with exports. America, no longer "number one" across the board, must modify its rich-country habits and learn to pay its bills. The challenge for leaders in both countries is to mobilize pragmatism, ingenuity, energy, and good humor in support of these tasks.

Three

Trends in the Japanese Economy

While U.S. and Japanese trade negotiators stall, blast, counter-attack, and compromise, changes which greatly overshadow trade are slowly unrolling in the world economy. These changes, in turn, are spurring far-reaching adjustments within each country's *domestic* economic system.

Japan's industrial profile is now undergoing its most significant transformation since World War II. The push for change is not concern for the alliance or pressure from other governments as much as the need to remain competitive in the wake of an external "shock": the massive yen/dollar realignment of 1985–86.

In September 1985, the so-called Group of Five formally agreed that "exchange rates should better reflect fundamental economic conditions than has been the case," and noted that for that purpose "some orderly appreciation of the main non-dollar currencies against the dollar is desirable."[1] Exchange markets took the cue. By the following spring, the yen had risen vis-à-vis the dollar by 35–40 percent—the first rise of such magnitude in nearly ten years. Whereas a dollar brought approximately 240 yen in early 1985, it could bring only 140–150 yen by 1987.

In Japan, the most immediate consequences of the rise of the yen, or *endaka*, were signs of a lengthy recession. By the spring of 1986, Japan's GNP had dropped half a percentage point—the first quarterly decline in eleven years—reflecting a fall in first-quarter exports of nearly 5 percent. Meanwhile, unemployment had climbed to a record 1.7 million, almost 3 percent of the work force—the highest percentage since the mid-1950s. As Japan appeared to lose ground to lower-cost producing countries, Japanese newspapers spoke of a significant "hollowing out" of the industrial base.

Policy Adjustment

Abrupt as it seemed at the time, the yen "shock" merely accelerated what was already a substantial rethinking of Japanese policy.

Until quite recently, the Japanese Government had assumed that a pattern of economic development driven by the excess of savings over domestic investment was good not only for Japan but also for the world. Annual White Papers issued by MITI and Japan's EPA, for example, placed Japan's capital exports in a positive and progressive historical context, comparing them to those of the United Kingdom and the United States in earlier times. Addressing a conference in Washington, D.C. in 1984, an EPA official noted that Japan, a debtor country until 1964, had become a "mature debtor" and then an "immature creditor," with a rough balance between rising household savings and a declining rate of corporate investment.[2]

A number of American economists share the view that the excess of Japanese savings over domestic investment is good for the world. Martin Feldstein, former chairman of the Council of Economic Advisers, has predicted that the excess of Japanese savings over domestic investment will continue, generating an ongoing capital outflow and thus a trade surplus for many years. He wrote in 1985, "In a world in which capital is scarce, we should learn to regard this as an advantage rather than a problem."[3] Manuel Johnson of the Federal Reserve Board has suggested that instead of pressuring Japan to save less, the global community should devise constructive schemes to make better use of Japanese capital.[4]

By the mid-1980s, Japanese leaders recognized that the rest of the world did not necessarily view Japanese savings in the same light. They realized that the structure of the Japanese economy was not fully in step with the goal of "internationalization," and that persistent trade surpluses and inadequate investment opportunities at home were an essential part of the problem. The government's policy of encouraging the emergence of world-class export-oriented industries while tolerating highly inefficient sectors had created imbalances in Japan's domestic economic structure.

These residual imbalances add up to a vast array of regulatory thickets and hidden trade barriers that stifle or retard the development of new markets in the fields associated with them. These obstacles might not matter so much in a small, weak country, but they are obsolete in a large economy like Japan's. They generate political friction not only within Japan, but also with the outside world, to the point where Japan cannot afford *not* to restructure its economy. Japan's trading partners appear less and less tolerant of what they see as an export-driven savings machine. Within Japan, importers, retailers, and larger companies are pressing for a relatively more open market, since the gradual deregulation of the economy gives them freer rein to seek foreign suppliers and thus lower their costs in Japan. Consumers, too, are becoming more active champions of deregulation and market-opening measures because they associate such measures with lower prices.

Not all of the tools to shape a more balanced and open economy are in the government's hands, but some are—notably tax policy, regulatory standards, and measures affecting the price of land, housing, and food.

In 1985, Prime Minister Nakasone appointed a special commission to explore ways in which to restructure the Japanese economy. The commission's formal title was cumbersome but suggestive: Advisory Group on Economic Structural Adjustment for International Harmony. For short, it was known as the Maekawa Commission, after its chairman, Haruo Maekawa, a former governor of the Bank of Japan.

What was unusual about the Maekawa Commission was that it explicitly tackled a number of difficult subjects and near-taboos. These included sky-high land prices, tax measures discouraging the purchase of private homes and the sale of land, long working hours, the subsidized and protected agricultural market, and "the behavior of private companies which tend to pursue expanded market share at all costs."

The commission's report, submitted to the Prime Minister in April 1986, went far beyond traditional calls for more aid and market-opening "packages," and was in this sense a landmark. It called for a "historical transformation" of Japan's traditional policies on economic management and the nation's life-style. Citing the need for "international harmony," the report called on Japan to assume "responsibilities commensurate with its economic position," to reduce reliance on exports, and to improve the standard of living at home. The measures recommended for government action included expansion of domestic demand, economic restructuring, improved market access, currency stabilization and financial liberalization, promotion of economic and scientific cooperation, and improved fiscal and monetary policy.[5]

Implementation of the Maekawa Commission's recommendations, however, has been uneven at best, and nil in some cases. Party elders, whom Nakasone characteristically bypassed in appointing the commission, feel no particular commitment to it. Opposition from predictable sources, such as the agricultural lobby, remains fierce. Maekawa himself has criticized the government for moving too slowly to stimulate domestic demand.

In September 1986, the government announced an economic stimulation package consisting of public works, lower interest rates, relief for small businesses hard hit by the revaluation of the yen, and a variety of other measures calculated to pump perhaps 3.6 trillion yen (roughly $22 billion) into the Japanese economy. To the extent that the government had a conscious overall goal, it was to prevent or delay the painful sectoral unemployment that America had known in the early 1980s.

A larger package, announced just before the Venice economic summit in June 1987, included stimulative measures valued at some 6.2 trillion yen (roughly $42.6 billion). This time around, the government intended to cover a substantial portion of the spending itself rather than rely on the private sector and on local governments. The new package once again featured large-scale public works along with major cuts in personal income taxes.

Neither package, however, contained relief for the urban consumer. Food prices are, if anything, going up, and there seems to be no near-term solution to the twin problems of land prices and the shortage of affordable housing.

Also missing from both packages was comprehensive tax reform. Under a tax reform package proposed in 1986 and debated intensely in 1987, interest on postal savings accounts would have been subject to a 20 percent tax, while taxes on high-bracket income would have been lowered. As part of that package, however, the government had included a sales tax—a feature vigorously opposed by shopkeepers, retailers, and consumer groups. Eventually, opposition parties brought the Diet to a standstill, forcing the Liberal Democratic Party (LDP) to withdraw the proposal.

Following at least one of the Maekawa Commission's recommendations, the government undertook a review of working conditions. In December 1986, it announced that it would seek to reduce statutory working hours from 48 to 40 hours a week—the first revision of the Labor Standards Law since its passage in 1947. There has also been talk about urging workers to use their allotted vacation time, but this initiative faces obstacles ranging from crowded resorts to social pressure.

On the financial front, restructuring has been revolutionary. For years Japan's financial markets were heavily regulated and largely closed to foreign participation. In May 1984, the United States and Japan signed an agreement providing for substantial liberalization of the Japanese capital market and a corresponding internationalization of the yen. Japan agreed to deregulate interest rates, create new market instruments, and improve foreign access to its lucrative financial marketplace.

Although a timetable for the deregulation of interest rates has yet to be established, the U.S. Government has expressed satisfaction with the progress achieved to date. The General Accounting Office, for example, noted with satisfaction in 1986 that "equal or national treatment has been achieved for foreign banks in Japan." Even the Tokyo Stock Exchange opened up, admitting six foreign firms as members in early 1986 and several dozen more thereafter. The U.S. Federal Reserve, in a deliberately calibrated response, gave approval in December 1986 to two Japanese investment houses to join an elite group of authorized dealers in U.S. Government securities—a move that met with some criticism in Congress.

To be sure, the Japanese Government did not agree to financial liberalization merely for the sake of international harmony. In large measure, it took steps corresponding to the interests of Japanese banks. In the late 1970s, the banks had been reluctant to purchase mounting public-sector debts at artificially low rates, and had demanded more flexible market instruments. In 1979, the Ministry of Finance responded by permitting the establishment of a market in certificates of deposit with freely moving rates. Bankers' acceptances followed several years later. The government proceeded with further liberalization in part because it recognized the need for a more efficient capital allocation process, given the weakness of the venture capital market, and in part because it realized that without further liberalization, Japanese financial institutions might face restrictions abroad.

Despite these unmistakable signs of progress, and regardless of who is prime minister, it is unrealistic to expect a significantly more rapid pace of change. It is becoming more difficult to locate—let alone obtain a consensus on—effective policy "handles" to retool the engine of Japanese economic growth away from exports. Even if everyone in Japan shares the Maekawa Commission's vision of the future, structural macroeconomic adjustment is necessarily a long-term undertaking. Such obvious "solutions" as providing low-cost food and housing require years of effort, not to mention courage on the part of politicians and bureaucrats.

Moreover, as a result of substantial deregulation, the government has less power to implement agreed priorities than it did twenty years ago.

On the other hand, many observers believe that consumer attitudes in Japan are finally changing. Consumers of the mid-1980s know that they are the ones bearing the burden of subsidies and protectionism. They realize that the high cost of living is not entirely due to natural factors such as the shortage of land, but also to conscious policies protecting the small farmer. They are reminded almost daily that they are not the prime beneficiaries of their own savings. They are joined by other groups in the society who also stand to gain from market-opening measures and deregulation—e.g., supermarket entrepreneurs who wish to bypass the inefficient distribution system and users of protected products, such as manufacturers of rice crackers, who are forced to pay high prices for their ingredients. The strength of this domestic coalition is a matter of debate, but, barring new international "shocks," pressure for some kind of reform is likely to continue.

Industrial Restructuring

The initial effect of the yen/dollar realignment has been severe for many firms in Japan's private sector. While certain industries—notably banking, construction, real estate, and electric utilities—continue to flourish, many others appear to be foundering.

The setback has been measured in dozens of minute ways. One survey found that in the six months ending in September 1986, the profits of 774 publicly traded firms dropped 43 percent compared to the same six-month period a year earlier. Another study calculated that the stronger yen had increased Japanese labor costs by $25 million, translating into 900,000 lost jobs. Still another study indicated that of the sixteen industries that had made a profit when the yen/dollar rate was 244:1, only two—computers and automobiles—would be profitable with the rate at 100:1.

The first line of defense has been corporate cost-cutting and even layoffs. While most companies will not go so far as to release workers presumed to be employed for life, they may well turn away from specialized, small-scale "Mom and Pop" suppliers. A survey conducted among 399 firms found that almost three-quarters of the companies had already taken steps in this direction or were thinking of doing so.[6] Larger firms are not likely to undergo the "hollowing out" of some of their American counterparts, but the landscape could be littered with the empty shells of smaller companies.

Anticipating both a higher level of manufactured imports and more investment in manufacturing overseas, MITI ran a series of trial calculations in 1986 to gauge how these trends might affect employment by the year 2000. It estimated that a 100 percent increase in manufactured imports would eliminate 550,000 jobs in the intermediate-goods sector and 500,000 jobs in the finished-products sector, and that a nominal growth rate of 12 percent in overseas direct investment would eliminate another 560,000 jobs.[7]

Still, the manufacturing sector would be far from moribund. For if Japan's streamlined companies incorporate low-cost imported components into their products—as they seem to have every intention of doing—they will remain competitive, possibly becoming more so. Moreover, according to MITI's projections, many of the lost jobs in the manufacturing sector are likely to be replaced in the information and services sector as Japan advances toward the "information society."

In the short term, however, many small and medium-sized firms are finding industrial restructuring painful and temporarily destabilizing. While they account for as much as one-fifth of Japan's exports, they lack the resources of their giant compatriots to help them through the adjustment period. As in America, however, small business wields disproportionate political clout, as indicated by the government's special relief package of 1986. Along with farmers and the huge construction industry, small and medium-sized enterprises account for much of the protectionism and resistance to restructuring that frequently thwart market-opening measures.

Should imports rise too rapidly or restructuring proceed too quickly, workers in these smaller enterprises could spearhead collective resentment against foreign pressure. Unemployed students could join their ranks. Japanese companies already seem to be cutting back on the hiring of new engineering graduates, a trend which could prove politically troublesome all by itself.

A rising tide of imports could also fuel resentment against South Korea, already seen as Japan's most competitive rival in many key areas. Some Japanese industrialists complain openly of the "boomerang effect": Japanese manufacturing technology transferred abroad, especially to South Korea, comes back to "bite" Japan in the form of low-cost exports of finished products. This trend may be impossible to check, inasmuch as

South Koreans clearly have no wish to remain mere subcontractors to the Japanese.

On the other hand, if Japan should somehow block the expected surge of imports from Asia, the result could be new political tensions with countries in the region. Already disgruntled by what they perceive as Japan's endemic resistance to imports, Asian exporters are unlikely to be bought off with foreign aid or revived expressions of pan-Asian solidarity. Political tensions within many Asian countries could rise as well, for these countries, like Japan, have relied in part on a growing export market for their postwar prosperity.

There are other reasons why Americans should think twice before urging the immediate and drastic restructuring of the Japanese economy. Currently, Japanese savings and investment finance roughly one-third of the U.S. budget deficit. A sudden drop in the level of Japanese savings would reduce Japanese net foreign investment, thus raising the level of interest rates abroad. Interest rates in the United States would rise quite sharply, exacerbating the debt problem and cramping the entire economy.

A second reason is that Washington will find it even more difficult to achieve its trade and financial objectives when Japan is in an economic slump. When the United States endured a crunching economic transition in the late 1970s and early 1980s, political attitudes stiffened and compromise became more difficult. When both economies are growing, economic conflicts are easier to resolve.

Looking at the last fifteen years of U.S.-Japan trade, economist Vincent Reinhart found that whenever Japan's real GNP grew faster than America's, U.S. exports to Japan increased at about the same rate as U.S. imports from Japan, and that when Japan's growth rate slowed in the late 1970s, the export-import balance fell wildly askew. He estimates that while the strong dollar accounted for perhaps a third of the soaring bilateral trade deficit of the 1980s, the slowdown in Japan's real growth accounted for as much as 40 percent.[8] The point is simply that Japan's economic slowdown, while perhaps gratifying to the "bashers," is not necessarily good news for America.

On the international front, Japan's industrial restructuring appears to have accelerated an earlier drive by Japanese companies to expand overseas investments and joint ventures. In the fiscal year ending March 31, 1987, direct investment overseas surged 83 percent to over $22 billion, up from roughly $6.5 billion in 1985. Almost half of this investment flowed to

the United States. Japan has become America's third largest foreign investor—after Britain and the Netherlands—and its largest foreign direct
investor. Japanese companies reportedly have close to 2,000 subsidiaries
in the United States—far more than in any other country.

Among the factors favoring partnerships between U.S. and Japanese
firms are: (1) U.S. antitrust restrictions—real or perceived—which sometimes make it easier for U.S. firms to team up with a foreign counterpart
than with an American competitor; (2) the desire on the part of Japanese
companies to establish a foothold in the huge U.S. domestic market; and
(3) the frequently complementary nature of the technology which U.S.
and Japanese firms can offer each other. While no one would agree on a
precise definition, America's national strength is said to lie in *product* innovation, while Japan's centers on *process* innovation. Those who have
surveyed the relevant technologies usually list incremental product improvements, rapid commercialization, process technology, and quality
control as typical Japanese advantages, and basic research, inventions
and new product breakthroughs, systems integration, customization,
and software as typical American advantages.

In any event, Americans are now welcoming—indeed, competing for—
the hefty Japanese investments flowing to the United States. Coalitions
between American and Japanese firms are forming almost daily. In semiconductor technology alone, close to one hundred corporate linkages
have reportedly been forged.

Some American companies in declining health have taken the attitude
"if you can't beat 'em, join 'em"—and let themselves be bought. National
Steel, America's sixth largest steel company, for example, is partly owned
by Nippon Steel and has a Japanese president. In the mid-1980s, Japanese
corporate acquisitions in the United States were proceeding at the rate of
more than twenty a year.

To date, however, Japanese investment in the United States has been
heavily skewed toward bonds, real estate (up from $385 million in 1984 to
perhaps $5 billion in 1986), and other nonmanufacturing assets.[9] Invest-
ment in manufacturing is still fairly small compared to the size of the two
economies. As of 1985, according to one count, perhaps 100,000 Americans were employed by some 440 Japanese-owned or Japanese-affiliated
manufacturing facilities.[10] Given the stronger yen and the ongoing threat
of protectionism in the United States, however, a new surge of Japanese
investment into the establishment or expansion of subsidiaries can be expected.

Thus far, Japanese investment has not met with the same degree of fear and underlying lack of rapport that met the influx of Arab petrodollars in the 1970s. Some Americans in business and government circles, however, are beginning to feel the same sense of threat that Europeans felt when U.S technology and investment appeared to be dominating Western Europe a quarter of a century ago. In 1986, Fujitsu's proposed acquisition of Fairchild's semiconductor division brought these concerns into the open. Many factors were responsible for the failed outcome, including a largely unrelated dispute over supercomputers, second thoughts on the Japanese side, and the publication of a report expressing alarm over the Defense Department's high degree of dependence on Japanese semiconductors. Some Americans viewed the episode as further evidence of their claim that Japanese companies are pursuing a predatory strategy of deliberately weakening American rivals and then buying them up. For their part, many Japanese felt that Japan was discriminated against, because Fairchild was already in the hands of a French firm. (The firm in question, however, was not an electronics company, and was merely holding Fairchild.) The U.S. Government never reached a final decision on the case, leaving unsettled a host of policy issues that will undoubtedly recur.

At a minimum, some Americans would like to attach more "strings" to the incoming wave of Japanese investment to ensure that the ensuing benefits are not simply siphoned back to Japan. Others speak of either restricting Japanese investment or requiring an American partner for investments in certain key sectors. Washington is now closely monitoring Japanese investments in highly visible industries, such as semiconductors, computers, telecommunications, machine tools, and aircraft.

To succeed in this new policy environment, Japanese firms operating in the United States may have to increase their contribution to training and to research and development, and speed up the transfer of Japanese manufacturing know-how. Not to do so would feed criticism that Japanese companies are simply taking advantage of raw American labor to evade trade barriers.

As Japanese direct investment in the United States grows, it becomes increasingly difficult to decide just who is "American" and who is "Japanese." As one Japanese official observed, "the lines of competition are being redrawn by new multinational groupings of industrial and commercial players."[11] This blurring of national lines has interesting policy implications. For instance, Congress has directed U.S. Government laboratories to give priority to "American" firms in releasing technology developed with federal funding. But nowadays the question is: Just what is an "American" firm?

Tokyo's problems with Washington could be exacerbated if Japanese investments are simply funneled to the Third World, without substantially benefiting either the recipient country or consumers in Japan. American firms often hold a much larger share of the market in Third World countries than they do in Japan, but they are facing substantial challenges from Japanese exports and the financing that facilitates them. Charges of "predatory" behavior associated with Japanese exports to developing countries could easily spill over into investment, especially if Japanese companies make use of their new overseas locations to launch further export drives.

Wherever they are, Japanese companies may need to cultivate a more genuinely multinational identity. Otherwise, stepped-up overseas investment could breed further resentment against what is widely perceived as a tendency among Japanese corporations and their employees "to carry the homogeneity and cohesiveness of Japanese society abroad, to form self-sufficient, exclusive communities."[12]

Skeptics say that Japanese companies investing abroad will never share their best technology with a noncorporate outsider, least of all a foreigner. This conclusion is too facile. Much depends on the nature of the technology and to whom it is to be transferred. A field study conducted in Thailand and Indonesia, for example, ranked Japanese firms ahead of U.S. firms in conducting extensive on-the-job, technology-specific training.[13] When it comes to sharing the "family jewels" with high-technology companies in the West, the Japanese tend to be more guarded. A prestigious U.S.-Japan study group implicitly criticized the one-way flow of knowledge to Japan when it called recently for "symmetrical access" in the domain of technology;[14] there is no doubt that Japan's lingering "catch-up" mentality does contribute to a kind of unconscious hoarding of know-how. Moreover, Japanese laboratories and research institutions do not have as much experience as their American counterparts in licensing technology abroad. Yet another consideration is the character of the intended partner; to the extent that an American company is perceived as a future competitor, its prospects of receiving relevant Japanese technology are naturally dimmer. In this respect, the Japanese are surely not unique. All companies—including the most competitive American ones—hold back their very best technology to some degree. There is nothing "unfair" about this; it is simply good business logic. In the corporate world, too, it seems, good fences make good neighbors.

Trends in Research and Development

The gradual restructuring of Japanese industry has affected not only employment and investment patterns, but also trends in research and development. Ultimately, the latter form of restructuring could affect the future of U.S.-Japan relations more profoundly than market-opening measures and other goals now sought by U.S. negotiators. For the only way a country can remain competitive in a world marked by rapid technological change is to continually design and produce new products—a dynamic process which requires ongoing and high-quality R&D.

Japan's total R&D spending in 1986 accounted for 2.8 percent of GNP, up from about 1.6 percent of GNP in the mid-1960s, and is growing at about 10 percent a year.[15] As a percentage of GNP, its R&D spending is higher than that of the United States and second only to that of West Germany. Despite the yen "shock," there are no signs of a slowdown. Indeed, Japan's Council on Science and Technology, which includes both government officials and private-sector experts, has called publicly for raising R&D expenditures to 3.5 percent of GNP by the 1990s.

Given Japan's priorities, it is not surprising that the private sector should fund some 80 percent of total R&D spending. Even during the peak years of MITI's influence in the early 1970s, the private sector accounted for three-quarters of total R&D expenditures. It is also not surprising that the purpose of Japan's R&D programs is overwhelmingly commercial, with only 5 percent or less devoted to defense goals.

A prominent example of the difference between U.S. and Japanese priorities was Japan's decision in 1986 to participate in the Strategic Defense Initiative. For domestic political reasons, government leaders—at least in public—felt compelled to duck searching questions about its military aspects and to emphasize its presumed commercial applications. This connection is not appreciated by American businessmen, who feel that Japan gives them enough to worry about as it is.

Along with the increase in spending has come a new emphasis on basic research. This trend confirms Japan's arrival as an advanced industrial country. Having exhausted the potential for merely applying the results of Western research, Japanese engineers have long since begun to improve upon it. Inventing new ideas is the logical next step. Many Japanese, stung by the label of "copycats," feel compelled to show that they, too, can win Nobel Prizes. (Actually, six have done so, four of them for achievement in science.) The share of Japanese prizewinners may be disproportionately small relative to the size of Japan's economy and research base, but breakthroughs leading to future Nobel Prizes have no doubt already been made.

The Japanese Government encourages the move toward basic research, but its resources are increasingly limited. Nevertheless, it still performs important functions. It attempts to distribute knowledge from abroad, and it promotes coordination among Japan's disparate and otherwise insular research establishments. Government funding for basic research concentrates on high-risk long-term projects that are deemed important to the future of the nation. Following the 1973 oil shock, for example, the government launched projects in areas such as energy conservation (the "Moonlight Project"), new energy sources (the "Sunlight Project"), and nuclear fusion. In 1981, the government-financed Research and Development Corporation of Japan established a new research system known as ERATO (Exploratory Research for Advanced Technology) to coordinate seven projects ranging from perfect crystals to "superbugs" (microorganisms that grow in extreme environments). More recently, the government has invited international participation in basic research, but institutional mechanisms must be established before this important initiative can bear fruit.

Contrary to the image of "Japan, Inc.," most if not all major Japanese companies no longer rely on government laboratories or universities for their basic research, and are increasingly reluctant to participate in MITI-funded projects. "We do it to keep MITI happy," said one corporate R&D director, "and to get a sense of what our competitors are up to, but we don't usually send our best people." While the big private companies still regard government sponsorship of high-risk projects as useful, they have largely grown out from under MITI, and their research funds often outpace those available to government agencies. Japan's largest companies spend a significantly larger portion of their sales revenues on R&D than the largest U.S. companies. Their leaders see R&D as a kind of lifeline to the future, to be funded regardless of this year's sales.[16] In the first half of the 1980s, corporate R&D spending doubled, with communications, electronics, automobiles, electrical machinery and appliances, chemicals and chemical textiles, pharmaceuticals, and steel leading the charge.

A somewhat negative reason for the emphasis on basic research may be Japan's concern that tapping into the intellectual capital of the United States—still the most scientifically creative country in the world—will no longer be so easy. Convinced that Japan is inhaling U.S. science and technology like a vacuum cleaner but offering little in return, some Americans speak recklessly of "cutting off Japan." Many Japanese may not know that it is almost impossible, legally and otherwise, for Americans to carry out this threat. They believe that Japan has to guard against the day when knowledge from the rest of the world is not as freely available as it is now. They favor as much self-sufficiency as possible, as soon as possible.

Japan's apparent drive toward total self-sufficiency in a number of leading-edge, high-technology sectors, especially the space program, next-generation military aircraft, and supercomputers, has elicited much criticism. The problem here is that Japan is behaving not like a poor relation, but like a rich country with no concern for the outside world. In effect, Tokyo is declaring that Japan has the right to spend its money on whatever it wants. Moreover, the drive toward self-sufficiency in crucial next-generation programs seems to be taking the form of excluding—or at least severely restricting—foreign participation in key sectors. This trend fuels charges that once again Japan is being "unfair" in areas where the United States is demonstrably competitive.

For Americans to say that such "go-it-alone" behavior is wasteful and unfriendly sounds patronizing to some Japanese. Why shouldn't Japan spend its money to become more self-reliant like other industrial nations? One answer to this quite legitimate question is that Japan is arriving on the R&D scene at a time when costs are high and markets are limited or even saturated. (Even the mighty Boeing company decided not to finance a new commercial passenger jet all by itself.) One might reasonably ask whether self-sufficiency in vastly expensive fields of technology makes sense for any country, and whether Japan's wealth might not be put to better use in other areas—to improve its housing, for example, or to accelerate the implementation of its defense plan.

In public, at least, the goals of basic research in Japan are typically described in terms of peaceful human values, not in terms of knowledge for its own sake or, heaven forbid, commercial gain. One representative of the Industrial Bank of Japan, for example, began a speech before the American Chamber of Commerce in Tokyo by defining high technology as "any new technology at the forefront in the pursuit of the three major values of our society: life, information, and energy."[17] Other goals often cited are "the desire for harmony between science and technology and society" and "the need for greater internationalization."

In 1985, Tokyo tentatively floated a proposal for a massive global research project on "human frontiers," aimed at a revolutionary breakthrough in scientific understanding of the human body. The project was subsequently withdrawn from international consideration, but Japan seems intent on pursuing it on its own, in cooperation with foreign scientists. Meanwhile, basic research related to pharmaceuticals, medical equipment, and biotechnology is receiving heavy emphasis, in part because of Japan's rapidly aging society. In general, research of a "life-enhancing" variety is especially popular in a society that remains skittish about military goals.

Another research theme is the "information society," which puts in a positive light the inevitable shrinking of Japan's manufacturing base. Armed with such buzzwords as "softnomics" and "informationalization," crystal-ball gazers in both the government and the private sector assert that the sheer momentum of global industrial development is already propelling Japan away from standard manufacturing toward high-technology, high-quality, information-intensive industry and services—and that the pace of this transition is accelerating. Indeed, the percentage of the total labor force employed in information-related industries rose from roughly 18 percent in 1960 to 30 percent in 1975. By the early 1990s, workers in the information and service industries are expected to outnumber those engaged in manufacturing.

Although some Japanese deplore the fate of "computer children," prematurely immersed in mechanical reasoning and swept up in a language-limited, communicating-by-computer craze, the majority hail the new "age of the intellect" and appear optimistic that the shift from manufacturing to information-intensive life patterns will generate both creative jobs and adequate leisure.[18]

Last but not least, futuristic research—in its more gimmicky form—tends to be popular with the general public because it introduces a tangible new reason to be proud of being Japanese. EXPO '85, held at Tsukuba ("Science City"), capitalized on this widespread public interest. Western firms, loathe to invest in a pavilion and inexperienced at popularizing their technology, largely passed up the chance to participate. Japanese companies, however, seized the moment and erected Disneyland-type exhibits featuring talking robots and enormous television screens. Japanese visitors came away eager to believe that technological leadership had passed into their hands at last.

Increased R&D spending and the emphasis on basic research have led to a surge in Japan's technology exports. Between 1950 and 1980, Japan entered into tens of thousands of technology licensing agreements at relatively modest cost, buying most of the relevant industrial and manufacturing knowledge in the world and selling relatively little. More recently, Japan's technology trade has become less one-sided.

In the decade 1971–81, Japan's technology exports rose from $60 million to $537 million, and the ratio of technology exports to technology imports increased from 20 percent to 67 percent. By 1983, new contracts for technology exports and imports appeared to be roughly in balance, at about $1 billion each way.[19] Sales to developing countries or to Japanese subsidiaries in those countries account for much of the growth in technology exports, with the bulk of licensing revenue coming from construction engineering, steelmaking, and other heavy industries. By the beginning of the 1980s, however, the United States was absorbing the largest share of Japan's technology exports. U.S.-Japan technology trade is still roughly 3:1 in favor of the United States, but new contracts in areas such as automobiles and electronics suggest that such trade will become more balanced in the future. For a country struggling to overcome its "copycat" image, this is no small achievement.

In sum, Japanese R&D is branching upward and sideways at a rapid pace while America's nonmilitary R&D remains sluggish. Unless Americans overcome their lingering complacency, pay more attention to getting into the marketplace the fruits of the technology that they pay for, and/or team up more closely with the Japanese, they may find themselves on the sidelines of future global competition.

While trends in Japanese technology will help to define the future, certain other adjustments may be less progressive. For instance, one can make the case that whereas the 1973 oil shock pushed Japan toward the future by forcing it to streamline and shed energy-intensive manufacturing, the 1985–86 yen shock has temporarily pushed the Japanese Government backward, forcing it to prolong its protection of the least efficient sectors of the economy.

Paradoxically, American pressure for greater liberalization, at least in the short run, counters the trend toward deregulation and the corresponding decline in the power of Japan's bureaucracy. This is because MITI and other government agencies are responsible for responding to U.S. Government requests, some of which add up to more rather than less intervention in the market. To settle a dispute with the United States, for example, internationally oriented officials from MITI, the Foreign Ministry and, to some extent, the Finance Ministry must band together to do battle against other ministries and their clients, whose concerns are more domestically oriented. Sometimes the goal is market liberalization;

at other times MITI's intervention aims at export restraints, targeted import levels, or some other outcome negotiated in advance by the two governments. While this reassertion of Japan's bureaucracy in economic decision making is often helpful to American interests in the short term, it may work against the long-run goal of privatizing and deregulating the Japanese economy.

Instead of politicizing trade disputes and inviting government-imposed solutions, it would be far better for the United States to identify groups within Japan that favor liberalization and work quietly with them as they seek to promote change from within. The success of a coalition strategy rests not only on shared interests, but also on mutual trust and close communication between Japanese and Americans on a person-to-person level.

Four

Patterns of Behavior

Differences in patterns of social behavior and styles of communication are as relevant to U.S.-Japan relations as transactions that can be more easily measured. While they do not cause tensions, they frequently exacerbate them. Americans and Japanese must come to grips with them if they are to communicate better than they have up to now.

To many Americans, the seemingly closed and slow-moving nature of Japanese society poses frustrating barriers, delays, and riddles. In a country known for its high standard of education and middle-class standard of living, where imported styles and ideas have been in circulation for decades, why do so many Japanese still seem uncomfortable with foreigners? Why is the whole decision-making process so time-consuming, murky, and apparently resistant to change? Why do even small market-opening measures seem to require outside pressure? Why does it take so long to establish a new business or win new customers? In these circumstances, how can Japanese society ever emerge from its opaque labyrinth of groups and obligations into the light and transparency of a "level playing field"? Common to all of these questions is group behavior, both real and perceived.

In the private sector, group behavior takes the form of well-defined corporate clusters or networks (*keiretsu*). Competition among them can be fierce, but it is hard for a foreigner to break in. The pattern carries over into overseas investment as well, for Japanese companies locating abroad often maintain their preference for Japanese suppliers, freezing out local firms. With the recent worsening of Japan's economic climate, relations within corporate *keiretsu* have reportedly become even more intense as suppliers and subsidiaries turn to their corporate "parents" for support. Japan's multilayered and arcane distribution system may also be becoming even more difficult to penetrate.[1]

Many Americans also complain that decisions in Japan are made in small groups from which non-Japanese are excluded. They find Japanese bureaucrats and businessmen "secretive," confiding nothing to foreigners but everything to each other. "There are no secrets in Japan" is a common expression, meaning no secrets among the Japanese.

Although the Japanese Government publishes a kind of official gazette, Japan has nothing that corresponds to the well-developed body of U.S. administrative law requiring open rule-making proceedings, prior publication of draft regulations in the Federal Register, and formal requests for comments. Americans seeking to open up new markets often find their path blocked by bureaucrats who suddenly dust off obscure health and safety regulations—or invent new ones. In response to their complaints, the Japanese Government recently allowed foreign companies to participate in selected advisory committees and other groups setting regulatory standards, but thus far only a handful of industries have been affected.

The same Americans who complain about closed-group behavior, secrecy in decision making, and obscure regulations note that Japanese interest groups—backed by key groups or "tribes" of politicians (*zoku*) who, in addition to their factional identity, have become closely identified with a specific issue, a particular ministry, or a given policy—hire expensive lobbyists in Washington who enjoy easy access to Congress and the White House. Against such "unfair" competition, small wonder they call on Washington to apply massive pressure.

It is easy to jump to the conclusion that obstacles and obfuscations are designed specifically to keep out the foreigner. In some instances regulatory roadblocks may indeed be manipulated to the disadvantage of the foreigner; in most others they also thwart new businesses and suppliers in Japan. Japanese who seek to break down closed-group patterns from within often quietly invite American pressure because it is the only way they themselves can overcome established barriers. Outside pressure not only brings short-term results, but also serves to bring an issue into the open. The process is well understood by those on both sides who engage in it. Unfortunately, this shadow play reinforces the widespread belief among Americans that Japanese society as a whole is secretive and reactive, and that without massive outside pressure nothing will change.

Even in private life, where "fairness" is not an issue, Japanese group behavior and its overt and stylized conformity makes some Americans uncomfortable. An American who went skiing with Japanese friends found that each time they got to the top of the ski-lift, they huddled in a group to choose the route that everyone would follow. An American engineer working for a Japanese company found that on a company trip his colleagues literally never left him alone and never expected him to make a decision by himself.[2]

Because Japanese seem to be less individualistic on the surface, they strike Americans as being less "human." Japan's Honorary Consul General in Denver, an American of Japanese descent, was quoted as saying, "I cannot overemphasize this point: American society is most receptive to individualists. And to Americans today the Japanese are a race of faceless machines."[3]

Clearly, Japan's group behavior and group mentality predate the "fairness" debate and go beyond taking advantage of economic competitors.

Origins of Japan's Group Mentality

Clans or groups of one kind or another are common to all human societies. But the hold of the group—especially the small, immediate in-group and its parent institution—seems to be exceptionally strong in Japan. As Japanese sociologist Chie Nakane and others have noted, small groups determined largely by school and college affiliations, year of graduation, place of employment, and date of entry into the hiring institution constitute the bedrock of Japanese society.[4] Corresponding suspicion is directed at nonmembers of the group, be they Japanese or foreign. In the words of an old Japanese saying, a newcomer without proper introduction is a "horse bone whose origin nobody knows"—that is, not fully accepted as a fellow human being.

The prevalence of group behavior in Japan is linked to a long tradition of group responsibility. For centuries, Japanese society was organized into groups consisting of five persons or households. The group was held responsible for the actions of individual members, such as the nonrepayment of a loan. The chief of each group was directly responsible to a higher authority. During the World War II, the Japanese Government revived the system, organizing groups of neighbors (*tonari-gumi*) to carry out activities ranging from distributing information to putting out fires. These groups were infiltrated by the secret police.

Scholars and experts have offered a wide array of explanatory concepts linking Japan's group mentality to other aspects of Japanese society and culture. One such concept attributes the group mentality to the cooperative effort required to maintain the complex irrigation and drainage system of paddy field agriculture. Another cites the central role of the clan in primitive times in caring for the welfare of the spirits of the dead. A third suggests that because Japanese value power and influence more than wealth, success is measured by group allegiance, and that rife factionalism is to be expected.[5] A fourth is based on Ruth Benedict's distinction (now belittled by many scholars) between Japan's culture of shame (*haji*), which relies on external sanctions, and Judeo-Christian cultures of guilt.[6] The somewhat related notion of "situational ethics" argues that the Japanese define "right" behavior in terms of the particular situation at hand.[7]

Crowding is also said to contribute to Japan's group mentality. Unlike America, Japan has no wide open spaces where a man can feel truly alone. According to this theory, if 121 million Americans were packed into a territory the size of Montana, they, too, would have a group orientation.

Finally, it is said, the relative homogeneity of Japanese society tolerates little diversity; people are rejected if they are different. The common saying in Japan, "A nail that sticks up will be hammered down," stands in striking contrast to the American saying, "The wheel that squeaks the loudest is the one that gets the grease."[8] In a heterogeneous society like America, people can afford to be individualistic without being labeled misfits.

Takeo Doi and other psychiatrists offer an entirely different interpretation of Japan's group behavior. They attribute the need for ongoing group reassurance to certain child-rearing practices, such as late weaning and sleeping in the same bed with the mother, which seem to encourage passive dependence even while fostering security.[9]

Whatever its origin, group mentality is deeply rooted in Japanese society. Neither things nor people float freely in Japan; like Lafcadio Hearn's house at the turn of the century, they are bound up in webs of long-standing loyalty and obligation.[10] A group can begin to function only when it has become a community in a deeper social and emotional sense, and a new group forced to assume a function quickly turns into a community.[11]

Even young Japanese retain a group orientation. When asked what kind of personal qualities they would like to be known for, young Japanese typically downplay individual skill and ability in favor of group-related attributes.[12]

Gifted individuals are supposed to let the rewards of talent flow back through them anonymously for the benefit of their group, company, or family. Even speaking about oneself—let alone of one's achievements—is considered inappropriate, at least for a subordinate. Thus, a Japanese child who had spent some time in an American school was reprimanded for writing an essay in the first person.

Being "different" is far worse. Students who speak a foreign language fluently sometimes find it best not to let that fact be known.[13] Alternatively, as a defense mechanism, they sometimes band together, thereby reinforcing the impression that they cannot fit in. Individuals endowed with an unusually strong personality often feel compelled to drop out or rebel in eccentric and ostentatious ways. Others may be subtly excluded or even bullied. The late Professor Hiroshi Wagatsuma of Tsukuba University deplored this polarization between Japan's group-minded majority and the "outcasts":

> Once a Japanese becomes too non-group oriented to comply with the major cultural norms, he/she will often have to find a place outside Japanese society. . . . It would be tragic for the nation if such a minority were made to remain a group of misfits.[14]

The Tension of Mutual Watching

One feature of Japan's group behavior that often unsettles Americans is a high degree of mutual watching, which has been attributed to an intense concern with one's standing in the group, combined with a habit of waiting to see what others will do.[15]

One purpose of mutual watching is tactical or competitive. From the game of *go* comes the expression *okame hachi moku,* freely translated as "he who is watching can see eight moves ahead," or "the bystander has the advantage." The expression means something more than "Monday morning quarterback"; it emphasizes the importance of anticipating what others will do in a competitive situation.

Mutual watching also serves to maintain a certain code of ethical behavior, formerly enforced in the village but now transferred to the workplace, the urban neighborhood, or—in well-publicized cases—the nation as a whole. The contrasting fates of popular singer Misora Hibari and comedian "Beat" Takeshi illustrate this ethical dimension of mutual watching. Because of the misdoings of her brother, Hibari found herself under pressure to behave in a repentant, humble way. When she went to the opposite extreme, she was stigmatized and barred from a number of radio and television stations and singing contests—even though she herself had committed no crime. Her ordeal was the modern equivalent of *mura hachibu,* or expulsion from the village, a kind of social death. "Beat" Takeshi, on the other hand, assaulted the staff members of a notorious magazine for hounding his girlfriend, but later apologized for causing a disturbance. Although his original action had met with widespread approval, his apology was a gesture that the public expected.

Mutual watching adds extra tension to what would otherwise be routine meetings between groups of Americans and Japanese. The Japanese watch for clues indicating who is the most senior person on the other side of the table, and what his intentions are. They also watch each other, noting—not necessarily with approval—who adapts most easily to the foreigner's style. Americans encountering Japanese for the first time may find this behavior disconcerting.

The only refuge from the tension of group vigilance lies in evening visits to bars and restaurants, where a man can finally relax. And relax he does—to an extent that surprises, amuses, and occasionally dismays uninitiated American observers. Liquor offers a particularly convenient excuse to escape from group obligations, for what a man does or says "under the influence" is not held against him.

Social Distinctions

Besides mutual watching, another consequence of Japan's group mentality appears to be acute attention to rank and status within established groups. Within an organization, for instance, an individual's rank is normally more important than his name. The director of a government office is addressed simply as *kachō.* An official might introduce himself merely as the director-general of a bureau, without mentioning his name. This emphasis on titles serves to establish an individual's rank within the organization, hence reinforcing group identity.

Seniority is also measured in minute and seemingly rigid ways. An age difference of merely a year between two people will identify who is "senior" and who is "junior" for the rest of their lives. Yet relationships may be described in familial, almost sentimental terms, such as *senpai-kōhai* (born first, born later) or *oyabun-kobun* (parent-child or, depending on the circumstance, boss-henchman or patron-protégé).

Paradoxically, such fine-grained distinctions may be a consequence of Japan's highly egalitarian education, income distribution, and life-style.

The phenomenon of finely graded rankings leading to harsh competition at all levels is "a pervasive feature of Japanese society," writes one Japanese educator. "The smaller the gap between an individual and his rivals, the greater the sense of competition."[16]

Like the group mentality itself, this combination of acute competition and hierarchical rank and status inhibits easy mingling between Americans and Japanese. Americans, of course, also observe rank and status, but not to the same degree as the Japanese.

One might expect the group-oriented, rank-conscious Japanese to be extremely class-conscious as well. Yet they are not, at least not now. Pre-Meiji Japanese society was divided into classes, with samurai at the top and merchants at the bottom. The Meiji Restoration wiped out these formal distinctions, but created its own class of aristocrats. These in turn were abolished by the American Occupation. While Japan's great families still form a kind of hereditary class, the rest of Japan's class structure crumbled so easily that one wonders whether it was well-rooted in the first place. It is possible that the Japanese shun explicit class affiliations because their loyalties tend to lie overwhelmingly with their immediate group and its parent structure. Another explanation might be that those who are eligible to be called "upper class" are too modest to identify themselves as such; in the words of one Japanese commentator, "some very well-heeled individuals are hiding out in the middle class."[17] Or perhaps today's Japanese shy away from class distinctions because their intellectual traditions shun formalistic concepts and divisive ideologies.

Class barriers are not unknown even among relatively egalitarian Americans, but they are fairly watery and often change within one generation. In any case, where class is concerned, today's Japanese have more in common with Americans than with Europeans. Indeed, Japanese companies list class-consciousness among European workers as an obstacle to successful investment in Europe.[18] Still, the Japanese differ significantly from Americans in their emphasis on rank and seniority, and the difference often inhibits easy mingling between them.

Responsibility and Order: The Role of Government

One thing that the U.S.-Japan dialogue has revealed is that the two countries differ in their perceptions of the role of government. On the whole, the American prescription is more limited than the Japanese.

This was not always so. In colonial America, government intervention was fierce, not only in matters of thought and religion, but also in the economic domain. Regulations covered the price and quality of bread, meat, bricks, firewood, and leather. The authorities imposed import and export taxes, inspections, and embargoes.[19] Americans resisted or evaded many of these government regulations—as witnessed by the Stamp Act, the Boston Tea Party, and the Whisky Rebellion. It is a myth to suppose that a free market took root from the day the Pilgrims landed.

Only in the latter half of the eighteenth century were Americans successful in doing away with much of this intervention. The opening of the West and the arrival of new immigrants and new currents of political thought made America, in Oscar Handlin's words, "a society without order."[20] The legitimate function of government was to maintain the peace, not the social order.

In the 1980s, American right-wingers have campaigned for a certain uniform moral order extending from the schoolroom to the bedroom. Yet Americans as a whole have a high tolerance for disorder in society. And to the extent that they desire order, they typically do not look to the government to bring it about. In this respect, Americans may be unique. As long as an American pays taxes once a year, he or she can literally disappear. By the same token, the government is not perceived to be particularly necessary. A New England saying goes, "Calvin Coolidge took a nap every afternoon—and the country prospered."

The extent of government regulation elsewhere in the world is quite different. In Sweden, a person who moves is supposed to register with the authorities. In Argentina, the government requires parents to choose the name for a newborn baby from a certain list. In America, such requirements would stir up outraged opposition. When Americans complain, "There oughta be a law," they are usually not serious; in fact, that phrase is the title of a series of cartoons.

In Japan, the scope of regulation and the associated attitude of the bureaucracy is quite different. During the Tokugawa Shogunate (1600–1868), the government decreed who could or could not use certain kinds of hair ornaments, sleeves, sandal thongs, umbrellas, and even toys. The menu and the serving dishes used at weddings were similarly regulated. Although government regulation was subsequently reduced, the notion that the government is responsible for maintaining social order, as well as the signs and symbols thereof, is a powerful historical legacy.

Even today, Japanese tend to hold their government responsible for almost everything that goes wrong. For example, while it did not occur to

Americans to blame the government when bottles of poisoned pain-relief capsules appeared on drugstore shelves a few years ago, the Japanese might well have blamed their government had such an incident occurred in Japan.[21] Similarly, should a child be injured at a construction site in Japan, chances are that the public will criticize the government for not preventing the accident. Small wonder that Japanese bureaucrats are fearful of doing anything that might attract public criticism on health and safety grounds. In 1985, LDP leader Kiichi Miyazawa (now Finance Minister) spoke candidly of Japan's dilemma:

> There is a dichotomy between a public hue and cry to scale down the size and function of the government . . . and the national tradition of holding the government responsible for everything, such as injuries or damages caused by consumer products.[22]

Where health and safety are concerned, American negotiators regard Japan's regulatory procedures as "unfair" to U.S. exporters. They have offered proof that product standards are rarely drawn up on the basis of final performance, but are based instead on detailed manufacturing techniques established by Japanese producers. An American manufacturer using a different technique may be told that his product is not safe or reliable enough for the Japanese consumer. U.S. negotiators argue that the Japanese Government has no business telling companies how to manufacture their products as long as the products are safe and reliable. In their view, more extensive standards of excellence and consumer protection or desirable economic behavior lie beyond the purview of regulation. Using these arguments, they have whittled away numerous regulatory barriers to U.S. products, especially telecommunications equipment.

Deregulation is also delayed by fierce bureaucratic turf battles. Contrary to the notion that "there are no secrets in Japan," Japanese bureaucrats in rival ministries do not share information with each other. Sometimes delays are due to competing jurisdictions, such as when MITI battled the Ministry of Post and Telecommunications in the case of "value-added networks"; sometimes they arise from the lack of coordination between ministries handling different sectors, such as automobiles and plywood. Deliberations can drag on for weeks and months, if not years, because no one in consensus-minded Japan is supposed to lose a fight—at least not overtly.

Arbitrary and excessive regulation, the elite status of bureaucrats, the lack of strong individual leadership, lifetime employment in the service of a single ministry, associated vertical loyalties, relatively narrow training, and ferocious turf battles add up to a major trade barrier. Characteristically, Americans want Japan to "do something" about this problem, and do it quickly. But it is difficult to change entrenched attitudes and patterns of behavior quickly. The government has sown the seeds of change in the name of deregulation and administrative reform, but the crop will take a generation or two to reach fruition.

Individualism

Individualism has been a central value in American society since the time of the Puritans. In challenging the claims of religious hierarchy, the Puritans stressed the competence of the individual; the distinctive note of Puritan teaching was individual responsibility, not social obligation. Puritanism also legitimized business and commerce as fields of Christian endeavor and linked them to the ideal of individual exertion rather than team effort. Individualism was not confined to Puritan communities; all the colonists left Europe when the idea of individual liberty was predominant and when the very choice of self-exile was a supremely individual act. Moreover, individualism opened up avenues to status and power, because authority in this new society grew from individual experience and talent, rather than from a castle or a monastery.

All of these influences and more reinforce the vitality of this cherished American ideal. Individualism looms large in what Stanford University professor Harumi Befu calls the "idealized American self," which tends to downplay outside influences on individual decision makers.[23]

To Americans, such sacred expressions as "enlightened self-interest," "the pursuit of happiness," and "equal opportunity" are definitions of freedom—the hallmark of a mature democracy—precisely because they take the individual as their reference point. Where overt individualism is discouraged, as in Japan, Americans suspect that freedom must be lacking as well.

The Japanese vision of individuality as a balance of rights and duties, of innovation and social cohesion, of talent and the betterment of the nation appears to fall significantly short of this concept of freedom. The first report submitted by Japan's Council on Educational Reform, for example, insisted that greater respect for individuality is inseparable from self-discipline and responsibility: "Oneself and others are interwoven."[24] There is little appreciation in Japan for the emotional power of the American ideal of individual rights, especially when these rights run counter to social prejudice. Bitterly critical American reactions to Prime Minister Nakasone's disparaging comments about U.S. minorities in the fall of 1986 prompted some thoughtful Japanese to engage in soul-searching, but the public at large was perplexed. For the same reason, some Japanese find it hard to understand why Americans tend to get worked up about Japan's treatment of its own minorities—notably people of Korean ancestry, but also the Dowa (formerly known as the *burakumin,* a group that has suffered social discrimination for centuries) and the Utari (Ainu aborigines, living mainly in Hokkaido).

To the Japanese—especially older ones—whose imagination is profoundly shaped by group ideals and values, Western "individualism" has certain derogatory connotations.

Many Japanese businessmen, for instance, view America's much-touted individualism as a cause of America's economic problems. They are appalled to hear that American workers refuse to work overtime or to go beyond their narrowly defined assignment on the grounds that to do so interferes with one's personal life. In their view, excessive emphasis on the individual adds up to laziness and indiscipline. Americans might call such behavior self-indulgent, but never "individualistic."

Japanese also tend to see "individualism" as a source of social problems. The high divorce rate in America, for instance, is seen not as a sincere (if misguided) search for love, but as a sign that individualistic Westerners need less emotional warmth and security than the Japanese. Westerners are said to treat relationships with friends and family like contracts, which, once they no longer satisfy needs, can be broken.

Fundamentally, the Japanese associate "individualism" with personal gratification and the pursuit of pleasure at the expense of social obligation. Possibly because young children in Japan are treated with indulgence, freedom of the individual to do what he or she wants is seen as childish. When "individualism" is combined with the idea of freedom, it suggests anarchy.

Just as many Japanese associate "individualism" with materialism and the pursuit of pleasure in today's America, so many Americans believe that Japan's group mentality breeds people who are dull, conformist, devoted to their work, and more or less alike. Yet group behavior by no means negates Japanese individualism and creativity; instead, it provides certain outlets for their definition and expression.

Japanese individuality is perhaps best understood in the context of developing a tradition from within. Zen Buddhism did its best to destroy consciousness of individuality and identity or—more accurately, perhaps—to merge them with nothingness. But most Japanese did not go that far. Instead, they developed a concept of individual fulfillment through the mastery and subsequent enrichment of living forms. As expressed in art, the arrangement of food, sumo wrestling, or social relations, this is the ideal of "life as art," a sophisticated unfolding of potential within a discipline, a bud of talent on a tree of tradition.

Many Americans, however, are not attuned to Asian cultures in their more subtle forms, viewing them as "traditional" and therefore unchanging. They are quick to see imitation and slow to see sophisticated innovation from within. But as rueful American businessmen have discovered, Japan's absorption of Western technology and subsequent innovation is a far cry from mere "copying." Its success owes less to piracy and the violation of copyrights and patents than to the flowering of individual talent.

To release that talent, Japanese companies sometimes put together special teams of engineers to explore all phases of a new project, from design through production. In such a setting younger employees feel less inhibited about challenging established ideas. The results—whether in cars, steel, or electronics—are well known in the West. In short, it is a mistake to equate overt individualism with the realization of individual talent; in Japanese industry at least, the latter is most likely to occur within a group.

Yet the contrast between Japan's group mentality and American individualism must not be exaggerated. In fact, Americans at all levels of society are more group-minded than they may realize. David Riesman's *The Lonely Crowd* depicts Americans yearning for the security of a group. In his classic study, *An American Dilemma,* Gunnar Myrdal observed a pattern of individual leadership and mass passivity. Others say that the hold of religious groups throughout American history can be explained in part by the need for security among Americans who feel rootless and adrift as a result of the disintegration of traditional structures.

In a well-known experiment, an image is shown to a group of people who are then asked to describe it. All but one are told to falsify what they see. The one unsuspecting person initially clings to his or her opinion, but eventually gives in and agrees with the others. When this experiment is administered to groups of Americans and groups of Japanese under similar circumstances, the outcome depends very much on the nature of the group. In a casual or one-time setting, supposedly individualistic Americans give in much more readily to group pressure than supposedly group-minded Japanese. This finding suggests that a key difference between the two societies is not the presence or absence of groups as such, but rather that Americans form and adapt to informal or short-lived groups more readily than the Japanese.[25]

Thus, Americans who happen to be riding the same subway or bus—even in big cities—will sometimes cooperate quite unexpectedly. Passengers in an elevator or trainees in a one-day seminar, even though they never expect to see each other again, will often strike up casual conversations or share a joke. In America, there seems to be less of an "invisible screen" inhibiting the individual from mingling with strangers than there is in Japan. Although the evidence is fragmentary and anecdotal, Americans are more likely to come to the assistance of a stranger who is a victim of a crime than the Japanese, who may stand by passively. The Kitty Genovese case—in which more than twenty New Yorkers heard the cries of a young woman being murdered but stayed in their apartments and did nothing—is at first sight an appalling exception, but no one actually witnessed the crime. More to the point, even after two decades, Americans still speak about the incident with shame and horror. However one chooses to characterize the difference between the two societies, Americans do things for other people besides themselves.

The Group as the Nation and the Cult of Uniqueness

As a people, the Japanese have always been intensely conscious of who is foreign and who is Japanese. While the physical features of today's Japanese reflect early waves of immigration from other parts of Asia, the ethnic content of the population has remained more or less stable for some fifteen centuries. The habit of thinking of people primarily in terms of foreigners and Japanese dates back almost that far. As early as A.D. 815, a survey of families listed naturalized foreigners (mainly Chinese and Koreans) in a separate category.[26] Two long spans of almost total isolation in Japan's subsequent history reinforced this habit. The first such period, from the end of the ninth century to the end of the twentieth century, nurtured and brought to flower a rich and distinctive culture that continues to shape Japan's aesthetic ideals. The second, from the early seventeenth century to the mid-nineteenth century, sealed off Japan from the universalistic ideas then gaining force in the West.

Even today, outside of the major cities, consciousness of foreigners is still pervasive. An American wandering into a coffee shop in the provinces may find the waitress calling a friend to say that an "honorable foreigner" (*gaijin-san*) is in the shop. In Tokyo's relatively cosmopolitan Roppongi section, two Westerners who recently entered a bar were told politely that no foreigners are admitted on weekends, only on weekdays.[27] The controversial practice of fingerprinting foreign residents of Japan is a more extreme example of an age-old spirit.

Underlying this intense consciousness of foreigners is a widespread notion that Japanese are different from everyone else, and that what is "different" is innate. The latent assumption is that Japanese culture is so unique that it is beyond the comprehension of foreigners. Many foreigners who speak Japanese have found that the more fluent they become, the more older Japanese will retreat behind a veil of obscure phrases. *Gaijin* (literally "outside people," usually Westerners) who are able to master the nuances of Japanese behavior may even find themselves objects of suspicion. Foreign residents in Japan remember wistfully a young American wearing a tee-shirt imprinted with the words (in Japanese): "I'm a foreigner . . . but I'm a human being."[28]

True, Americans might not trust an outspoken, back-slapping Japanese either, but their reasons for doing so would be different. Americans do not feel particularly defensive or fearful when they discover that a foreigner has successfully penetrated American culture. Many middle-aged and older Japanese, however, will try to hide things from foreigners. When a foreigner stumbles upon a hidden truth, they will say, "You are discovering all our secrets."

This cult of uniqueness inspires seemingly endless fascination with the nature of the Japanese people (*Nihonjinron*). By one count, some seven hundred books on this subject appeared between 1946 and 1978; today, there might be a thousand. New theories about the supposed uniqueness of the Japanese brain, or nose, or tolerance of alcohol, or some other characteristic find an instant audience.[29] Higher scores for Japanese children on comparative IQ tests tend to be interpreted in racial rather than motivational or socioeconomic terms. Some older Japanese are even said to believe that such things as body temperature and the length of pregnancy are different for Japanese. A Japanese smoker, frustrated by the international trend toward no smoking in public places, even wrote an angry letter to his newspaper insisting that "Japan is different from other countries!"[30]

Some Japanese believe that group solidarity based on innate Japanese-ness is only common sense. Others refuse to admit there is a problem. Whatever form it takes, this cult of uniqueness has the effect of projecting onto the nation as a whole the clannish, closed-group attributes that Westerners tend to resent. If the biggest group of all—namely, Japan it-self—is closed to outsiders and impossible for foreigners to understand, what hope is there of penetrating smaller groups within it? Japanese who say that Americans don't try hard enough to adapt to Japanese conditions have yet to grasp the emotional depth of American frustration and dis-couragement—and to recognize the realities behind it.

The Japanese Government has acknowledged that these attitudes add up to significant nontariff barriers to foreign trade and investment, not to mention an insularity that is anachronistic in today's transnational world. It has charged the Ministry of Education with the task of revising the school curriculum to promote a more international perspective. Current plans call for an increase in the number of foreign teachers and foreign students. According to a Ministry of Justice report, the foreign student population has more than doubled during the decade ending in 1984. Prime Minister Nakasone has suggested a further increase in the number of foreign students, from the present level of about 14,000 to 100,000 by the year 2000. Meanwhile, many Japanese companies have instituted "in-ternationalization training" programs.

"Internationalization," however, faces mixed prospects. At present, Japanese children returning from abroad tend to face strong pressure to conform once they are back in Japanese schools. When a sixth-grader who had spent six years in America asked questions or expressed opinions in class, other students called him a show-off and jeeringly told him that he should return to America. Far from defending the child, the teacher told the boy's mother, "Your son has a big problem because he doesn't act like other Japanese."

"Internationalization" is also hampered by the relatively small number of foreigners in Japan. According to the same Ministry of Justice report cited above, the number of foreign residents in Japan rose by 12 percent in the decade ending in 1984, but the total still falls well below one percent of the population. The category registering the largest growth was enter-tainers, of whom 90 percent are Filipinos and South Koreans. Of the estimated 841,000 foreigners residing in Japan, only about 6 percent come from North America or Europe.

To be sure, generations are changing, and attitudes will change with them. Young people in Japan today have had more exposure to foreigners than their parents had. Their attitude toward foreigners seems to be somewhat more tolerant and relaxed, even disinterested. They appear to be more open-minded on the subject of marriage to foreigners, for example. Surveys have found that over half of the respondents in their thirties accept the idea, while only about a third of those in their forties approve.

Young Japanese currently studying abroad are also likely to make a difference. Some 300,000 are studying in the United States; about 50,000 are in West Germany; and another 50,000 or so are in the United Kingdom. They represent a small minority, but they are likely to assume positions of leadership when they return to Japan. Similarly, Japanese company executives returning from extensive service abroad are beginning to find themselves valued and promoted instead of subtly stigmatized. This trend could have highly favorable implications for future business relations between Americans and Japanese.

In the long run, Japanese society will become less group-oriented as less clannish generations grow to maturity. For the foreseeable future, however, patterns of behavior in Japan and America are unlikely to change quickly. Decision making will still be lengthy and group-oriented in Japan, and erratic and individualistic in America. Neither Japan's regulatory mind-set nor the social attitudes behind it will melt away quickly. Americans will still prefer disorder to social discipline. Both sides will have to acknowledge their differences without undue criticism, strive to build on the complementary strengths of the two traditions, and patiently cultivate long-term personal ties.

Five

Styles of Leadership and Communication

In addition to group behavior, differences in styles of leadership and communication tend to complicate the management of disputes and inhibit personal friendship between Americans and Japanese.

Japan's relatively passive and decentralized leadership, combined with its distaste for confrontation, results in a pattern of decision making that some Americans see as frustrating at best and "unfair" at worst. Many Japanese have corresponding difficulty coming to terms with the way Americans behave. For all their knowledge about Americans, they find it difficult to deal with them face to face.

Skeptics have argued that problems of communication are just a smoke screen. In an internal corporate memorandum describing the ups and downs of negotiating a business deal in Japan, a battle-scarred American executive confided: "Consensus, lack of understanding, lack of knowledge of English are more often than not excuses to buy time, to draw you out, to have you bid against yourself, etc., etc." It is true that institutional interest groups—including the Japanese Government—sometimes exploit varying and even contradictory images of Japanese culture to achieve their own ends. And many Japanese may well go along with culturally approved behavior—such as the search for harmony or loyalty to their group—because they derive tangible benefit from doing so, not because they actually conform to a (mythical) homogeneous society.[1]

Nevertheless, who people "actually" are may be less significant than who they *believe* they are and what they choose to express. The brief and highly superficial comparison of characteristically Japanese and American styles of leadership and communication presented in the following pages does not aim to promote "understanding" in the sense of uncritical acceptance of the social and cultural status quo in either country. It merely highlights certain culturally rooted differences that exacerbate current tensions in U.S.-Japan relations.

Styles of Leadership

Passive and Collective Decision Making.   To use a mischievous metaphor, the characteristic American response to a world crisis is to jump up on the table and make a speech, while the characteristic Japanese response is to crawl under the table and quietly build a consensus.

Events in the aftermath of the Soviet invasion of Afghanistan, the revolution in Iran, and the military crackdown in Poland confirm the profound difference between Washington's rapid-fire initiatives and reactions and Japan's slow and relatively passive style of decision making. White House staffers with a domestic political orientation swiftly entered the decision-making scene. They urged the President to show the American people—and, of course, the Kremlin—that the United States was not simply going to conduct business as usual. Since cutting off exports was something the President could do almost overnight, export restrictions quickly rose to the fore. Even in Washington, doubts were expressed that export controls would accomplish their intended purpose. Yet export controls, however unwise they might be, lent themselves nicely to America's predilection for instant response.[2]

To a greater or lesser degree, all the allies dragged their feet. In group discussions and in public, Tokyo remained passive, letting Europeans take the lead in arguing with Washington. Hoping for more active and visible support, many Americans grumbled that the Japanese were not behaving like allies. Many Japanese, on the other hand, complained privately that the United States was imposing its will—once again—on Tokyo to serve its superpower interests. Some were even convinced that the United States was secretly pursuing commercial goals, halting the exports of its allies only to clear the way for its own later on. In the end, Japan's support for American export sanctions was more consistent than that of any other ally with major business interests at stake—an outcome that was noted and appreciated by the White House but lost on the public at large.

In meeting the need to "do something" quickly, the President of the United States can draw on a large staff, a strong national and local party organization, and far-reaching powers of appointment—none of which is available to the same degree to the Japanese Prime Minister. Still, the preference for action seems built into American culture. The itch to "get things moving" (in John F. Kennedy's oft-used expression) springs directly from America's characteristic sense of newness and universal mission. Americans seem to have so much proselytizing energy, so much of a desire to change the world, that they regard resistance to their efforts abroad as a denial of talent and virtue, not merely of profits. For people with such a mission, stagnation in others is viewed as "an anti-historical force, an obstacle to the realization of the American character in its profoundest dimension."[3]

Japan, of course, is hardly "stagnant." On occasion, Japanese decision makers have shown themselves capable of taking action quickly. In 1973, for example, a statement sympathetic to the Palestinian cause appeared with almost indecent haste after the imposition of the OPEC oil embargo. The decision to share with the United States intelligence related to the shooting down of the Korean aircraft in 1983 crystallized almost overnight. On the whole, however, caution and passivity vis-à-vis other countries, a profound mistrust of one-man leadership, and a corresponding emphasis on consensus-building at home seem to be the norm.

The Japanese style of decision making is best understood not as a conspiracy against foreigners, but as a long-standing historical legacy. As early as the seventh century, scholar-statesman Prince Shotoku urged his countrymen to avoid "wanton opposition." Echoing the Confucian respect for harmony, he stressed that decisions on important matters should always be discussed with many people.[4] The profound changes ushered in by the Meiji Restoration of 1868 were guided not by a single charismatic leader, but by a group of clan leaders from Satsuma and Choshu, and later by a group of elder statesmen known as *genrō*.

Collective leadership was similarly responsible for the rise of Japanese militarism in the 1930s; one looks in vain for a Japanese equivalent of Lenin, Mussolini, or Hitler. At a time when the rest of the world thought that Japan was single-mindedly bent on world conquest, groups within Japan were groping in confusion for direction.[5]

Today, when the world is changing so quickly, Japan's passive and collective leadership style often irritates even the most sophisticated Westerners. The former president of a major multilateral lending institution recalled that in more than two hundred top-level meetings he had chaired, the Japanese delegates "never once—never *once*—spoke before the Americans." Their reticence clearly annoyed and bothered him.

"But it's *our* culture," responded one Foreign Ministry official when this point was raised. Most of the time, however, it may not be culture so much as style that is at stake.

Building a Consensus.   Americans who chafe at Japan's snail-like decision making may turn to "outside pressure" only to find that their target is not available to be pressured: bureaucrats are closeted in intra-ministerial meetings or consultations with the Diet; business leaders are tied up in the time-consuming mechanics of forging an internal consensus.

In all democracies, of course, civil servants must cater to their parliaments to promote needed legislation, to secure adequate funds, and to avoid criticism in the press. In Japan, however, working-level staff officials seem to spend undue amounts of time preparing for discussions in the Diet, rehashing material that their bosses have been over many times before. The net result strikes the impatient American as a kind of paralysis, a sticky web of daily political niceties, at a time when managing U.S.-Japan relations cries out for high-quality attention.

When asked the reasons for these extraordinarily time-consuming exercises, government officials tend to answer vaguely that "the Japanese people prefer harmony." One official's response was more explicit: a confrontation in the Diet is seen as a personal failure, a sign of inadequate preparation or proof of insufficient effort. When a confrontation occurs, he added, subordinates are blamed—and blamed heavily.

To avoid open confrontation, therefore, government officials will spend a great deal of time negotiating compromises behind the scenes, not only with the various factions of the ruling Liberal Democratic Party, but also with the more moderate opposition parties. Consensus-building of this sort, known as *nemawashi* (literally, "root-binding," or preparing the roots of a tree before it is moved), glues a decision together and lends it durability—a quality that one cannot always count on in Washington or in U.S. corporate headquarters.

"That's a great idea—let's do it!" exclaimed a middle-level Japanese businessman to his American joint-venture partner. "But," he added sheepishly, "you'll have to give me a few months, so that I can conduct *nemawashi*, avoid a fight, and make my superiors believe it is their idea." The American was not pleased because the business environment was changing rapidly. Shortly thereafter, however, his own company started having second thoughts about the venture. Eventually it backed out.

In foreign policy, such stop-and-start behavior takes a toll on U.S.-Japan relations. Washington may make decisions more rapidly, but to the Japanese it is not always clear that the decisions will outlast individual decision makers. In retrospect, it is surprising that U.S. foreign policy blips and reversals—from neutron bombs to withdrawal from Lebanon, from grain embargoes and Soviet gas pipelines to on-again, off-again troop withdrawals—have not bolstered the "go-it-alone" faction in Japan more than they have.

Styles of Communication

Differences in the style of leadership are natural expressions of differences in the style of communication. These contrasts do not determine the underlying U.S. and Japanese tensions and interests at stake. They nevertheless influence the likelihood of rapport and trust between individuals engaged in managing them. They come into play not only when Americans and Japanese are seated at the negotiating table, but also when they talk more informally. Some of the more striking differences between American and Japanese styles of communication are outlined below.

"Wet" and "Dry".   Many Japanese are fond of saying that they are a "wet" people, whereas Westerners are "dry." By "dry" they mean that Westerners attach more importance to abstract principles, logic, and rationality than to human feeling. Thus, Westerners are said to view all social relations, including marriage, as formal contracts which, once they no longer satisfy individual needs, can be terminated. Their ideas of morality are generalized and absolute, with little regard for the particular human context. They have a cut-and-dried reaction to minor slights and injuries, shrugging them off rather than brooding over them. Accordingly, they are not particularly sensitive to emotional nuance. Being "hunters" or "nomads" (*shuryō-gata*) rather than "farmers" (*nōkō-gata*), they are always on the move. They make casual friends then let them go, minimizing or avoiding lifelong emotional obligations.

By contrast, the "wet" Japanese are said to attach great importance to the emotional realities of the particular human circumstances. They avoid absolutes, rely on subtlety and intuition, and consider sensitivity to human feelings all-important. They notice small signs of insult or disfavor and take them deeply to heart. They harbor feelings of loyalty for years, perhaps for life, and for that reason are believed to be more trustworthy. Some go as far as to say that Japanese are simply "more emotional" than Westerners.[6] Ironically, many Americans who have faced a row of impassive, reserved, and apparently unyielding Japanese across the negotiating table believe that it is the Japanese—at least the men—who have less human feeling.

The term *naniwa bushi* exemplifies this "wet" quality. In the literal sense, it refers to long story-poems from the Osaka area which typically center on tragic conflicts between duty and romantic love or between family ties and loyalty to a clan leader. Many Japanese listeners are moved almost to tears by these age-old themes. In modern use, the term is applied to persons who are open-minded, generous, and capable of appreciating another person's position, even when that position is neither logical nor rational. A negotiator who adopts a rigid position, recites a familiar catalog of grievances, and appears to have no understanding of Japanese concerns is said to lack *naniwa bushi*. Such a person is judged to be neither effective nor trustworthy. The comment has nothing to do with being weak-minded or conciliatory. In Japanese eyes, the ideal U.S. negotiator combines tough-mindedness—based on a realistic, long-term, and consistent definition of national or corporate interest—with those "wet" qualities so highly valued by the Japanese.

Ingrained Vagueness and Nonverbal Communication.   As one might expect in a culture that values intuition and sensitivity to human feeling, communication between individuals is characterized by ambiguous language, nonverbal signals, and silence. Such ingrained vagueness frequently frustrates Americans, who wonder if the Japanese are manipulating them. In fact, many if not most of the same patterns of communication prevail when Japanese are talking to other Japanese.

Distaste for explicit statement dates back at least a thousand years. For Lady Murasaki's Prince Genji and his fellow courtiers of the Heian period, the refined expression of feeling lay through imagery, understatement, and exquisite subtlety.[7] To let fall elegant but elliptical fragments of poetry and double entendre was considered the height of good taste. Instead of expressing his feelings in words, a lover immortalized in a tenth-century poem "does not speak his love / Yet feels its waters seething underneath."[8]

Many Japanese believe that subtle and intuitive communication is unique to Japan. Yet in George Apley's Boston or Winston Churchill's England, mention of one's school or club, or friends in common, spoke paragraphs. Nevertheless, geographic isolation, a high degree of linguistic and cultural homogeneity, and the strong influence of Zen Buddhism have left their mark. Over the centuries, Japan's insular, self-contained society naturally developed subtle means of transmitting shared values.

Silence, in particular, holds an honored place among Japan's cultural ideals. Nobel Prize-winning novelist Yasunari Kawabata is said to have remarked that, to a Japanese, truth lies in what is implied, not in what is stated. Understanding the words is useless without understanding the silences between them; verbal communication supplements nonverbal communication, not the other way around. Anthropology professor Masao Kunihiro has written that Japanese words are like dots in a picture: it is up to the listener to connect the dots with lines and to fill in the remainder.[9] In the face of pain and suffering, the Japanese ideal is "to endure without words" (*gaman-suru*); even joy and pride should be masked.[10]

At press conferences, the late Prime Minister Ohira would remain silent for the first few minutes while reporters waited patiently. Finally, an older reporter might ask, "How are you today?" Ohira's typical response might be, "I feel fine this morning, but I don't expect to feel so well this afternoon." Reporters would piece together what was going on from such cryptic remarks. With foreigners, Ohira's trait was something of a disadvantage; he was nicknamed "Ah-san" because he was so inarticulate. Prime Minister Nakasone is far more talkative, but whereas the Japanese admire him for his ability to communicate well with foreigners, they trust him less than they trusted Ohira.

To the dismay of some Japanese, especially older ones, Americans seem to talk all the time. Whereas long stretches of silence are not uncommon when a group of Japanese meet or dine together, Americans would feel compelled to fill the void. One American businessman advised that the "first and most important rule" of communicating with a Japanese counterpart is to let him do the talking. He noted: "Americans have a national and natural tendency to use expressions like, 'Sorry to interrupt, but in America we . . .' or phrases like, 'That's not the way we do it in the States—let me tell you how we would handle that situation.'"[11]

By Japanese standards, Americans not only talk too much, they also touch other people too frequently. To be sure, Japanese men who have had too much to drink can often be seen hugging each other clumsily or staggering off with their arms around each other. Yet as a form of normal interpersonal communication, touching appears to be twice as common among Americans as among Japanese.[12] By now, most Japanese have become accustomed to shaking hands with Americans. But they are uncomfortable with other customs, such as the affectionate pat on the back and (in the case of women) the light kiss on the cheek. To the relief of some Japanese, Americans have learned not to clap them on the shoulder— even if they did drink together and crack silly jokes the night before.

Paradoxically, Americans tend to recoil more than Japanese when a stranger intrudes into their space. They are uncomfortable with the anonymous touching of the sort experienced in a crowded subway. They find the covert touching and fondling that some Japanese women are subjected to in a packed subway car to be particularly offensive. City-dwelling Japanese, by contrast, seem to retreat into an imaginary private space behind an unseen screen. They are accustomed to being literally pushed in and out of subway cars, and they don't seem to mind if a stranger standing next to them leans against them for a good bit of the ride. In public, they endure high levels of noise; indeed, noisy chatter seems to be the rule rather than the exception, invading the grounds of even the most serene temple.

Although many Japanese claim that their national culture is unique, the intuitive and subtle qualities that characterize the Japanese style of communication resemble what the West sometimes considers a "feminine sensibility." Authors ranging from nineteenth-century English novelists to contemporary feminists have expressed the belief that women tend to be better at sensing people's feelings, probing delicate situations, gathering emotional information, and devising subtle means of approaching a sensitive topic. This viewpoint runs the risk of sexism and reverse prejudice and should therefore be treated with considerable skepticism. Yet the analogy between Japanese—men as well as women—and Western women may not be as fanciful as it seems, for Japanese literature and language took flight in an age when women were prominent and when cultural values were almost effeminate. During the Heian period—the period that produced *The Tale of Genji*—virtually every noteworthy author writing in Japanese was a woman. The late Ivan Morris' classic study of the Heian court lists no fewer than fourteen.[13] While men studied and wrote in Chinese, the language of scholars, priests, and officials, women developed the vernacular literature. The great seventeenth-century scholar Motoori Norinaga, who revived and inspired the study of Japan's indigenous culture, religion, and history, confirmed this feminine influence.[14] So has America's foremost translator and interpreter of Japanese literature, Donald Keene, who wrote:

> The melancholy of a rainy evening, the preciousness of beauty that would soon fade away, the unspoken overtones of a casual remark, and other characteristics of the feminine sensibility of the Heian period became the heritage of the entire Japanese people.[15]

In short, vagueness, nuance, and occasional silence are not ploys to keep Americans at arm's length. They may have that effect, but they are better understood as long-standing cultural ideals.

Pragmatism and "Situational Ethics".   Together with "wetness," ingrained vagueness, and nonverbal expression, the Japanese style of communication is noted for its nonjudgmental, case-by-case nature. From earliest times, observers have documented the relative absence of abstract concepts, moral absolutes, and definitive judgments based on purportedly universal standards. No single set of ideas reigns supreme. The distinguished political theorist Masao Maruyama has described Japanese ideas as "disjointed," lacking a "coordinating axis."[16]

At the turn of the century, Lafcadio Hearn noticed that Japanese courts weighed each case on the basis of individual circumstances, and handed down judgments that were based not on codified rules, but on what he called "moral common sense." Such decisions often included rewards for good conduct as well as punishment for bad behavior.[17]

A best-seller in Japan, *The Japanese and the Jews,* has labeled this case-by-case approach to human problems "Nihonism" (*Nihon* is one of several words for Japan). The author argues that whereas Western law is based on abstract ideas of universal applicability dating back to biblical times, and specifically to the notion of a covenant with God, Nihonism is based on "logic beyond logic . . . the importance of pragmatic action." It relies on "human experience instead of on a covenant or body of dogma." This "genius in pragmatic politics," the author reasons, is (predictably) unique to the Japanese, who are unburdened by the notion of contract.[18]

Comparing present-day Americans to Moses may seem a bit fanciful. Still, because we live in a secular age, it is easy to overlook the contribution of religion to the fundamental structure of daily thought and expression in both countries.

Except for a few minor episodes during the era of bloody civil war four hundred years ago, Japan did not experience the religious controversies that wracked the Western world for centuries. As the great cultural historian Sir George Sansom observed, "The Japanese as a people were spared the pains of *odium theologicum.* Lacking a metaphysical bent, they never developed a fervent interest in transcendental problems and mistrusted speculative philosophy. Their outlook has been practical and intuitive rather than intellectually rigorous."[19] Consequently, the main currents of Japanese religious thought shun or downplay reason and logic in their Western sense.

The contrast between Japanese pragmatism and Western rationalism in extreme form is illustrated by the Zen Buddhist concept of enlightenment (*satori*):

> *Satori* may be defined as an intuitive looking-into, in contradistinction to intellectual and logical understanding. . . . In logic there is a trace of effort and pain. Logic is self-conscious. . . . Zen abhors this.[20]

This is not to say that the Japanese lack a sense of right and wrong. On the contrary, their vocabulary is rich with concepts such as faithfulness, loyalty, and benevolence, illustrated with homilies and cherished feats of heroism; cynicism and amorality are noticeable for their absence. It is merely that in defining right behavior, they tend to emphasize "situational ethics" rather than individual responsibility based on reason and absolute norms.[21]

Perhaps Japan was lucky to bypass the violence committed in the name of God. But out of the great religious tremors in the West emerged a profound faith in "reason" and "logic" as means of regulating human behavior and achieving individual fulfillment. Here is how historian Clinton Rossiter described the impact of reason on early American thought:

> Rationalism was a way of thinking that cherished reason as the path to valid knowledge; assumed the worth and dignity of man, as well as his ability to use reason in the search for happiness and truth; proclaimed a benevolent, dependable, gentlemanly God; and therefore stood forth in its most developed form as an enlightened protest against tradition, dogma, superstition, and authority.[22]

Whether these ideals are culturally predetermined or universally valid lies well beyond the scope of this book. Suffice it to say that their universal aspect is characteristic of American thought. Describing seventeenth-century Americans, Rossiter wrote: "Few people in history have been more given to public moralizing, to proclaiming a catalogue of virtues and exhorting one another to exhibit them than the American colonists."[23] Even today, Americans tend to believe that the path to truth lies through the application of reason and logic, as they define them. They consider their approach to be right, moral, and universally valid, and feel frustrated when they find that the Japanese do not see things in the same light.

The Problem of Problems.   In pursuit of their concepts of reason and logic, Westerners tend to break down complex material into analytically manageable segments, to examine them critically, and to learn through disagreement. Underlying this pattern of thinking is what one expert in intercultural communication calls "the problem of problems"—that is, a tendency, especially among Americans, to approach every subject in terms of a "problem" to be solved.[24] American businessmen and government officials are likely to arrive at a meeting with a proposed solution to a "problem." That is considered both constructive and efficient. They will assume that the Japanese have arrived similarly prepared to spend most of the time debating the "problem." To save time—a typical American concern—many Americans tend to proceed directly to the areas of disagreement rather than take the time to establish a common framework or common priorities.

When their Japanese counterparts fail to state their position at the outset, Americans tend to conclude that they are simply stalling. In a sense this is true, for Japanese negotiators typically spend considerable time fishing for clues to the other side's position. Their idea is that once the two sides have sized up the situation, they can work out a compromise to satisfy everyone's needs and desires in that particular context. They are puzzled and dismayed by the American notion of a "fallback" position, which suggests that the opening gambit is not a genuine option.

As an illustration of the differences in approach, one MITI official cited the example of two people dividing an orange—an example borrowed from conflict-resolution expert Roger Fisher. "The American approach would be to cut it in half, right?" he asked. But suppose, he added, one person wanted to eat the orange and the other wanted the peel for making marmalade. His point was that, to obtain maximum satisfaction, the two people should go through the time-consuming process of sounding out each other's needs and intentions at the outset rather than open with an explicit negotiating objective or demand.

In the course of a negotiation, Americans expect give and take as a normal means of arriving at a better course of action. Constructive criticism, even disagreement, is not taken personally—especially when laced with humor. Unless they are accustomed to Americans, however, Japanese find it difficult to understand, let alone engage in, a style of communication that mixes debate with friendly insults, pointed jokes, and argument for its own sake. They find it embarrassing, offensive, and even threatening when a senior person is contradicted by a subordinate, especially if the two are not close in age. To challenge even a small portion of another person's presentation shows disregard for that person's feelings and implies disharmony and lack of consensus. Depending on the context, Japanese may even conclude that the American style of solving problems is a crude way of telling other people how things should be done.

"Honne-Tatemae" and Good Intentions. In the Japanese emotional context, sensitivity to human feelings may require doing or saying something (*tatemae*) that does not necessarily correspond to one's private thoughts or intentions (*honne*). Most Japanese accept and recognize this

duality as valid and appropriate, a mark of human maturity. They associate it with the legitimate needs of the group and the reinforcing role of each person within it. Americans, however, feel betrayed when something a Japanese appears to have agreed to or promised turns out to be quite different. *The Economist* once labeled such behavior "the Japanese art of lying." Even Japanese occasionally feel manipulated.

A Japanese phrase book put out by a major Japanese company explains:

> *Tatemae* . . . is used in connection with a view made from an accepted or objective standpoint. *Honne* has the meaning of one's true feelings or intentions. . . . This doesn't necessarily mean anyone is lying. There is a delicate but important difference between *tatemae* and *honne* which comes up in any situation where a person must consider more than one's own feelings on the matter.[25]

Unfortunately, failure to understand *honne* and *tatemae* has bred such mistrust that some Western visitors feel they cannot believe what a Japanese person says.[26]

The art of the white lie is, of course, no stranger to the West. But particularly since the 1960s, Americans have been taught that it is hypocritical, even unhealthy, to restrict self-expression. They are taught to "be yourself," "let it all hang out." Ironically, such candor tends to make the Japanese suspicious. To many Japanese, the failure to observe *honne* and *tatemae* smacks of insensitivity, selfishness, and bad taste. They find American behavior so unpredictable that social rules designed to avoid embarrassment do not apply. Some of them look for new "rules," such as cracking jokes at the outset or calling an American partner by his first name, and adjust accordingly. Yet in private they sometimes criticize Americans for being informal when they should be formal (e.g., telling jokes during a daytime business meeting), and formal when they should be informal (e.g., discussing business at a bar at night instead of singing songs). In fact, Americans are simply being themselves.

A *tatemae*-type apology by a Japanese evokes skeptical responses among Americans. For example, many Americans were quick to doubt Prime Minister Nakasone's sincerity when he issued an apology for his disparaging remarks about U.S. minorities. Conversely, many Japanese find it reprehensible that Americans do not apologize when an American airplane crashes in Japan, a Japanese is mugged in an American city, or an explosion claims the lives of seven astronauts. Americans might respond that they see no need to apologize when they don't feel responsible.

The Japanese concept of *sei-i* (sincerity or integrity) comes into play here. *Sei-i* does not connote "sincerity" in the sense of genuineness (as in "I was sincerely glad to see him.") Rather, it is an attribute of a disciplined, trustworthy, and ethical person who is free of passion or ambition, and who believes in and carries out the manifold obligations imposed by the Japanese code of behavior. Such a person would respect and act out the distinction between *honne* and *tatemae* in carrying out the obligations imposed by the particular context.

Even in daily encounters, expected behavior varies with the circumstances. Some visitors from a major U.S. company, for example, were impressed with the bluff and hearty manner of a Japanese plant manager in his factory. Later, when they accidentally encountered him on the street, they were puzzled by his reticent and embarrassed behavior. Yet he was being sincere; the context had changed.

Given this interpretation of sincerity, good intentions, in the American sense, may be irrelevant. Of course, the Japanese will sense and appreciate a good "heart" or "spirit" (*kokoro*). But unless they have had substantial exposure to Western mores, they will unconsciously expect Americans to conform, at least outwardly, to certain rules of behavior. Americans need not "genuinely" adhere to or respect these rules; token observance of them is a sign of appropriate, and therefore sincere, conduct on their part.

Many Americans instinctively understand what is expected of them and do respond with sensitivity and tact. Unfortunately, a few arrive in Japan with the notion that they must "play the game"—that is, trap or be trapped by the allegedly devious Japanese. American literature abounds with the smart con man as hero, the shyster who swindles money and disappears into night. In Japan, where strangers are noticed and closely watched, almost no one disappears. The success of any enterprise in Japan rests on long-term relationships based on trust. Mistaking *tatemae* for untrustworthiness would be foolish, for it is just the opposite. Regrettably, some Americans continue to do so, thereby arousing corresponding mistrust among Japanese.

Problems of Language and Expression.   Last but hardly least among the barriers to effective communication between Americans and Japanese is language. In a typical meeting between Americans and Japanese, even a casual listener is struck by the difference in the way language is used.

Few American business executives and government officials speak Japanese and few of their Japanese counterparts are truly fluent in English. Americans, sensing the tension, may try to break the ice with humor and aggressive informality. The Japanese may try to go along with the general banter, but often only the junior employee by the door understands English.

Beyond basic comprehension, there is the challenge of translation. As English and Japanese are two of the world's most difficult languages, translation from one to the other is like scaling a cliff: an amateur cannot bluff or guess; one misstep and he or she falls off. English words adapted into Japanese can make matters worse, for they are often shortened or distorted to the point of being unrecognizable: *waapuro* for word processor, *pasokon* for personal computer, or *depaato* for department store.

The observance of various levels of politeness in spoken Japanese requires careful choices among a variety of styles: humble/honorific, formal/informal, men's words/women's words, and so on. The signal that is conveyed by switching from "vous" to "tu" in French is but a tiny fraction of the myriad signals that can be conveyed through carefully chosen words in Japanese. Even the Japanese sometimes have difficulty threading their way through the maze of verb forms and honorifics.

Without knowing the language, some Americans incorrectly conclude that the Japanese are incapable of speaking to each other as equals. That is a myth; to do so merely requires a certain set of words and phrases. Another erroneous American idea is that the Japanese language has no word for "no." But Americans are often unprepared to recognize the subtle signs of disagreement.[27]

The intricacy of Japanese grammar lends itself nicely to such polite circumlocution. Japanese grammar strikes the neophyte as slippery, if not downright hazardous. One American student of Japanese has embroidered on this difficulty with mischievous humor:

> I found that if I got one word in the wrong place, the whole sentence would change itself materially. . . . The sentence doesn't go to pieces, exactly. It takes on new life—all the words revise themselves, the nouns, as likely as not, become verbs, the verbs adjectives, and here and there a word shudders so that it becomes a different thing. I have seen cases in which a word has disappeared altogether.[28]

A more fundamental difficulty than grammar is the subtle, indirect style of discourse discussed earlier. Much of what is said cannot be truly captured in translation, and much of the meaning depends on what is left unsaid. When President Nixon asked for restraint on Japanese textile exports to the United States, Prime Minister Sato reportedly replied with a phrase that was translated variously as, "I will take appropriate measures" or "I will deal with it in a forward-looking manner." To a Japanese, however, the phrase meant "I will try to do something even though I know I can do very little" or "I will try my best to find a good solution, but I cannot promise." President Nixon was reportedly angered by Sato's subsequent inability to act.

Similarly, when the Japanese Government asked permission for its nationals to visit their relatives' graves on Okinawa, then held by Americans, the reply was something like, "Let's think about it." Accustomed to the subtlety of the Japanese language, newspapers in Japan assumed that the United States had turned down a humanitarian request and made quite a fuss about it. In fact, the response had been positive all along.

Sometimes a seemingly simple phrase is given widely different interpretations by Japanese and Americans. Shortly after taking office, Prime Minister Kakuei Tanaka compared Japan's relationship with America to "the air we breathe." He meant the relationship was quite natural, but some Americans interpreted his words in the sense of free and abundant, to be taken for granted.[29]

Other phrases which appear clear and unambiguous to Western minds may conjure up deep emotional associations for the Japanese. In writing about defense, for instance, Japanese journalists have to choose carefully the equivalents of English terms with explosive implications, such as "militarism," "revising the Constitution," and the like.

In one fateful case, translation that arguably misconstrued ambiguity changed the course of history. Responding to the Allied Powers' call for unconditional surrender in the Potsdam Declaration of 1945, Prime Minister Zenko Suzuki used the word *mokusatsu,* whose more common meaning is "to ignore or to treat with silent contempt." Another possible interpretation, however, is "to remain in wise and masterly inactivity." A group of contemporary Japanese historians have concluded that Suzuki used the word in the latter sense.[30] Whether their reading of his response is correct or not, the Allies read rejection in the word, and carried out their threat of "prompt and utter destruction" by dropping the atom bomb on Hiroshima and Nagasaki.

The Japanese, of course, have the same problem in reverse. With its irregular verbs, multiple tenses, and confusing prepositions, the English language is a nightmare for foreigners—even for those who have studied it in school. In Japan, high school English courses, geared toward the all-important university entrance examinations, emphasize fine points of grammar rather than the ability to converse. Students are asked to translate, for example, the sentence: "Stripped to their essentials, man's major problems have always hung on the necessity of making adjustment to the irresistible force of change."[31] Among students who have little use for English on a regular basis, proficiency in spoken English is therefore extremely low. Informal reports suggest that Japanese housewives, free from examination phobia and motivated to learn conversational English, are now the best students of the spoken language.

In a survey that asked native speakers of English and Japanese to describe their impressions of their own and each other's languages, each group felt its own language was "warm" and the other's "cold." Native speakers of English described the Japanese language as "vague," "polite," "formal," "abstract," and "repetitious"; native speakers of Japanese described the English language as "mechanical," "harsh," "practical," and "concise."[32] Japanese women say that they feel assertive, and even aggressive, when they speak English.[33]

The use of Chinese characters in written Japanese makes for even greater difficulty in communication, reinforcing the impression among Americans that Japanese culture is impenetrable. In their zeal for educational reform, American Occupation authorities initially tried to do away with written Chinese in Japanese schools. To have succeeded would have been tantamount to cultural murder. Calligraphy, with its fluid, vertical lines, can convey a wide range of tone and meaning. To write beautifully is, in George Sansom's words, "to solve fundamental problems of art." Small wonder that nineteenth-century traditionalists seeking to block Western influence rejected the cramped, sideways writing of the West, which they called "crab writing."[34]

True fluency in Japanese and a knowledge of the written language may be out of question for most foreigners not brought up in Japan, but the ability to master a basic vocabulary and carry on a polite conversation is not. According to one survey, enrollment in Japanese language courses at American universities increased dramatically from the mid-1960s to the mid-1970s—even though enrollment in modern languages as a whole actually declined during that period. As of 1985, more than 16,000 Americans were studying Japanese. Courses related to Japan are both more numerous and more popular. Whereas approximately eighty schools offered a Japanese studies program in 1968, roughly two hundred do so now.[35]

While U.S. banks and investment firms are hiring some of these graduates, the manufacturing sector appears to be disinterested. With some exceptions, international business managers seem to be of the opinion that knowledge of foreign languages and cultures is less important than basic business skills, such as marketing and finance.[36] Accordingly, a very small percent of students holding advanced degrees in Japanese studies enter American industry. Apparently, more are being hired by Japanese companies.

Attitudes Toward the Study of Culture and History. Japan's catch-up mentality and the associated thirst for knowledge show up in a certain "vacuum cleaner" approach to American firms. Japanese businessmen who are considering approaching an American company tend to be thoroughly briefed on its corporate history. A large firm seeking a long-term association with a U.S. company may even assign a junior employee to monitor all available information about the company in question and serve as an in-house historian, personnel locator, and guide. Often, this person ends up knowing far more about the company assigned to him than the visiting American who represents it.

By contrast, many Americans tend to downplay or even ignore the need for in-depth homework prior to negotiating with Japanese. Not only do they often fail to collect and study detailed information about the company they are dealing with, but they also frequently guess at or gloss over basic information about their own companies—percent of exports, annual sales, and so forth. They see nothing wrong in asking each other for such information in the presence of the Japanese.[37]

Even Americans most directly involved with the Japanese tend to be relatively ignorant of Japan's culture and history. Since Americans did not consider Japan to be very important a decade or two ago, the average business executive learned nothing about Japan in school or college. Today, books on Japanese business practices are widely read—indeed, a small industry has grown up around the subject—but in-depth knowledge of Japan is still relatively rare.

The typical American business executive, banker, lawyer, or government negotiator does not consciously refuse to study Japanese history and culture for fear of becoming or being perceived as too "soft"—although that is sometimes a danger. It is rather that such preparation is somewhat alien to America's own cultural traditions. Compared to Europeans or Japanese, Americans pursuing a career outside the humanities tend to display a curious indifference to cultural and intellectual topics.

In Thornton Wilder's quintessentially American play *Our Town*, a pretentious lady asks in a shocked voice, "Is there no *culture* in Grover's Corners?" She is clearly out of place. Even in America's big cities, "high" culture does not pervade the moneyed classes to the same extent that it does in Europe or in Japan.

By contrast, a good number of Japanese company executives pride themselves on their practice of or interest in the arts, whether Japanese or Western. Business magazines regularly print columns on chief executive officers who are connoisseurs of painting or skilled calligraphers. To be featured in these articles is not only good public relations for the company, but also a mark of individual prestige. All forms of "high" culture find a ready audience in Tokyo.

The late chief executive of an American company with many joint ventures in Japan described his reaction to this contrast in these words:

> When I first arrived in Japan, like many other businessmen, I thought of culture as a mere cultivation of aesthetic sensibilities, and of sociology and anthropology as abstruse academic specialties of very limited application. . . . But experience changed my original view.[38]

Similarly, the Dutch-born chairman and chief executive officer of a major advertising agency, who had been a prisoner of the Japanese during World War II, deplores the relative lack of interest in Japanese culture on the part of most American companies. For him, culture "extends to Japanese business practices and the nuances of the Japanese language."[39]

Most observers agree on the relatively low status of culture in American society, but not on its cause. The late historian Richard Hofstadter traced it to the influence of Puritanism, with its hatred of finery, its emphasis on direct expression, and its suspicion of intellectual activity in general.[40] Others cite the high degree of social and geographic mobility, characteristic of both the westward expansion and the subsequent waves of immigration. Alexis de Tocqueville considered it a consequence of equality, which "not only makes Americans equal in fortunes, but to some extent affects their mental endowments, too." He wrote, "There is no class in America in which a taste for intellectual pleasures is transmitted with hereditary wealth and leisure and which holds the labor of the mind in esteem."[41]

Others attribute the low status of culture in American society to the nature of American capitalism, which puts a premium on assertiveness and downgrades "culture" as soft and effeminate. Some feminists speculate that one effect of the Industrial Revolution in the West was to move the "real world" out of the home into the factory, leaving behind culture— along with housework—for the woman. Until fairly recently, drawing, a knowledge of music, and fluency in French were considered essential to the education of a well-bred young woman, but not a young man.

To be sure, many of America's great cultural institutions have been established through the generosity and interest of successful businessmen. And cultural programs, made possible by grants from corporate sponsors, have greatly enriched educational television. Indeed, some American businessmen have developed extraordinary sophistication and taste in the arts. But rare is the top-ranking American corporate executive or lawyer who can wield a brush or compose a poem with the skill of some of his Japanese counterparts.

This characteristically American approach to culture contributes to frequent oversights. For example, an American invited to a restaurant by his Japanese hosts may not know that he is seated in the place of honor in front of the *tokonoma,* or raised area in a tatami room. He may overlook the special care his hosts have taken to select a menu reflecting the season or featuring local specialties. He may not appreciate that the teacup or lacquerware presented as a souvenir is a sample of local craftsmanship. By now, many Japanese have become used to American behavior and do not take offense. Still, for Americans to overlook small, subtle expressions of Japanese courtesy only reinforces the image of Americans as a casual and insensitive people.

More serious—and probably harder to cure—is a certain tendency among Americans to ignore or dismiss history. "No nation learns fewer lessons from its own errors of the past than the United States," commented an article in *The Times* (London) in 1985. Most of America's allies, including Japan, would agree with this statement.

Americans still display an almost anti-historical instinct associated with their vision of the New World. Describing America's great migrations, Oscar Handlin wrote that Americans in the nineteenth century believed that the country would move in new directions of its own because "its people were a new people . . . emerging from the experience of life on a new continent."[42] This sense of newness continues to lend flexibility and verve to American society. On the other hand, one of the consequences of the relative lack of interest in history on the part of America's leaders is that every crisis or political upheaval tends to come as a surprise. Another is that American leaders often think that the way to handle a foreign policy problem is to offer military support for one group or another.[43] These instincts feed on both the preoccupation with national security and the characteristic desire to "do something" in response to a crisis.

When it comes to U.S.-Japan relations, unfamiliarity with Japanese history and tradition puts Americans at a serious disadvantage, for it leads them to ignore certain deep-seated and continuing influences on Japanese behavior at home and abroad. Asked to identify major historical influences on Japan's behavior, few Americans can go back much further than Pearl Harbor. Yet a historical perspective helps to explain Japan's catch-up mentality, its closed-group behavior, its pattern of regulation, and its global outlook.

With time and effort, those who now indulge in "bashing" and brooding can overcome these obstacles and learn how to "fight within the family." Japan may have to speed up its decision making and overcome its fear of expressing disagreement. The United States may have to become more cautious, better informed, and more mindful of the need for a durable consensus. To the extent that both societies adjust in these ways, they can get on with the task of solving their shared problems as industrial democracies.

Six

Society and Politics

espite numerous and profound differences in their historical and cultural development, the United States and Japan now face many similar challenges as industrial and postindustrial societies: a rapidly aging population, higher levels of divorce, dislocations arising from the transformation of smokestack industries, the need to adapt educational standards to meet the requirements of a high-technology society, and so forth. Identifying and comparing notes on these problems can serve to broaden and strengthen U.S.-Japan relations, partly because "misery loves company"—even international company—and partly because each society can learn something from the other's experience.

At the same time, the twin revolutions in transportation and communications have brought large numbers of Americans and Japanese with little or no international experience into the foreign-policy arena, once the near-exclusive preserve of diplomats and experts.

Thus, if only for purely practical reasons, those with a stake in the U.S.-Japan partnership must gain a deeper understanding of social and political trends. How the two societies and their respective political systems evolve will largely determine the national identity of their respective foreign policies—and hence the future of U.S.-Japan relations.

Society

Social trends in Japan that may strengthen the U.S.-Japan relationship include the entry of women into the professional work force, somewhat more relaxed attitudes toward work, efforts to liberalize the educational system to encourage more individual creativity, greater balance between government officials and elected politicians in the exercise of political power, and a long-term trend toward political moderation among the electorate. As a result, Japan's hitherto closed-group society is gradually "spreading out"—becoming more open, more fluid, more pluralistic, more tolerant, and more genuinely democratic—in short, less different from American society. Over time, this transition may help to ease the frustrations of foreigners and overcome perceived differences between Japan and the rest of the world.

At the same time, Americans seem to be reverting to certain values and attitudes that resemble more closely those held by the Japanese. After the spasms of the 1960s, America seems to be settling down and pulling itself together. Young people seem to be more interested in jobs than in political causes or social rebellion. Values upheld in Japan, such as careful workmanship and attention to detail, now receive more respect in the United States. The work ethic has been partially revived and renewed. Educational standards are being raised—boosted in part by unflattering comparisons with Japan's and in part by the influx of Asian immigrants, for whom scholastic achievement represents the key to success.

Aging.   The Japanese Government describes the future of Japanese society in terms of three broad trends: "internationalization," the "information society," and the "aging society."[1] Internationalization and the information society represent goals as well as trends. The aging society is already a reality.

In Japan, as in other postindustrial societies, a rising standard of living tends to increase life expectancy and reduce the birthrate. Over time, the obvious result is more old people and fewer young people.

As the society moves from what the Japanese call the "fifty-year life-style" to the "eighty-year life-style," the government has postponed the onset of old age by coining the label "age of fruition" for people in their fifties and sixties. Finding meaningful and constructive activity for people in their "silver years"—seventy years and over—has taken on the character of a national dilemma, if not a crisis.

The numbers illustrate the problem clearly. Japan's working-age population will climb until 1995, and then taper off. By the year 2000, the ratio of working people to people over 65 is expected to drop from 7.5:1 to 4.3:1.[2] After 2015, over 20 percent of the population will be 65 years or older. By comparison, people aged 65 or over constitute 15.6 percent of the population of Western Europe in the mid-1980s, a figure considered quite high by today's world standards.

As might be expected in a capitalist society, the economic sphere has taken the lead in adapting to Japan's rapidly aging population. Industries and services catering to the elderly—dubbed the "silver industry"—already account for annual sales of approximately 21 trillion yen, equal to those of Japan's automobile industry.[3] Older people are also prominent customers of the growing leisure industry. Partly to accommodate them, the number of restaurants, museums, hotel rooms, and cultural services mushroomed in the 1970s and is still expanding.

On a gloomier note, the Ministry of Health and Welfare estimates that expenditures for medical care will more than triple by the early twenty-first century. It is hard to see how Japan will be able to shoulder the burden of an aging society without redirecting at least some of its resources from productive investment toward social welfare. This reallocation is bound to affect Japan's future economic performance and the future of U.S.-Japan relations. The popular American perception of Japan as a nation of vigorous, healthy "workaholics" is likely to change as well. Many Americans admire this energy, but some seem to resent it. In the decades to come, aging will no doubt drain off some of Japan's vitality.

Women in the Work Force. The entry of large numbers of women to the workplace is another feature common to industrial societies. Meeting the social needs associated with the rise of women is a challenge facing leaders in both Japan and America.

As early as the 1950s, the proportion of Japan's working women employed outside of small family businesses or family farms began to rise. Today, more than two-thirds of Japanese working women hold regularly paid jobs in professional settings. Put another way, women hold more than one-third of these jobs. The proportion of married women in Japan's work force rose from roughly 33 percent in 1962 to almost 60 percent in 1982.[4]

Nevertheless, work-related sex discrimination is still perfectly open in Japan; one sees it everywhere, from explicit corporate policy to male- and female-only want ads. Many factories still offer menstrual leave to their female workers, and are only beginning to dismantle limits on overtime work. Young female employees are expected to speak with girlish voices and to act cute (*kawaii*); their employers typically expect them to spend a few years serving tea and running elevators before leaving to get married.

For Japanese women who manage to enter the professions, opportunities for upward mobility are far fewer than those enjoyed by their American counterparts. The contrast shows up most strongly at the middle and upper-middle levels—the ranks from which tomorrow's leaders will be drawn. Resistance to professional women is greatest in larger and more established companies, banks, and government agencies, where employees are expected to stay for life. Many women are simply unwilling to commit themselves, especially when the job entails assignment overseas.

Well over half of Japan's professional women are married. Even if they stay on the job, they find working life difficult to combine with child-rearing. For one thing, working hours are still not very flexible, and meaningful part-time jobs are hard to come by. The habit of working late and drinking with one's colleagues on weekday evenings also interferes with the demands of a family. Moreover, babysitters are not readily available. Although the number of day-care centers is increasing, most working women must rely on their parents or parents-in-law to mind the children. Even this solution has limits, for today's mothers are under great pressure to help their children succeed in Japan's rigorous education system. Many of these "education mamas" attend classes themselves so that they can better assist their children with homework—a time-consuming task not easily entrusted to anyone else.

The tradition of taking care of the elderly at home compounds the difficulties of Japanese working women. Roughly 65 percent of Japan's old people live with their children, compared with only 40 percent in Sweden and less than 10 percent in France. Even those who are bedridden tend to live at home. In any case, the responsibility of taking care of old people is left overwhelmingly to women, especially the daughter-in-law.[5] As women enter the work force in ever larger numbers, and as the number of old people in the population increases, the problem of caring for the elderly has become acute.[6]

To date, men have offered little help to working wives, mothers, and daughters-in-law. Japanese men are simply not expected to participate in weekday family life, let alone share the housework. Except on Sunday, they are rarely at home during their children's waking hours. (Compared with America, Japan places less weight on the need for caring, participating fathers.) Nor are men expected to carry the burden of taking care of their own parents. Wives often prefer it that way, believing that a husband around the house just adds to the burden. "A husband who is healthy and away from home is best" is a common saying in Japan. One nickname for husbands is "big trash."

In some ways, prospects for the working woman in Japan have improved. In 1985, the Diet finally passed an equal opportunity law banning—or at least urging the elimination of—most forms of job discrimination. Major catalysts included self-consciousness in the face of publicity and world public opinion. (The law was passed at the tail end of the United Nations' Decade for Women.) While progressive leaders of both sexes deride the law for having no "teeth," one can make the case that the mere passage of the law in a society that emphasizes consensus and downplays litigation was a landmark.

Some companies and banks have recently adopted special arrangements to facilitate the employment of women, such as instituting a leave system for women wishing to return to work after several years' absence. A number of electronics firms now permit married female employees to work from computer terminals installed at home. As in America, public affairs, advertising, retailing, communications, computer technology, and other fields born of the "information society" are among those most receptive to women's career advancement. Fields with more flexible working hours, such as real estate and the travel industry, are also accommodating to Japanese women. More women are even starting their own businesses.

In the United States, the concept of equal employment opportunity for women has now gained widespread acceptance. Although subtle discrimination remains, formal and explicit barriers against equal treatment for women have fallen away sharply, to the point where all-male bastions are the exception rather than the rule. While this progress is quite recent, it reinforces American perceptions that the Japanese are "unfair."

Actually, the difference is less absolute than many Americans believe. The fact is that American society has not fully adjusted to the influx of women into the professional work force either. America may lead in the treatment of career women in middle-level positions, but standard measurements reveal that in both countries, females are heavily represented at the bottom of the job ladder and grossly underrepresented at the top. Relatively few women sit in the U.S. Congress or the Diet; fewer still are senior scientists or presidents of major companies.

Juggling family life and a career is a problem for American women as well. In America as well as Japan, men share the consensus that the society should reproduce itself, but the difficulty of balancing work and family is considered a "woman's problem." A report issued in 1986 by a panel of prominent American labor, corporate, and academic leaders noted that the American workplace has failed to adjust to dramatic changes in the society. According to the report, less than 10 percent of American households consist of a husband who works and a wife who stays at home with the children. Women with children under the age of three and those whose youngest child is between six and thirteen years of age constitute 50 percent and 70 percent, respectively, of the U.S. labor force. Yet jobs are still structured in traditional ways, with the result that "the majority of Americans are finding that their work and family lives increasingly come into conflict."[7]

Divorce.   The higher incidence of divorce is another problem associated with rapid economic change.

Statistics show 1.4 divorces per 1,000 people in Japan compared with almost 5 per 1,000 in the United States.[8] While the percentage of Japanese couples seeking divorce is steady or even declining, the absolute number of divorces has risen. This trend is alarming because some 70 percent of divorcing couples have children of school age or younger. According to one estimate, divorce affected 200,000 Japanese children in 1985, triple the number twenty years ago.[9]

Divorce may be responsible for the increase in the number of households and the decline in the average number of members per household in Japan. According to the five-year census report released at the end of 1985, the number of households has increased to over 38 million, nearly a 6 percent increase since 1980. In the same five-year period, the average number of members per household fell from 3.25 to 3.18. The birthrate during this period dropped to an all-time low—0.7 percent, substantially lower than the 1.9 percent of the early 1970s and the 2.9 percent of the early postwar years.

For women who do not have aging parents to take care of, divorce, fewer children, and more job opportunities add up to more money and more independence. These women will clearly have more time and incentive to branch out into activities of their own. Sooner or later, as they become more serious about careers, their male colleagues will no doubt pay more attention to their opinion as professionals.

Even now Japanese men are amazed to find that Westerners perceive Japanese women as weak and subservient. They point out that Japanese women traditionally hold the power of the purse, dominate life at home, and exercise subtle but constant manipulation. "So what if they are trained to be subservient to their husbands in public?" snorted a steel executive. "Japanese women are tough, tough, tough! Why can't Americans see that?"

Work and Leisure.   Many Americans believe Japanese are "workaholics," driven by group pressure and fanatic loyalty to their companies.

At the opposite extreme, many Japanese—especially businessmen and government officials—seem convinced that Americans are lazy on the job and only minimally loyal to their employers.[10] Labor unions are the object of special contempt.[11] Although it is hard to prove, these stereotypes almost certainly distort business decisions on both sides—for instance, by deterring Japanese companies in the United States from fully trusting and promoting American managers.

Actually, polls taken in the two societies strongly suggest that the difference in attitudes toward work and leisure is less a national or cultural gap than a gap between generations within each country.

To be sure, the notion that sheer effort in itself is a good thing is widespread in Japan. Absenteeism is remarkably low, even among younger workers. In a study of twelve industries, a Japanese authority on labor economics found that the average rate of attendance exceeded 99 percent.[12] On average, white-collar workers, or "salarymen," take only half of their paid vacations.[13] While this work pattern is not always efficient, it can lead to eventual success on a grand scale. Japan's success in improving American technology can be traced in part to sheer perseverance on the part of Japanese engineers. "They brute force everything," remarked an American semiconductor analyst, with appalling grammar but considerable acumen.

In both countries, the relative prosperity of the 1960s accentuated dissatisfaction with work and society among the young. After the oil shock of 1973, signs of "greening" receded somewhat in Japan;[14] by the end of the decade, they had receded in America as well. The "yuppie" phenomenon—the rise of young, upwardly mobile professionals with materialistic values and moderate or conservative political views—is common to both countries.

Japanese commentators refer to the younger generation as the "new human species" (*shinjinrui*). The term means different things to different people, but in general it implies that young people are less idealistic, less committed to work and sacrifice, more self-centered, and (to use American slang of the 1960s) more "cool" in both a pejorative and an admiring sense. Some blame the older generation, citing bad influences ranging from permissiveness to educational pressure. American journalist Frank Gibney, for instance, believes that young people in Japan are simply "underled" and "overdirected."[15]

The attitudes of Japan's young people, although often volatile on other topics, are remarkably consistent when it comes to work and leisure.

Younger Japanese men are ostensibly less loyal to their companies, less competitive, and less committed to work for its own sake. When asked in polls if they want "more leisure," younger respondents typically answer in the affirmative.[16] The Japan Recruit Center, a private firm that compiles data on hiring, found that 72 percent of male college graduates in the mid-1980s describe themselves as oriented more toward "home" than "the company." This trend, nicknamed "my home-ism" (*mai hōmu-shugi*), dismays older Japanese, who do not distinguish between spending time at home with children and indulging in an unprincipled life of leisure and consumption. They consider "my home-ism" a sign of laziness: "The younger workers do what they are told and not one iota more," scolds the author of a book on newly hired corporate employees.[17]

Polls also indicate a surprisingly low level of job satisfaction across the board. A cross-national survey found that the Japanese rank with the British as among the least satisfied in terms of a match between jobs and values.[18] Similarly, a survey conducted by a major Japanese newspaper in six Japanese and six American firms revealed that two-thirds of the Japanese respondents felt overworked and almost all of them felt underpaid. Three-quarters of the American respondents chose work over family and community as the source of lifetime satisfaction—leading the newspaper to conclude that Americans are "just as workaholic as Japanese."[19]

Survey findings must be taken with a grain of salt, because many Japanese appear to have a penchant for responding pessimistically to polls. The "my home-ism" of a salaried employee in his twenties may well give way to greater dedication to work when he reaches his thirties and forties. The managing director of one high-technology company's research laboratory asserted that enthusiasm was as high as ever among his young recruits.[20] All the same, such companies may be the exception. Less dedication to work seems too pervasive to dismiss.

Conversely, Americans are more committed to work than many Japanese commonly believe. Even though American workers do not normally want to put in much overtime, Japanese companies who hire them report that they work hard and well in good management settings. College professors also note that American students are far more concerned with work and career than they were fifteen years ago.

Common to both American and Japanese workers are energy, ingenuity, a "fix-it" instinct, and eagerness to learn. So is a demonstrated competence. Americans may be a bit more impatient than Japanese—or any other people for that matter. (Titles of popular books, courses, and newspaper articles are indicative: "The 30-Minute Gourmet," *The One-Minute Manager,* and "Sushi in Three Hours.") But their competence is seldom in doubt. As one Englishman put it:

> They work at it: the garage hands and the salesmen, the corporation executives and the scientists. We laugh at their "how-to" obsession. . . . But the bottom line is that Americans are constantly changing to grapple with their future. They want to learn.[21]

Education.   Education is another field where two relatively extreme patterns seem to be moving a little closer to the middle. Paradoxically, changes on both sides were prompted in part by the same need—to keep pace with the demands of economic competition. Americans have tried to integrate some of the rigor of Japanese education into their system, while the Japanese are trying to introduce some elements of American creativity into theirs.

Education has been valued in Japanese society for centuries. Building on this tradition, Meiji-era leaders upgraded education to a pressing national priority. Believing that human resources could partially overcome the lack of natural resources, they designed an educational system to meet the challenge of catching up with the West.

The spirit behind this commitment to high-quality education persists to this day.[22] Japanese schools are turning out perhaps the most highly educated young people in the world. Schools offer a rigorous but relatively well-rounded curriculum, featuring not only the traditional academic subjects, but also sports, various extracurricular activities, and trips. Japan's high school students hold the world's highest test scores in mathematics and science. Graduates are not only educated but educable, capable of being trained throughout their career. A study team sponsored by the U.S. Department of Education reported in 1987 that Japanese children succeed in large part because they are taught diligence and attention to detail in a well-ordered and purposeful environment.[23] One of the advantages enjoyed by Japanese companies is the rich base from which to recruit tomorrow's first-class engineers and skilled workers.[24]

On the other hand, it appears that only the better schools encourage limited discussion and debate in the classroom. Learning by rote, pressure to conform, unwillingness to ask or be asked challenging questions, lack of attention to the individual needs of students (especially gifted stu-

dents), and preoccupation with "examination hell" are among the handi-
caps cited by the critics.

Many thoughtful parents and educators in Japan and in the United
States recognize that American schools have one enormous strength:
a climate that fosters considerable individual creativity and self-
expression.[25] They believe that these qualities are keys to the growth of
knowledge on which the future depends. And from this perspective they
have come to the conclusion that Japan must reform its educational
system.

The National Council on Educational Reform, appointed by Prime
Minister Nakasone in 1984, was charged with examining these complaints in a broader context. From the outset, the council undertook to
look at the development of students as full human beings. It found much
to criticize: the lack of appreciation for nature, the disappearance of moral
education (whose reintroduction is bitterly opposed by the teachers'
union, which is not represented among the council's members), and lack
of parental supervision (read mother's absence from home) in two-career
families. It even found fault with the emphasis on science and technology, seeing not progress but rather "the spread of materialistic ideas, the
absence of feeling, an excessive emphasis on an empirical approach and
on quantifiable values, a lack of reference for the sublime, less contact
with nature, and a lack of due regard for the dignity of life."[26] Because of
such comments, the council came to be seen as unduly traditional and
unenthusiastic about modern education in general. Unlike other commissions appointed by Prime Minister Nakasone, this one seemed to offer
relatively little guidance for the future.

Perhaps the clearest example of the council's "traditional" outlook was
its assessment of individualism and creativity. While it initially appeared
to embrace these concepts as central goals of reform, the council ended up
expressing strong reservations about them. It rejected, for example, the
word *kojin-shugi* (one of several words for "individualism") because it
connotes selfishness. In the same vein, the council criticized any interpretation of individuality that implies an "imbalance between the assertion of rights and the awareness of responsibility."

The council had little to say about a concern of many parents and
educators: the intense academic pressure on the young, which some associate with the much-publicized problem of bullying (*ijime*) and occasional suicide among adolescents. A child's performance on examinations will virtually determine his lifetime career pattern. The council dealt

gingerly with these complaints and with related complaints about the in-famous examinations governing entrance to Japan's top universities; it criticized "excessive competition," but stopped far short of recommend-ing more well-rounded admissions criteria.

Nevertheless, signs of change have appeared. Several of Japan's major universities have established special programs geared to students return-ing from abroad that de-emphasize standard examination results and give credit for fluency in a foreign language. This trend is now spreading to the schools. One reform under discussion would shift the beginning of the school year from April to September, thus making it easier for foreign teachers and students to spend time in Japan and for Japanese students to go abroad for schooling. There is also talk of more flexibility in the class-room, with greater opportunity for debate and self-expression. But it is difficult to judge how far and how fast long-standing patterns will change. Certain after-school tutoring programs already emphasize creative methods in preparing students for examinations. Further pro-gress in this direction is likely as today's young people become tomor-row's teachers.

While these changes are occurring in Japan, American education is moving in the direction of more discipline and academic depth. In 1983, a Presidential commission on American education saw "a nation at risk," threatened by "a rising tide of mediocrity that threatens our very future as a Nation and a people."[27] It warned that today's children will be the first generation in modern American history to fail to meet or exceed the edu-cational standards achieved by their parents.

Although the commission's gloomy findings have been challenged, there is no doubt that American education is stumbling in some important respects. To rectify the situation, a number of states are seeking to up-grade teachers' qualifications, raise teachers' salaries, and re-emphasize the "three Rs"—reading, writing, and arithmetic. Recognizing that break-throughs in knowledge depend not only on individual creativity but also on team effort, some schools are experimenting with learning through teamwork in the classroom.

American students are more diverse than their Japanese counterparts, and the American educational system is far more decentralized. For these reasons alone, significant differences in educational philosophy will re-main. Nevertheless, in education, as in other fields discussed earlier, Japan and the United States are discarding outdated attitudes and be-havior and are beginning to move closer to each other.

Politics

Just as the two societies face many social problems and challenges common to the industrial and postindustrial age, so the two political systems operate in a roughly comparable environment. Above all, both are functioning democracies.

The structure and process of Japanese politics are quite different from those in the United States. In America, two major parties take turns in the White House; in Japan, the LDP has ruled almost without interruption for forty years. The spectrum of political representation in Japan is more extreme, owing to the presence of sizable and active Socialist and Communist parties. Yet Japan's political parties, compared with political parties in the United States, are organized more around personalities than issues. Hence the prevalence of factions and personal support organizations and the relative weakness of local party organization.[28] Party discipline is also much stronger than in the United States.

Japan has what is sometimes called a "one-and-a-half party system" because all of the opposition parties combined cannot seem to break the LDP's long-running majority. (As of 1987, the LDP held 304 seats out of 512 in the Lower House.) Although voters have signaled dissatisfaction with LDP policies by voting for candidates from other parties, they seem to stop short of actually wanting them to take power.

The legislative process presents another contrast. In Japan, emphasis is always given to building a consensus between the government and the Diet, among the parties, and within parties before draft legislation is submitted. Absent are such features of American politics as filibustering, up-and-down votes, bolting ranks, and public criticism of individuals in authority. Although showdowns are sometimes inevitable, the LDP takes great pains to avoid the appearance of exercising the tyranny of the majority.

Resolutions, like laws, are introduced and passed in the Diet only after intense compromise and consensus-building. Typically, they are adopted when parties cannot agree on specific legislation or when the LDP feels the need to appease opposition parties. Because resolutions usually embody vaguely worded but symbolically important compromises reflecting extensive discussion, they tend to acquire a status almost as binding as law. Resolutions relevant to U.S.-Japan relations include those urging the government to observe the ban on possession, introduction, and manufacture of nuclear weapons and to restrict the use of space to peaceful purposes.

In the United States, by contrast, any one of the 535 members of Congress can introduce a bill. Bills are often a means of initiating a debate, not resolving it; only a very small number ever make their way into law. Resolutions are also more transient and haphazard than they are in Japan; they are often drafted and passed hastily in response to a major news story of the moment. For members of Congress, resolutions offer a cheap way of going on the record without commitment to do anything further in the way of binding legislation.

These differences in the legislative process often exacerbate U.S.-Japan tensions. Although the Japanese press appears to be getting more selective in its coverage, it still tends to give undue publicity to minor bills and resolutions in Congress. Misunderstanding how the system works, many Japanese overreact to the fireworks of the American legislative process, confusing introduction with final passage and rhetoric with substance. Americans, for their part, find the Japanese system opaque and snail-like. Even the most progressive Japanese discourage Americans from pressing for reforms that require action in the Diet, however obvious the need.

Another difference between the two systems lies in the demographic make-up of political constituencies. Whereas large parts of America are still rural, a fact reflected in political representation, very few rural districts as such are left in Japan. Depending on the yardstick used, only 22 to 24 out of 130 Lower House districts (electing 76 to 91 out of 512 members) now qualify as "rural." It is true that the reapportionment of Diet seats lags way behind the urban sprawl of the 1950s and 1960s, but Japan's overrepresented districts are no longer primarily agrarian; they are more like suburbs or provincial towns, or perhaps like America's northeastern districts. As a result of the decline of rural representation, the agricultural lobby in Japan, which has acted to restrict the sale of a number of products from abroad and maintain high price supports, has gotten weaker.

As the number of full-time farmers and agricultural laborers has shrunk, a new class of provincial businessmen and related interest groups has sprung up, spawned by the spread of industrialization in general and the extension of vast public works projects to rural and suburban areas. The construction industry has become particularly powerful. Its open resistance to foreign participation in the construction of the planned Kansai International Airport on the outskirts of Osaka is an ongoing source of U.S.-Japan tension.[29]

These dissimilarities tend to obscure a number of commonalities between the two political systems, including a drift toward centrism, a shift in the balance of power from the bureaucracy to the legislature, and—above all—a flourishing democracy.

Until the mid-1960s, postwar Japan's political life was marked by ideological polarization and conflict. The major opposition parties—the Socialists and the Communists—often took extreme positions and employed obstreperous tactics.

In the following decade, a more ideologically pluralistic, democratically mature, multiparty system emerged, with middle-of-the-road parties—notably the Komeito (Clean Government Party) and the Democratic Socialist Party—enjoying a rise of support. This development, along with the ongoing strength of the Socialists, obliged the LDP to respect what became known as "parity between conservatives and progressives." The handling of disagreements evolved from heated arguments and occasional fisticuffs to backroom compromises over drinks.[30]

The 1980s have witnessed a further decline of political extremism and a corresponding shift toward moderate/centrist positions. Fewer voters in Japan now call themselves either "progressive" or "conservative"; more voters—especially those in their twenties—call themselves "independent."[31] Annual polls have registered an increase in the percentage of voters who believe that "national policy corresponds to the people's will," which seems to be another way of saying that the Japanese are satisfied with the status quo.[32]

Opposition parties have taken advantage of this drift toward centrism, forcing the LDP to compete against them for the support of urban voters on bread-and-butter issues. The public now tends to see the LDP as experienced, pragmatic, and committed to stability, rather than as conservative or pro-farmer. Competition for leadership in the post-Nakasone era among three "new leaders"—Noboru Takeshita, Shintaro Abe, and Kiichi Miyazawa—is unlikely to alter this perception.

In the United States, too, centrism and moderation have gained ground. The left wing of the Democratic Party has lost a certain amount of credibility, while the right wing of the Republican Party has partially burned itself out or strained the tolerance of the public. Whoever succeeds Ronald Reagan is likely to pursue middle-of-the-road policies supported by moderates in both parties. Political leaders in both countries will pursue the "yuppie" vote, which is typically moderate to conservative.

In both countries, parties and interest groups that have traditionally been oriented to the working class as such are losing the support of blue-collar workers. Unions have suffered a sharp drop in membership, reflecting both the smaller percentage of blue-collar workers in the labor force and the attraction of job opportunities in nonunionized companies and regions. Partly because of this decline, the unions' political influence has waned considerably.

Another point of similarity is the increasingly complex maneuvering between the legislative body and the executive branch. Over time, Diet members as well as members of Congress have acquired real expertise in particular issue areas. There is, for example, a "defense *zoku*," which acts as an oversight group. Like their Congressional counterparts, some of these watchdogs have been around for years and wield considerable influence.

The enhanced political power of the Diet corresponds to a gradual erosion in the power of the government bureaucracy in favor of elected politicians. Several factors have contributed to this shift. One such factor transcends the political process as such: the bureaucracy has lost power because the gradual deregulation of the economy has reduced the number of available bureaucratic levers, such as postwar controls over the allocation of foreign exchange. The sheer size and vitality of the private sector has dwarfed government-funded industrial projects. New economic actors have grown out of infancy and are chafing at protective regulations. Although the government still enjoys great prestige and attracts some of the country's most elite graduates, it has lost much of its grip on Japanese society and hence on the country's elected leaders.

Another factor is the legacy of the Tanaka era. Security issues have always generated intense activity in the Diet, but until the late 1960s Japan's elite bureaucrats ran economic affairs more or less on their own. During his tenure as prime minister, master politician Kakuei Tanaka interfered to a greater extent than had his predecessors with the daily work of the ministries. His colleagues in the Diet continued the practice.

Budget deficits arising from Tanaka's lavish spending programs on public works projects and social welfare also incited Diet members to take a more active interest in the work of the ministries. By the late 1970s, Japan's budget deficit as a percentage of GNP was the highest of all the industrialized countries. In reaction, the Finance Ministry initiated strict austerity programs and sharply curtailed "pork-barrel" spending, forcing politicians to compete for ever-smaller sums of money for their districts.

Yet another factor contributing to the power of the Diet was the Lockheed scandal of 1976, in which Tanaka and several others were indicted and eventually jailed for accepting bribes in connection with aircraft procurement. The ensuing revelations shook the foundations of Japanese politics, bringing about a situation not unlike that following the Watergate scandal in the United States. In the aftermath of Watergate, Congress—already soured on U.S. involvement in the Vietnam War—became permanently distrustful of the executive branch. The expansion of the Congressional staff dates in large part from that period, as legislators chose to rely on their own sources of information and advice rather than on the administration.

Tanaka's effective withdrawal from the political scene, following a severe stroke in 1984, created a leadership vacuum in the LDP's largest faction, thus bringing into greater play several smaller and weaker factions. Since none of them could command the same power, Tanaka's collapse had the effect of strengthening the LDP's cross-factional Policy Research Committee, thus enhancing the institutional role of the LDP as a whole. Although the committee commands a staff far smaller than the vast number of U.S. Congressional aides, it now stands alongside the factions as a durable fixture in the overall structure of the LDP.[33]

Over time, the larger policy-making role of the Diet may ease some of the tensions in U.S.-Japan relations. Diet members already maintain direct contacts with members of the U.S. Congress. Being politicians, they tend to understand each other quite well, and are skilled at judging what is politically necessary and at figuring out how to get there. As politicians are generally more sensitive to the concerns of their constituents than bureaucrats, consumers and other underrepresented groups in Japan may have more of a voice than before. Coalitions with selected Diet members may also help Japanese businessmen and their potential American partners cut through the bureaucratic maze. All in all, the more active role of the Diet reflects the trends toward pluralism already evident elsewhere in Japanese society, and is a generally positive development in U.S.-Japan relations.

Democracy.   The single most important commonality of the two political systems is democracy. To a great extent, democracy is what the U.S.-Japan alliance is all about.

Democracy is not an alien concept grafted onto the skin of Japanese society by the American Occupation authorities after World War II. For almost sixty years following the Meiji Restoration of 1868, Japan nurtured its own democratic seedlings, adopting a form of limited parliamentary democracy patterned largely on German and French models. In the late nineteenth century, there was lively debate between advocates of constitutional monarchy and those favoring more direct forms of democracy. Although fragile, these seedlings sprouted further between 1910 and 1925, during the period of "Taisho democracy."

Throughout those sixty years, however, anti-democratic weeds sprouted as well. For some Meiji-era reformers, democracy in the sense of genuine pluralism and debate was wasteful, debilitating, and unfocused. Japan, like China, had no time for such political luxuries; catching up with the West required too much work. Democracy was rowdy and chaotic, a waste of the national spirit.

This attitude gained ground in the 1920s; the introduction of universal male suffrage in 1924 was overshadowed by the Peace Preservation Act, which aimed to intimidate political candidates and stifle opposition. The hardship of the Depression strengthened the anti-democratic forces. As Japan edged toward war, the seedlings were crushed and their cultivators imprisoned or silenced.

The imposition of democracy on postwar Japan was, to say the least, a contradiction in terms. Democracy was thrust upon it, sincerely but heavy-handedly. While Americans believed deeply in democracy, they also had other motives—notably winning the Cold War and repelling the Communists. In 1948, the then Secretary of the Army asserted that the purpose of building democracy in Japan was to deter "other totalitarian threats which might hereafter arise in the Far East."[34] Takeshi Watanabe, then in charge of liaison between the Finance Ministry and the Occupation authorities, later said that America's "foremost preoccupation" was to keep Japan in the Ameerican camp without paying much in the way of economic aid.[35]

In these circumstances, it is hardly surprising that many Japanese became somewhat ambivalent about democracy. Some critics faulted the Occupation authorities for being arbitrary and high-handed in their purge of the rightists; on the other hand, they asserted that the Americans did not go far enough. Although democracy became a cherished idea, the understanding of it left something to be desired. Intellectuals frequently contrasted democracy with feudalism, which was presumed to be its opposite; for a while, they debunked everything traditional. The voices touting *demokurashii* became self-righteous and shrill; far from promoting democratic styles of thought, they found comfort in Marxist slogans and rejected pragmatism as chaotic and wasteful. Instead of reason and logic, one found ideology and extremism. Instead of loyal opposition, one found pitched battles.

These tremors came to a head in Japan's radical student movement of the 1960s.[36] Although student leaders called their demonstrations "democratic action," they were inspired less by a spirit of genuine democracy than by a much-admired Japanese ideal: the doomed hero futilely defying authority and dying a noble death. A MITI official who was a student with politically moderate views in those days confesses that it took him ten years to come to respect and appreciate the true meaning of the word "democracy."

Today, liberals and progressives in the universities and the press recoil from symbols reminiscent of Japan's militarist past. Many criticized Prime Minister Nakasone's official visit in 1985 to the Yasukuni Shrine and the revival of Founder's Day—commemorating, respectively, soldiers killed in action and the establishment of the imperial institution by Emperor Jimmu in 660 B.C. For similar reasons, many also opposed the lifting of the ceiling on defense spending, wondering why Americans seem so unconcerned about renewed militarism and so confident about the future of democracy in Japan. Some even suspect a double standard: "I often ask my American friends why they are so sensitive to signs of a Nazi revival in West Germany yet so willing to forgive former military collaborators and their protégés in Japan," complains journalist Yukio Matsuyama.

Others doubt that militarism poses even a potential danger. They acknowledge that Japan has a right-wing "lunatic fringe," complete with noisy sound trucks and occasionally nasty incidents. But the population at large, and the younger generation in particular, seems to have little attachment to the symbols of militarism. Like the "Me Generation" in America, Japan's young people are said to favor easy, eye-catching options and the pursuit of personal pleasure. Their attitude is hardly conducive to the patriotic self-sacrifice evoked by militarism.

Even relatively benign national symbols, such as the Emperor, for example, seem to have little or no appeal for the young. A poll analyzing attitudes toward the Emperor on the sixtieth anniversary of his reign revealed that 70 percent of respondents in their twenties registered no special feeling, and even indifference. For older Japanese, on the other hand, the Emperor is a cherished symbol of national unity; for right-wing nationalists, the imperial institution is a special focus of reverence and devotion.

As poll results are variable, a more meaningful index of democracy is the strength of democratic institutions. One of these institutional safeguards, a multiparty system with free elections, has already been mentioned. Another is a free press or, more generally, the freedom of expression. In this respect, too, Japan seems to have come of age as a functioning democracy.

The Japanese press has a complex, emotional history. Pressured, threatened, and even physically attacked before the war, Japanese newspapers gave in to the militarists and ended up supporting the war with apparent conviction. Partly because of this experience, some say, the press today suffers from a kind of institutional guilt complex. The brief period of censorship imposed by the American Occupation seems to have had a similarly destabilizing effect. Since then, the press has been bursting with pent-up views and emotions, which are often biased and subjective. News articles tend to be laced with editorial innuendoes.

Today, the three major national newspapers (*Asahi Shimbun*, *Mainichi Shimbun*, and *Yomiuri Shimbun*) serve as self-appointed watchdogs of the nation. Although they prod the slow-moving and faction-ridden LDP, individual reporters practice a form of collusion with the politicians whom they cover. There is little in-depth investigative reporting of the sort encountered in America.

One promising trend is that the three major dailies have branched out and away from each other. In the past they tended to be unanimous and automatic in opposing the government's position; now editorial opinions give evidence of greater sophistication and political diversity, ranging from somewhere left of center to slightly right of center. Another trend is more debatable: television appears to be overtaking the print media as the major source of news for the Japanese public. This shift is somewhat disturbing because viewers are unlikely to retain much from short news spots—especially as they are often doing something else while the television is on. Moreover, television coverage of complex issues is inevitably transitory and superficial. On the other hand, the trend could be healthy if it encourages viewers to form independent opinions.

At what point is a country judged to be truly democratic? More than forty years after World War II, many Americans and not a few Japanese still doubt the sturdiness of democracy in Japan. They note that in the postwar period, democracy has coincided with economic growth, and wonder how it would fare in the face of adversity.

On the worrisome side, Japan still lacks a system of checks and balances. In a society bathed in consensus and residual hierarchy, there are few cultural valves to shut off the flow of pressure to conform. Resistance to the abuse of power is often weak or nonexistent. "A big tree protects you in the presence of authority," runs a Japanese saying. Another one goes, "If something long tries to coil around you, resign yourself and let it happen." Japanese society gathers momentum slowly, but once it embarks on a course of action it has difficulty stopping or reversing course. Japan's new arrogance seems to typify a kind of industrial nationalism, not particularly compatible with militarism but not particularly sympathetic to liberal and democratic values either.

On the other hand, key democratic institutions are not only well-rooted but blooming. It is less clear that democracy has been fully internalized at the level of the individual, but the trends seem healthy and appear to give no cause for concern. Democracy in Japan may not exactly resemble democracy as practiced in the model New England town meeting, but neither does democracy as it is practiced in most other societies. If democracy means making decisions through the free and public exchange of different points of view, then democracy in Japan is thriving in its own way and in its own style. Professor Gerald Curtis of Columbia University puts it this way:

> The truth is that Japan like the United States has woven the threads of democratic political life—civil liberties, open elections, competitive politics, and responsible government—into the fabric of the nation's social structure to create a stable political system that echoes universal values and behavior while at the same time being utterly unique.[37]

Democracy is associated with the essence of the Western alliance, and in particular with America's global goals and values. Japan's evolution toward democracy, intertwined as it is with economic prosperity, has sent a strong signal to the rest of Asia. Those Japanese who support democracy in its truest sense are generally the same people who are most supportive of a free and open trade and investment climate, a cooperative security relationship, and a larger role for Japan in global development. For all these reasons, the United States has—or ought to have—a special interest in the future of democracy in Japan. This is not a paternalistic assertion left over from the Occupation, but a solid conclusion based on the realities of the world today.

Americans obviously do not control the fate of Japanese democracy; whatever they do—even "Japan-bashing"—will not cause it to collapse.

They do have an influence, however, on the Japanese perception of external threat. In the current economic and political climate, many Japanese see the Soviet Union as a lesser danger than the specter of Western Europe and North America ganging up on Japan to choke off its lifeline, trade. If relations deteriorate to the point where that specter appears to be materializing, and tensions reach the boiling point, the least democratic and least progressive elements in Japan are bound to gain a larger following. "Japan-bashing" clearly feeds the perception that such a deterioration is in fact occurring.

This is not an argument for inaction on America's part or for excuses on Japan's. The point is simply that the U.S.-Japan alliance is and must remain a community of values. To the extent that Americans and Japanese overcome barriers to communication and trust and believe that they share common social and democratic values, they will learn to cooperate more fully with each other as true partners in a common global endeavor.

Seven

Adjusting to New World Roles

J apan and the United States not only have a great deal in common as industrial societies; they also have many similar objectives in foreign policy and national security. In fact, with the possible exception of Mrs. Thatcher's Britain, Tokyo probably comes closer to sharing Washington's views on world issues than any other U.S. ally.

Until fairly recently, however, certain attitudes and values associated with the lingering "rich/poor" images identified earlier in this book precluded the development of a full-fledged U.S.-Japan partnership in foreign policy and defense. In the early postwar years, economic recovery was a matter of survival. For the sake of rapid economic growth, Japan kept defense spending to a minimum, stayed out of foreign conflicts, and relied on the security umbrella extended by the United States.

Reinforcing this poverty-driven economic orientation was the loss of confidence stemming from total defeat in World War II. Japan had entered the European-American colonial game too late; its policy of conquest and expansion had come to ruin. It was left with bitter wartime memories and a profound reluctance to venture forth again into international politics. Foreign-policy goals extending beyond Japan's borders— and the military power needed to back them up—were not only luxuries, but frightening reminders of the past. Accordingly, Tokyo's foreign-policy goals were limited and its instruments few.

Similarly, foreign-policy goals articulated by the United States and its European allies, such as containing Communism and aiding economic development in the Third World, seemed remote and largely irrelevant to Japan's immediate tasks. In any case, the means of carrying them out— from development assistance to military aid—were either inappropriate or beyond reach.

For several decades after the war, both Tokyo and Washington seemed to prefer that Japan remain a junior partner in the alliance and leave the pursuit of global political-military goals to others. At first, it seemed only natural that Tokyo should rely so heavily on the United States: America was militarily and economically strong and Japan was shattered. Washington really did not need Japan's help abroad.

Indeed, as late 1976, Japan's stated policy was to resist "limited and small-scale aggression" and to rely on both Soviet-American détente and U.S. protection against large-scale aggression. Wary of renewed militarism and mindful of the benefits of the U.S. security umbrella, Tokyo took the position that "for the time being," annual defense spending would not exceed one percent of Japan's gross national product.

Also in 1976, Tokyo extended its policy of barring arms sales to Communist countries, countries targeted by United Nations restrictions, and countries involved in international disputes—the "three principles of arms embargo"—to a general ban on exporting anything military to anyone, anywhere. Under the new policy, the government banned, for example, the sale of semi-finished pipe intended for artillery tubes to South Korea and of hand grenade pins to the Philippines.

Yet in the space of a few years, Japan began to broaden its foreign policy beyond a weak defense posture and a single-minded quest for resources. As both Tokyo and Washington have begun to adjust to Japan's new wealth, the partnership has become far more equal.

Common Threats and Interests

At the Williamsburg summit of 1983, the world witnessed an implicit extension of the Western security alliance to include Japan. On that occasion, Prime Minister Nakasone joined the leaders of the industrialized Western nations in announcing that "the security of our countries is indivisible and must be approached on a global basis."[1] Barely two years earlier, then Prime Minister Zenko Suzuki's reference to a U.S.-Japan "alliance" had produced a minor uproar, leading to the resignation of the Foreign Minister.

At the London summit in 1984, Prime Minister Nakasone expressed support for the deployment of intermediate-range nuclear forces in Europe and for other self-strengthening measures. No longer passive observers, Japanese diplomats sought to ensure that arms control agreements centered on Europe did not lead simply to a corresponding buildup in Soviet Asia. By 1986, the Japanese Foreign Minister could speak publicly, as an involved and knowledgeable ally, of the global strategic implications of Soviet SS-20 missiles—without the political brouhaha that would have erupted five years earlier.

In defense and foreign aid in particular, Tokyo has taken slow but significant steps to develop the resources and instruments in response to new global threats and interests.

Both Washington and Tokyo agree that the strategic balance in Asia is generally favorable. Nevertheless, both are concerned about the Soviet Union's steady military buildup in Asia since the late 1970s. This buildup includes the deployment of a new generation of offensive weapons, including two Kiev-class aircraft carriers, Backfire bombers, and SS-20 missiles; the stationing of up to a division of ground combat forces plus Mig-23 aircraft in Japan's Northern Territories since 1978, as well as of an estimated 370,000 soldiers along the Sino-Soviet border, where troops are transported along a new network of roads and railways; a Pacific fleet of perhaps 700 ships and 130 submarines, many of which took part in unusually large-scale exercises in the western Pacific in 1986; and access to air and naval facilities in Vietnam and, through the Indian Ocean, to facilities in Ethiopia and South Yemen.[2] Whatever Japan can do to thwart the effectiveness of this buildup is of obvious value to American forces. For example, Soviet SS-N-18 missiles launched from Delta III-class submarines in the Sea of Okhotsk are capable of hitting the continental United States. Japan's ability to blockade the Soya, Tsugaru, and Tsushima straits through which Soviet vessels gain access to the Pacific and the major Soviet base of Petropavlovsk in the Kamchatka Peninsula would "bottle up" Soviet vessels, and thus buy precious time, as well as free up at least some U.S. forces for deployment elsewhere.

Another shared interest is maintaining the strategic balance in the Korean peninsula. In South Korea, stability has been strained by periodic political tension and rapid economic growth. Since the mid-1970s, North Korea has pumped 20–25 percent of its GNP into defense, virtually doubling its ground forces. Still, South Korea has been gaining ground, and is generally judged capable of achieving parity with North Korea by the early 1990s.

Since 1960, Japan has provided support for U.S. military activities in Korea. Tokyo's current support ranges from large amounts of economic assistance to Seoul to helping to maintain U.S. based in Japan that would be used—after prior consultation—in a Korean contingency.

China is not viewed as a military threat. All the same, Japan is in no hurry to see China transformed into a major military power. Tokyo shares with Washington a positive assessment of Peking's swing toward economic and political moderation.

Tokyo and Washington also share an interest in preserving stability in Southeast Asia, where the countries known collectively as the Association of Southeast Asian Nations (ASEAN), with the possible exception of the Philippines, seem both politically and economically resilient. Vietnam's continued presence in Cambodia, however, is a source of potential conflict and subversion. Hoping that the prospect of economic prosperity in the region might encourage Vietnam to pursue peaceful collaboration, Tokyo has apparently stood behind Japanese companies seeking new business opportunities in Vietnam—a move that has drawn criticism from ASEAN.

Japan's relationship with Western Europe is far from what it could or possibly should be. In retrospect, it is unfortunate that Japan did not or could not take the initiative to build a stronger political relationship with Western Europe before trade problems became acute. As matters stand, Japan has a problem of "damned if you do, damned if you don't." Tokyo's political initiatives are seen as efforts to buy its way out of trade frictions, but failure to take such initiatives only reinforces Europe's view of the Japanese as "economic animals."[3]

In light of Japan's dependency on the Middle East for roughly two-thirds of its total oil imports, and its sizable petroleum-related investments in the region, conflicts in the Middle East weigh heavily on Japanese thinking. Like many of America's other allies, Tokyo maintains a dialogue with the Palestine Liberation Organization and does not go nearly as far as Washington in its support for Israel. Even so, the region as a whole causes few real disagreements between the two capitals. Washington supported Tokyo's intense but ultimately unsuccessful effort in 1980 to find a solution to the Iran-Iraq war, and welcomed its quiet aid for covert and circuitous U.S. efforts to secure the release of American hostages in Lebanon. All things considered, the Middle East constitutes only a partial exception to the substantial commonality of views on international political and security issues prevailing in the two capitals.[4]

The New Activism I: Defense

The relatively low level of Japan's defense spending has been an issue in the "fairness" debate. Some Americans assert that by concentrating its resources on economic growth and industrial exports and relying on the

United States for its security, Japan has been enjoying a "free ride" at American expense.[5]

Yet even *before* the Nakasone-Reagan era, Tokyo had begun to make larger contributions to maintaining U.S. forces in Japan and to selected force improvements of direct and tangible value to the United States. It had also begun to shift toward active participation in joint defense activities with the United States. The Guidelines for Japan-U.S. Defense Cooperation, adopted in November 1978, provided for the participation of Japanese forces in joint training exercises with the United States.

In 1980, for example, Japan's Maritime Self-Defense Force took part for the first time in the Pacific rim naval exercise known as RIMPAC. In 1981, the Ground Self-Defense Force and the Air Self-Defense Force followed suit in joint exercises with their American counterparts. These low-key and relatively invisible activities provided U.S.-Japan defense forces with valuable hands-on experience, significantly enhancing cooperation in pursuit of common security interests.

Cooperation in sea-lane defense also began in 1981. At the time, experts in both capitals had suggested that Japan upgrade an existing Japan Defense Agency guideline to the status of a national policy—namely, that Japan would assume responsibility for defending its sea-lanes to a distance of 1,000 nautical miles. In 1982, following a series of classic exercises in ambiguous communication—marked by complicated maneuvers designed to satisfy domestic political interests on both sides—Tokyo proposed a joint study on the subject.[6] Because Japan had foresworn collective self-defense and limits itself to individual self-defense, two conditions were attached to the actual exercise of sea-lane defense: that U.S. vessels must be engaged in an effort to defend Japan, and that the commercial vessels being defended are bearing vital supplies. Despite these two conditions, improvements undertaken in the name of sea-lane defense—such as improved early warning, air defense, and antisubmarine warfare capability—serve the common security of both countries.

Tokyo's decision in 1986 to participate in the controversial Strategic Defense Initiative program is a particularly meaningful symbol of enhanced cooperation with the United States in the interest of global security. In earlier years, Japan's sensitivity to nuclear weapons and its long-standing commitment to the peaceful use of space might easily have precluded participation in SDI. For Tokyo to have responded positively, despite strong objections from the Soviet Union and dissent from members of Prime Minister Nakasone's own party, required not only the usual study groups and visits to U.S. laboratories, but also internal lobbying, consensus-building, and vision of unusual proportions. To be sure, participation was strongly backed by Japanese industry, which saw opportunities for commercial gain. Even so, the government delayed the actual announcement of its decision until after the LDP's landslide victory in the 1986 elections. In announcing its decision, the government declared that SDI could contribute to the deterrence capability of "the West as a whole, including Japan," and placed participation in SDI in the context of enhancing defense cooperation under the U.S.-Japan Security Treaty.[7]

Against this backdrop, it seemed inevitable that Japan would outgrow its self-imposed defense-spending limitation. Toward the end of 1986, after several false starts, planned defense expenditures finally broke what Prime Minister Nakasone called the political "sound barrier"—more or less avoiding a sonic boom. In the context of slower GNP growth induced by the revaluation of the yen, the new level of 1.004 percent of GNP is not significantly higher than the old. Politically speaking, however, it symbolizes the end of an era.

Washington has been uncharacteristically patient in the face of the one percent ritual, wisely avoiding the annual Kabuki drama associated with it. Rather than interfere publicly in a highly symbolic domestic debate, Washington has usually preferred to press quietly for speeding up the pace of agreed force-modernization programs. Visiting Japan in 1982, Secretary of Defense Caspar Weinberger skirted the one percent issue by remarking that Japan, with its economic vitality, was capable of reaching the level of self-defense already endorsed by the Prime Minister; in other words, it was incumbent on Japan to carry out its own decision, not a decision imposed by Washington. In a similarly diplomatic tone, the Pentagon's 1986 report to Congress on allied burden-sharing noted that whereas previous five-year defense plans had been regularly underfunded, the Japanese Cabinet's approval of full funding for the first year of the 1986–90 plan represented an "appropriate, significant step forward."[8]

Japan's defense expenditures now rank seventh in the world and second among nonnuclear nations. Per capita defense spending reached $187 in 1987—rapidly catching up with the estimated NATO average of $242—and is projected to exceed $200 by 1990. By the beginning of the 1990s, Japan's defense spending is likely to exceed that of the United Kingdom and France.[9] Even though some of these numbers are driven up by the rise of the yen, Japanese defense outlays are still considerable. One percent of a very large number is still a large number.

Meanwhile, Tokyo has steadily increased its contributions toward the upkeep of American bases in Japan. Annually, Japanese taxpayers contribute roughly $1.8 billion (in 1987 dollars), or $39,000 per American soldier.[10] Moreover, despite the severe shortage of open space, Japan provides a variety of basing arrangements for roughly 46,000 Americans at some 118 military facilities. These arrangements include home port facilities for the Commander of the Seventh Fleet and an aircraft-carrier battle group, headquarters for the Fifth Air Force and the Ninth Army Corps, basing and cost-sharing for forty to fifty F-16s at Misawa in northern Japan, and facilities on Okinawa for one Marine Corps division and one Marine air wing (the only Marine Corps presence in the western Pacific).

This large U.S. presence saddles the Japanese Government with political as well as financial costs. Hardly a week goes by without some local criticism of housing arrangements, night-landing practices, or other dislocations associated with the U.S. military presence. Nevertheless, the presence of U.S. troops is seen as a reassuring symbol of America's commitment to the defense of Japan and, indeed, of the entire region. The American presence also serves as a buffer or lubricant between Japan and its neighbors, loosely uniting various countries in the region that probably could not achieve unity through their own efforts. In this respect, American troops in Japan serve the defense goals of all friendly Asian nations.

As the world's only victims of the nuclear bomb, the Japanese retain a special emotional aversion to nuclear weapons. The self-imposed ban on the possession, introduction, and manufacture of nuclear weapons is still sacred. In earlier years, the visit of U.S. naval vessels suspected of carrying missiles with nuclear warheads—it is U.S. policy to neither confirm nor deny that a given vessel carries nuclear weapons—inevitably set off antinuclear demonstrations.

In recent years, however, the nuclear question appears to have become blurred and defused as a radicalizing issue. Perhaps the Japanese have become resigned to the existence of nuclear weapons. Perhaps they are now assured that no Japanese prime minister will allow nuclear weapons on Japanese territory in the foreseeable future. Perhaps they see only a remote danger of conflict with the Soviet Union, and consider direct engagement with North Korea unthinkable. Clearly, Tokyo and Washington have handled the issue with delicacy and finesse. In any event, the Japanese are not losing sleep over "no first use" and the use of tactical nuclear weapons on the battlefield—issues which remain highly relevant to the defense of South Korea. In 1981, former Ambassador Edwin O. Reischauer's revelation that U.S. vessels visiting Japan had on occasion carried nuclear arms caused a political storm, but the furor died down without further consequences.[11] In 1985, an effort by Japan's antinuclear activists to block the visit of a U.S. ship carrying nuclear-capable Tomahawk missiles failed to attract mass support.

Signs of Japan's new activism in defense, more tangible than either the now-defunct one percent limitation or the political quiescence of the nuclear issue, are coproduction and technology transfer programs with the United States. These programs, a major pillar of U.S.-Japan defense cooperation, have become increasingly controversial.

A major problem with coproduction is cost. Nearly half of Japan's limited defense budget is eaten up by personnel costs. Only about one-quarter is available for the procurement of new weapons. And much of that is absorbed by domestic production, which now includes armored personnel carriers, tanks, self-propelled howitzers, and a variety of aircraft, missiles, ships, and launchers.

As the market is small and exports of military equipment are prohibited, the unit cost of items produced in Japan tends to be high when compared with mass-produced, off-the-shelf-items. Japan does not derive as much "bang for the yen" as it might if it simply bought more equipment from the United States. This is the major argument advanced by the United States (and on occasion by the Japanese Finance Ministry) in support of direct purchases of major weapons systems such as the next-generation fighter-support aircraft known as the "FSX."

On the other hand, coproduction ensures standardized and interoperable equipment, a crucial consideration in light of the distance between the two countries. It does not make sense to ship every piece of equipment requiring minor repair all the way across the Pacific. On-ground repair facilities in Japan could serve other countries and theaters of operation in Asia. Besides, Japan has a reputation for manufacturing high-quality equipment and maintaining it conscientiously. American-made weapons are not always cheaper in terms of life-cycle costs.

Perhaps the most significant argument for coproduction is that it would preclude a more costly "go-it-alone" approach on Japan's part, which would freeze out U.S. suppliers and intensify pressures to export Japanese-built weapons in the future. Because of "big-ticket" items, such as the F-15, well over half of Japan's defense production in dollar terms is currently licensed from American companies.[12] Japan's more nationalistic leaders resent the large scale and high visibility of these programs and chafe at the associated licensing controls. Even if the United States were to adopt a restrictive coproduction policy, it is by no means clear that Japan would obligingly purchase more from American defense suppliers. Indeed, Japan's not unjustified concern that the United States may be an unreliable supplier is one of the reasons why supporters of greater self-sufficiency appear to be gaining ground in Tokyo. All this argues not only for occasional coproduction, but also, where appropriate, for joint development of next-generation weapons, drawing on each country's best technology.

Some Americans have become increasingly wary about releasing advanced technology to Japanese companies, fearing that technology transferred for military purposes will come back to haunt American manufacturers in commercial markets. In 1982, for example, a high-ranking Commerce Department official reported after a trip to Japan that American F-15 fighter planes and commercial corporate jets were being built in adjacent bays. (Ironically, that particular jet turned out to be a commercial failure.) For the same reason, U.S. industry circles have voiced concern about Japan's participation in SDI.

Some Defense Department officials worry that American technology transferred to Japan will end up in the Soviet Union or that Japan's own technology will be illegally exported to the Soviet Union. It is commonly said that next to America, Japan is the number-one target for Soviet agents. An American company selling a supercomputer to the Japanese, for example, could not consummate the sale without lengthy government-to-government discussions on special security measures. Such precautions seemed justified in 1987, when investigators uncovered a major violation involving the export of sophisticated milling machines that can help to produce quieter Soviet submarines. The case had major political repercussions: while Tokyo took steps to tighten its laws and prevent future diversions, the U.S. Congress sought to punish the offending company by restricting the import and sale of its products.

On the whole, however, Japan has a good record of protecting classified or otherwise sensitive information. Allegations that Japan is a "sieve" with respect to technology transfer to the Eastern bloc appear to stem partly from misinformation, and partly from differing U.S. and Japanese perceptions of what should be restricted. In recent years, American definitions of what should be withheld have encompassed virtually every aspect of manufacturing, from technology and equipment for the construction of gas pipelines to a truck factory.

Instead of restricting coproduction, the United States has recently sought to encourage the flow of defense-related technology in the other direction—from Japan to the United States. In 1983, the two governments agreed to permit the export of Japanese military technology to the United States and to promote the transfer of dual-use technology (technology capable of both commercial/civilian and military application).[13] Partly to encourage this policy, the Defense Department sponsored two study teams to identify and assess those fields of Japanese technology that might be applicable to defense. The two fields chosen were electro-optics and advanced manufacturing. During his trip to Japan in April 1986, Secretary of Defense Caspar Weinberger stressed that in the era of high-technology defense, "there are few opportunities for deterring Soviet power more promising than combining Japanese and U.S. technological capabilities."[14]

Japanese leaders see technology as an attractive candidate for cooperative efforts because it is complex, diffuse, and therefore relatively safe as a political issue. Japanese companies are interested because they see a potential for entry into a large and hitherto untapped market, and because they are interested in learning what the Americans are doing. American companies seem to be just as interested in gaining access to Japanese technology. Many preliminary discussions along these lines have already taken place.

As of mid-1987, however, only a handful of transfers of military technology have been approved. Even proposed transfers of dual-use technology—of far greater interest to U.S. companies—have encountered some difficulties. Japanese inhibitions include fear of publicity, unwillingness to submit homegrown technology to U.S. export controls, and reluctance to assist potential American competitors in developing products for the commercial market. On the American side, firms are either unaware that Japan has anything to offer in the defense field or afraid that their customers in the U.S. military services might resist foreign technology despite high-level support for two-way technology transfer. Still, the idea behind the new policy is both valid and constructive, symbolizing as it does a more equal U.S.-Japan security partnership based on complementary strengths.

Strategic Dimensions

Many factors besides national pride help to explain why, for virtually the first time since World War II, Japan now seems prepared to make modest but tangible contributions to political-military and security goals whose scope far transcends its geographical boundaries. Not the least of these is a sophisticated cadre of politicians and officials who have now reached senior positions. These people have repeatedly taken the initiative to deepen public awareness of security concerns and to convince the Japanese public that positive contributions to global security are in Japan's national interest.

Personality-conscious Americans are quick to give credit to Prime Minister Nakasone, a wartime naval officer and former Defense Agency director who is known to be enthusiastic about expanding Japan's defense capabilities. The first prime minister since 1972 to serve two consecutive terms, Nakasone has shown himself capable not only of communicating confidently with Western leaders, but also of undertaking bold initiatives that have won plaudits in the West and at least grudging praise at home.

This interpretation greatly exaggerates the power of the prime minister. Decision making in Japan is widely diffused throughout the political and administrative system. Key decisions often originate with middle-level office directors who command information and resources. (For example, the decision to raise the one percent ceiling on defense spending was engineered and pushed through by key politicians and government officials behind the scenes.) For all of his personal drive and for all of his celebrated "Ron-Yasu" friendship with President Reagan, Nakasone could never have succeeded in nudging Japan toward a more active political-military role had it not been for his predecessors' tangible steps in support of a more active defense posture.

More directly responsible for Japan's emerging activism was the perception of Japanese leaders in the mid-1970s that both the global and the regional balance of power had begun to shift in a negative direction, and that these negative trends were offset in part by positive political trends in Asia. The former made additional contributions to security seem more urgent; the latter made them seem less dangerous.

One negative trend was the apparent deterioration in the strategic balance between the United States and the Soviet Union. The increased U.S. vulnerability to a Soviet first strike led Japanese leaders to question the whole concept of deterrence and to worry that the U.S. defense commitment might no longer be there for the asking. Also of concern to thoughtful Japanese policymakers were the Soviet Union's stepped-up activities in the western Pacific, eastern Siberia, and the Northern Territories, along with its hostile reaction to the 1978 treaty of friendship between Japan and China, which contained a clause opposing "hegemony" (the Chinese codeword for Soviet behavior). Political rumbles in the Philippines, the extension of Soviet bases in Vietnam, and the Vietnamese invasion of Cambodia were disturbing, and continuing tensions in the Korean peninsula lay just across the water.

Meanwhile, Moscow's invasion of Afghanistan jarred comfortable conclusions that the Soviet Union had become a status quo power. The Solidarity movement in Poland flared up—and was put down, illustrating both the long shadow of Soviet power in Eastern Europe and the inability of the West to do much about it. The much-publicized weaknesses of the proposed Rapid Deployment Force also raised doubts about American capabilities in Europe and in Japan. Commenting on the overall strategic balance, the Japan Defense Agency White Paper of 1983 described the international situation as "harsh, complicated, and fluid."[15]

Even less reassuring was Washington's "swing strategy," which was intended to enhance the mobility and flexibility of U.S. forces. Like rival siblings, Europe and Japan each began to fear that, in a crisis, the United States would abandon it for the sake of the other. Americans would swing either toward Asians for their money or toward Europeans for their supposed common heritage. In 1984, U.S. Under Secretary of State for Political Affairs Lawrence Eagleburger spoke of a "shift" in relations toward the Pacific region, adding, "more and more of our attention is going to be drawn toward the Pacific." Subsequent concern in Europe was such that Deputy Secretary of State Kenneth Dam was compelled to issue a statement reminding the world that the United States is a global power with global interests. "Europe gains, not loses from strengthened U.S.-Asian ties," he said. "We do not have the luxury of choosing to care about one region more than another."[16]

On a more positive note, the whole subject of defense became less frightening to the Japanese public, possibly because the danger of war in the region seemed to have receded with the normalization of relations between the United States and the People's Republic of China and the end of U.S. military involvement in Vietnam. Both events seemed to signal that a modest increase in Japan's defense capability would be seen as less dangerous and provocative than it would have been at a time of high tension and conflict. Peace in the region meant that Japan was less likely to be dragged into a war as a result of its security relationship with the United States.

These positive and negative developments were reflected in the positions adopted by Japan's political parties. By the early 1970s, both the Komeito and Democratic Socialist Party had come out in support of the Self-Defense Force (SDF) and the U.S.-Japan Security Treaty. A special committee on national security was established in the Diet in 1980. In 1984, even the Socialist Party inched toward accepting the SDF: Party chairman Masashi Ishibashi held that the SDF, while unconstitutional, exists according to law.[17] For Japan's left-wing parties, this seemingly inconsistent pronouncement was progress indeed. The new chairman of the Socialist Party, elected in the wake of the 1986 general election, has continued to sound this more pragmatic note.

For all of these reasons, the Japanese public—still strongly pacifist in its emotional orientation—gradually became reconciled to the SDF and even accepted the likelihood of modest increases in defense capabilities. This drift was exactly what Japan's defense strategists had hoped for; indeed, they had helped to push it along.

The New Activism II: Foreign Aid

Running parallel to Japan's evolving defense policy has been the expanding role of foreign aid. Although Japan entered the world of foreign aid only recently, it has become a significant aid donor, funding development projects all over the world.

Not counting reparations, Japan did not become an aid donor until 1965, when it joined the Development Assistance Committee (DAC) of the OECD. In that year, Tokyo acceded to a U.S. request for aid to Korea and Taiwan, and to the Lower Mekong Project (then seen as an important part of the Johnson Administration's strategy in Indochina). Japan's positive response to this request was partly influenced by the impending return of Okinawa, held by the United States since the end of World War II. By 1965, Japan was already lifting its head above economic recovery and seeking full national sovereignty, of which control over Okinawa was a symbol. In joining the community of aid donors and demonstrating that it was a responsible partner in Asia, Tokyo hoped to cultivate goodwill in Washington.[18]

With the reversion of Okinawa essentially accomplished in 1971, Tokyo was free to shape its foreign policy in pursuit of raw materials and overseas markets where Japan could earn the foreign exchange to pay for them. Even before the return of Okinawa, Japanese companies had re-built themselves into vigorous exporters. Eyeing huge Siberian energy re-serves, and citing the separation of economics from politics (*seikei bunri*), Tokyo established institutional trade arrangement with the Soviet Union despite the latter's occupation of the Northern Territories. Japanese com-panies also began massive energy and petrochemical investments in Iran. In 1971, these efforts culminated in the establishment of the Iran-Japan Petrochemical Corporation.

In this context, aid became a component of a broader economic policy of promoting trade and access to energy and raw materials. Export financ-ing, semi-concessional credits, and other forms of assistance followed closely in the path of the companies. Relying on that famous Japanese combination of close communication and subtle policy signals, major Japanese banks edged toward countries with energy, raw materials, and/ or promising domestic markets.[19]

The result was a form of diplomacy that aimed at establishing an economic presence all over the world without openly taking sides, if at all possible, in local conflicts. This policy, nicknamed "resource diplomacy," struck most Japanese as extremely appropriate. The safe and peaceful pursuit of economic goals symbolized Japan's total rejection of military ambitions. Besides, Japan still saw itself as a small, vulnerable nation with no natural resources and therefore never far away from poverty. (The oil shock of 1973 reinforced this self-image. Some of the officials who most strongly resist today's market-opening measures were responsible for coping with the oil shock and the desperate days that followed.)

But Japan soon began to bump into the limits of "resource diplomacy." In 1967, Japan registered its first postwar balance-of-payments surplus. By 1969, Japan's textile exports had become a major issue in bilateral trade with the United States. Around this time, members of Congress and even President Nixon began to resent what they perceived as Japan's "free ride" in defense.

From then on, criticism mounted against the self-serving nature of Japanese foreign aid. In 1974, Tokyo encountered hostile fire in the DAC and anti-Japanese demonstrations in Asian capitals. The first proposal to double Japan's official development assistance (ODA) took shape shortly after foreign pressure gathered momentum. Since then, there have been three doublings, the last of which was announced in the fall of 1985 and shortened from seven years to five in 1987. Between 1974 and 1984, Japan's ODA nearly quadrupled. In 1984, its contribution came to about

$4.3 billion, second only to the United States' $8.7 billion. Japan now contributes roughly one-fifth of the funds made available for the loan programs of the World Bank. It is also a major contributor to the Asian Development Bank. If Tokyo fulfills its promises, untied Japanese aid in the period 1988–91 will amount to $30 billion.[20]

Despite these increases, Tokyo has been criticized for giving "too little, too late." Indeed, Japan's ODA as a percentage of GNP is relatively low: 0.29 percent in 1985, as compared with the OECD goal of 0.7 percent. (America's official development assistance in the same year was only 0.24 percent.) Moreover, Japanese foreign aid contains a low "grant element": 79.5 percent in 1983, as opposed to 94.4 percent for the United States and an average of 91.2 percent for all DAC donors.

The critics are not confined to non-Japanese. Both the first and the second group of Japanese and American "wisemen" (known officially as the Japan-United States Economic Relations Group and the United States-Japan Advisory Commission, established in 1979 and 1983, respectively) called for major new aid efforts. In 1986, the all-Japanese Advisory Group on Economic Structural Adjustment for International Harmony (the "Maekawa Commission"), whose domestic recommendations were described in an earlier chapter, called not only for more aid, but for a higher grant element, untied aid, restraint on mixed credits, debt relief, lower interest rates, technology transfer, acceptance of more students from developing countries, and easier adjustment for Japanese returning from aid-related assignments abroad. Former Foreign Minister Saburo Okita has also been a particularly outspoken champion of expanded Japanese aid.[21]

Japan is not the only country offering tied aid (aid with tangible and intangible links to exports) and mixed credits (a mixture of concessional and nonconcessional loans designed to sweeten export bids). Moreover, its record in using these devices shows some improvement. But the very existence of tied aid in the context of a massive capital surplus continues to draw heavy fire in aid circles. Given the economic hardship associated with the yen/dollar realignment, however, tied aid and mixed credits are unlikely to fade away entirely.

Because Japan was the greatest beneficiary of the fall in oil prices in late 1985 and early 1986, it came under even greater pressure from the aid community to raise the level of its contributions. When it announced in the World Bank's Development Committee that its share of the soft-loan budget would fall, reactions were harsh. "It's inconceivable how a country with the biggest trade surplus and foreign reserves could take such a position," muttered a European delegate.

On the positive side, Japan's contribution as a share of total aid from OECD countries rose from 10 percent in 1974 to 15 percent in 1984. Foreign aid is much more popular in Japan than in the United States. In a series of public opinion polls conducted between 1981 and 1984, roughly 40 percent of the respondents supported higher levels of aid.[22] In one 1986 survey, 55 percent of the respondents favored giving more aid to developing countries.[23] In the United States, by contrast, foreign aid enjoys the support of only a tiny minority.

Takeo Fukuda, who became Prime Minister in 1976, was a strong supporter of aid to the then five members of ASEAN—Indonesia, Malaysia, Singapore, Thailand, and the Philippines. In what came to be known as the Fukuda Doctrine, the Japanese Government declared: Japan (1) would not become a military power; (2) would expand its economic, cultural, and political ties with ASEAN; and (3) base its policy toward Asia on mutual understanding and (it was implied) warm emotional ties. The Fukuda government also pledged a total of $1 billion for industrial projects in ASEAN's five member countries. As a result, Japan replaced the United States as the largest aid donor to Asia and contributed in no small way to the stability of the region.

Japan was one of the few major countries to remain in contact with the governments of Indochina after the United States pulled out in 1975. Tokyo suspended aid to Vietnam in 1979 after the Vietnamese invasion of Cambodia, but it stepped up aid to Indochinese refugees, if only as an alternative to accepting them as immigrants. In March 1986, Prime Minister Nakasone announced additional aid for the new Aquino government in the Philippines. All in all, Japanese assistance to developing countries is not what it could or arguably should be, but it is still considerable.

In the late 1970s, another set of developments began to steer Japanese foreign aid in a direction that coincided neither with "resource diplomacy" nor with the needs of the poorest of the poor. Chief among them was the shift in the global balance of power described earlier. This time around, American requests—and Tokyo's generally favorable replies—mirrored political and strategic challenges far beyond Asia.

In 1980, for example, shortly after Moscow's invasion of Afghanistan, Washington asked Tokyo to provide more aid to Pakistan and to strategically important countries in the vicinity of the Persian Gulf. Japan complied with these requests. Fully 30 percent of Japan's foreign aid now goes to countries far beyond East Asia: Pakistan, Egypt, Turkey, Somalia, Kenya, and the Sudan.

As Japan's aid to strategically important countries increased, the proportion allocated to Asian countries declined. Asia's share of Japanese aid fell from about 80 percent in 1976 to less than two-thirds in the mid-1980s. China entered the rolls as a major recipient in 1982, but the share of aid allocated to the now six countries in ASEAN—Brunei is now a member—fell to about 30 percent. South Korea is an exception. Japanese aid planners had previously judged that the Koreans had outgrown the need for concessional assistance on economic grounds. The South Korean Government, however, argued that Japan more or less owed Seoul extra assistance because of the latter's contribution to regional defense. For essentially political and strategic reasons, Prime Minister Nakasone wanted to improve ties with Seoul. In 1983, during his historic visit to South Korea, he resolved the conflict largely in Seoul's favor, and the two governments subsequently agreed on a seven-year, $4-billion aid package.

The gradual diversification of Japan's aid program during the 1970s signified that Japan, like the United States, was well on its way toward using foreign aid for political and strategic purposes, including the maintenance of global as well as regional stability.

Initially, Tokyo described this new orientation in characteristically vague language. In 1980, pursuing a policy developed under his predecessor Masayoshi Ohira, then Prime Minister Suzuki created a Cabinet Council on Comprehensive Security. Prompted by the usual desire to placate Washington, factional politics, and bureaucratic jockeying, the government coined the phrase "comprehensive security" in an effort to satisfy many different groups at the same time—all in the context of a very real historical evolution.

In general, comprehensive security signifies that true security must rest on economic and political strength as well as on military power. Japan, a country that had explicitly renounced regional or global military ambitions, was thought to be uniquely suited to round out the pursuit of security through nonmilitary means.[24]

Many Japanese liked the idea of foreswearing further military contributions to global security. They saw in comprehensive security an implicit division of labor in which America contributes military might and Japan contributes money. Others criticized comprehensive security for precisely that reason. They saw it as an excuse to keep defense spending low and to rely on U.S. protection and leadership to an extent unbefitting an economic giant. The official American position seemed to be that comprehensive security was fine, provided that Japan continued to contribute more to its own defense as well as to assist developing countries. As long as there remained a comfortable consensus along these lines, Japanese leaders saw no need to dispel the vagueness. The more nebulous the stated policy, the more Tokyo could get away with.

As far as the defense component of the security equation is concerned, the relationship between what the Japanese Government says—at least publicly—and what it does remains ambiguous. Where aid is concerned, however, words and deeds have become quite consistent. The reasoning is explicit: economic disorder in developing countries may give rise to political and social instability, eventually leading to international tension or triggering regional conflicts. Since development assistance contributes to the easing of tensions, Japan has been increasing its aid to those areas which are important for the maintenance of world peace and stability.[25]

Limits on Further Spending

To achieve simultaneously all of these goals—economic, humanitarian, and political-strategic—would require substantial resources. In 1986, for example, Chairman of the Board of American Express James D. Robinson III called publicly for additional Japanese aid on the order of $60 billion—some 13 to 16 times the current level—which he calculated would bring total Japanese spending on aid and defense into line with corresponding American expenditures.[26]

At least in the near future, budget restrictions will preclude meeting such gargantuan aid targets. As Japan's goals have branched out, the government's financial resources have shriveled or at least failed to bloom. In light of Japan's budget problems, the overall doubling of ODA may be particularly difficult to achieve. The bulk of Japan's financial resources lies in the private sector, not in the hands of the government. While the rest of the world criticizes Japan's ostensibly stingy behavior, the Japanese Government is preoccupied with keeping the lid on government spending—a goal that Americans are in no position to criticize. Until budget-cutting began in earnest a few years ago, Japan's budget deficit relative to GNP was larger than that of the United States. For several years, expenditures in every category except foreign aid and defense were either frozen or cut. Just as the budget came back into line, new pressures arose.

As described in Chapter 3, the Japanese Government found it necessary to stimulate the economy in 1986 and 1987—both to offset business losses associated with the revaluation of the yen and to stimulate domestic demand as a way of increasing imports. This meant allocating huge sums for public works, consumption, and investment, not for foreign aid.

Other factors stifling a positive response to proposals to raise overall aid levels include doubts in some circles about the effectiveness of aid and sensitivity to foreign criticism that Japan is trying to buy its way out of difficulties with its trade partners. Japan's foreign-aid experts, like their American and European counterparts, now recognize that the limited absorptive capacity of certain developing countries—not to mention frequent corruption—is an obstacle to externally funded projects. The government's report on official development assistance for 1985 observed that "the effective implementation of aid is becoming an increasingly pressing matter."[27]

The role of private philanthropy in supplementing Japan's official aid program is a new and interesting subject for discussion. In the last few years, Japanese corporations and foundations have increased substantially their contributions to international exchange and cooperation, but most of these contributions concentrate on science, technology, and medicine.[28] The government has floated several proposals aimed at making loans to developing countries more attractive to the private sector.

In pressing Japan to increase its aid contributions, American critics might follow the example set by the Pentagon in its handling of the one percent limit on defense spending—to hold the Japanese Government to the fulfillment of its own stated policy instead of demanding that it meet overall numerical targets. The official policy includes something far more beneficial than aid: access to the Japanese market for the manufactured goods of developing countries. In 1985, however, Japan absorbed no more than an estimated 7.4 percent of such exports, while the United States took 63 percent. The Japanese Government cannot change these figures by fiat, but it can move more speedily to create a climate in which manufactured goods from developing countries will be made available to Japanese consumers.

Japan's defense spending, like its foreign aid, also faces limits. Economic and budgetary constraints rule out a major increase in military outlays. Moreover, partly for historical reasons, and partly for lack of a "safe" vision of Japan's role in the world, the Japanese public still tends to recoil from anything that smacks of projecting power abroad. For all these reasons, the government is likely to move cautiously and slowly in the political-military arena for some years to come.

The United States is also facing a slowdown. As the severe macro-economic distortions associated with trade and budget deficits will necessarily occupy Washington's attention, past and present tools of U.S. foreign policy—defense spending and foreign aid—are bound to be subject to new restraints.

For both countries, a combination of economic slowdown and political-military limitations underscores the need to use existing resources selectively and wisely. For Washington, this means putting aside amateurism and ideology, concentrating on fundamental, long-term national and international interests, and devising measured and credible policies in pursuit of those interests. For Tokyo, the tasks are to define and articulate a constructive foreign-policy vision based on a positive sense of purpose, and to implement that vision by drawing more imaginatively on Japan's key assets—technology and people.

Japan Needs A Global "Identity"

The effort to define Japan's new role in the world inevitably raises the question of Japan's identity as a nation.

In America, the word "identity" as applied to individuals or to a group is associated with a coherent set of autonomous values and a sense of pride and separateness. Americans speak of "developing" or "asserting" one's identity, as if it were something to be thrust forward.

By contrast, Japan's postwar identity was benign and faceless, deliberately passive, modest, and retiring. The Yoshida Doctrine of the 1950s cast Japan's role in the world in negative terms: Japan would stay out of the limelight of power politics, foreswear national ambitions, and concentrate on rebuilding its domestic society.

The Japanese Government's outlook for the rest of the century, *Japan in the Year 2000,* defines Japan's future role in the world in essentially negative terms: Japan must abandon its obsession with "catching up," its self-image as a small nation, and its heavy reliance on exports.

It is harder to define a positive vision. As early as 1980, then Foreign Minister Saburo Okita declared an end to what he called a "passive" foreign policy and called on Japan to participate in the creation of world conditions rather than merely react to them. Despite much debate, however, there are no clear signs of a coherent alternative to the Yoshida Doctrine. The Maekawa Commission, the U.S.-Japan Advisory Commission, and other such groups all agree that Japan must open up its markets and contribute more to global development, but they spell out long-range economic goals that are hardly unique to Japan. In the absence of an international identity based on a coherent set of postwar Japanese values, Japan presents several faces to the world at the same time, choosing to downplay the occasional contradiction.

Vagueness is often useful in the context of domestic politics; as described in Chapter 5, vagueness is partly a matter of leadership style. When it comes to policies centered on political or strategic goals, vagueness also has special tactical advantages. To obtain acceptance by the Diet or the public, government spokesmen typically omit or downplay controversial aspects of the decision at hand, de-emphasizing its political-military implications. Through these means the Japanese Government has gradually and successfully won public acceptance of the more activist, strategically oriented policies described above.

Vagueness is not so well-received abroad, however. U.S. Government officials who are familiar with Japan may know what is really going on, but many Americans in both the public and the private sector tend to be suspicious. Whenever Tokyo edges out of diplomatic obscurity, they see nationalism and economic opportunism rather than an enlightened self-interest that encompasses genuine concern for the welfare of other countries. Alternatively, if Tokyo remains passive, they complain that in foreign policy Japan has no principles.

As a tactical matter, Japan could ease these suspicions by finding and articulating a new global identity and a foreign-policy vision. But more is at stake than tactics. Japan has become a major world player. Its new role calls for a stronger international personality and a more broad-minded, outward-looking foreign policy based on a healthy definition of its goals for the rest of this century and beyond. It needs a sense of purpose and some sense that the goals so chosen are broadly compatible with national values and strengths.

In the context of the debate about Japan's identity and its goals, four approaches stand out. Two are highly visible but politically marginal, and two are quite influential. In shorthand, the approaches on the political margin might be labeled "residual pacifism" and "martial nationalism," while the two with more general appeal might be called "material nationalism" and "liberal internationalism." While protagonists of these different approaches carry on a furious debate in the popular magazines, leading politicians—notably Prime Minister Nakasone—sometimes borrow from all of them.[29]

At one extreme, the strong pacifism of the early postwar years still exerts a certain emotional appeal. High school textbooks extol the United Nations and stress contemporary Japan's commitment to peace in a benign and idealistic way. This vision has lost ground in recent years, but it lingers on in certain newspapers, university circles, and left-wing political groups.

Residual pacifists shrink from the idea that Japanese foreign policy should become more visible, more active, and more responsive to the security concerns of the Western alliance. They oppose the policies of Prime Minister Nakasone and regard a resurgence of militarism and right-wing nationalism in Japanese society as a greater danger than the Soviet threat. They believe that a stronger defense industry will generate more money for right-wing politicians, whose goals are inimical to democratic values. In their view, Japan's foreign policy lacks institutional checks and balances and, as a result of the familiar consensus process, could swing toward an unrestrained political-military expansionism comparable to Japan's export drive in earlier years.

At the other extreme, champions of martial nationalism preach values and encourage attitudes associated with fervent patriotism and military virtues. Their favorite vehicle is a sound truck blaring martial music and hortatory speeches. They favor a significant arms buildup, partly because they believe that only military power can bring Japan self-respect and the respect of the world. Some martial nationalists are even convinced that Japan should acquire nuclear weapons. The press fears and attacks this school of thought. So do the liberal internationalists (described below), who fear that a revival of Japanese militarism would destabilize Asia and threaten their own proposals for modest self-strengthening.

The material nationalist approach to the world is unabashedly mercantilist. Its protagonists have no particular interest in military spending, except to the extent that it enhances the development of new technologies. They believe that Japan should behave like a "merchant country" (*shō-nin-kokka*), trading with everyone and seeking maximum gain for Japanese economic interests. Their patriotism takes the form of an underlying concern with national survival—a vestige of the "Japan is poor" mentality—combined with strong competitive instincts and a certain indifference to other countries' problems. This insularity and narrow self-interest is what the West finds so irksome and contemptible, and it is already breeding a backlash that undermines the mercantilists' own goals.

Finally, there are the liberal realists or liberal internationalists, who reject the mercantilists' narrow definition of national interest and want Japan to assume a larger share of global responsibility. An example of their outlook is the report of the Comprehensive Security Study Group, published in 1980, which recommends that Japan adopt a stronger defense posture, cooperate more closely with Western allies, and channel more aid to South Korea, Southeast Asia, and the Middle East in the interest of promoting political stability.[30] Liberal internationalists also favor efforts to open up Japan's domestic market and to improve the lot of Japanese consumers. Their approach is the most compatible with that of the Western democracies, in mood as well as in substance, because it appears to be rooted in realism, self-respect, moderation, and commitment to democratic values.

Liberal internationalists clearly bear most of the responsibility for Japan's recent contributions to shared political-military goals. In the process, they have gained domestic allies here and there—among the media, members of the Diet, and certain corporate circles—notably those who stand to gain from an open trade and investment climate. Relatively speaking, this group feels most comfortable with foreigners; many among them have lived abroad or at least traveled extensively. It is within their ranks that Americans seeking new business opportunities are most likely to find coalition partners.

Some liberal internationalists advocate a more active foreign policy, for they believe that Japan can bring fresh talent and unique resources to the solution of global problems. They make the point that Japan's new wealth—specifically, "information" and the technology behind it—is an important asset in the game of international politics, and a form of power hitherto denied to nations lacking an offensive-weapons capability.[31]

The uncertainty and debate surrounding Japan's past and present role in the world tend to surface in connection with highly symbolic events. One such event was Prime Minister Nakasone's official visit to the Yasukuni Shrine in August 1985—the first official visit by a prime minister since World War II. The shrine honors 2.4 million soldiers killed in various wars, not just World War II, but among those honored are General Tojo and thirteen others who were labeled "Class A war criminals" by special postwar tribunals. The visit provoked such intense criticism from the Japanese press and other Asian countries that Nakasone has not re-peated the gesture.

The controversy over the Yasukuni Shrine highlights the difficulty of developing a healthy nationalism. The symbols of the nation are highly charged. Yet it may be time for democratic, liberal, and internationally minded groups in Japan to take the lead in facing the past and working with these symbols instead of against them. Otherwise, the right wing will monopolize them, leaving the moderate forces with no patriotic plat-form of their own. The task is not to suppress nationalism, which remains a potent political force in all countries, but to redefine it in constructive in-ternational terms.

From this perspective, it may be a good sign that today's Japanese seem to be coming to terms with their country's role in World War II in a serious and open-minded way. The 1980s have seen a marked increase in the publication of declassified documents, diaries, memoirs, and books on the war and the years immediately preceding it. Outside of the schools, candid discussion of the war is more extensive than at any time in the last four decades.

These signs of self-searching could lead to a healthy confidence and na-tional self-awareness rather than to warmed-over guilt and/or right-wing defensiveness. As Japan faces the future, its renewed national self-re-spect need not be antiforeign in character. On the contrary, to the extent that young Japanese respect themselves and their country, they may grow up free from the lingering feelings of dependence that hobble and otherwise complicate Japanese approaches to U.S.-Japan relations.

Japan, Asia, and the West

As today's Japanese seek to shape a constructive foreign policy for the fu-ture, they talk of forging closer noneconomic ties with other nations. At the same time, they seem ambivalent about the two most logical candi-dates for a closer relationship: the rest of Asia and the West.

Japan shares with the rest of Asia a legacy of values and culture from China. Yet Japan's emotional identification with other Asian countries is problematic. Japan's identity, such as it is, is closely associated with race, language, and geography rather than with a set of clearly articulated values. The Japanese nation was just "there," so to speak; it was not a community founded consciously upon certain values. It had known wars, but no revolutions; it had a philosophy, but no universal and exclusive ideology.

Following the Meiji Restoration, enthusiastic reformers believed that Japan could and should forge a new or revived national identity. They sought out Western values and practices, and attempted to apply them to the tasks of modernization and self-strengthening. Their rallying cry was "Leave Asia and enter Europe" (*datsu a nyū ō*). Others, however, clung to "Asian" values and groped toward a latent pan-Asian identity.

For a while, this dualism was overshadowed by the quest for military power. Japan's military victory over China in 1895 symbolized the break with tradition: the relatively young and vigorous student had overtaken the aging, paralyzed teacher. Its subsequent victory over Russia in 1905 shattered the myth of white superiority, proving that Asians could beat the West at its own game. When Japan annexed Korea in 1910, not a single Western government protested. Later, Japan emulated the West in extracting ever greater extraterritorial concessions from China.

The "Asian/Western" dualism in Japan broke down in the 1920s and 1930s. One catalyst was the U.S. Immigration Restriction Act of 1924, passed by Congress in a massive, mindless reaction to Asian immigrants. Largely forgotten by most Americans, this law and its openly racist intent seemed to confirm Japanese suspicions that the Western powers would never admit Japan to the community of nations on an equal footing.[32] Japanese leaders were driven back upon a purely "Asian" policy and theater of operations, with fateful consequences.

Today, Japan has no real need to choose between Asia and the West. It enjoys passably good relations with all countries in Asia. With the exception of Indochina, they in turn enjoy good relations with Western Europe and North America.

Asia is the natural frame of reference for Japan's new, activist foreign policy. The Foreign Ministry's first postwar annual report, or "Blue Book," issued in 1957, listed "Japan as an Asian country" as one of the three basic principles of foreign policy. The other two were support for the United Nations and cooperation with Free World countries.[33] These principles are now firmly lodged in an overarching U.S.-Japan alliance.

References to Asia continue to appear in key Japanese foreign policy statements and speeches. If anything, these have become more supportive in the mid-1980s. In early 1986, Foreign Minister Shintaro Abe described Japan's policy toward Asia in terms of the warmth of heart-to-heart encounters, backing up his statement with a pledge of more aid. For their part, many Asian countries now look to Japan as a model for their own development.

Still, Japan's attitudes toward other Asian countries—and vice versa—are mixed. That Japan shares with them a racial and cultural heritage is beyond dispute. Like England, however, Japan is an island nation whose sense of identity does not seem to lie wholly with the continent. "Despite their often-heard claim of affinity with 'fellow Asians,'" wrote the managing editor of *Nihon Keizai Shimbun*'s English-language weekly in 1986, "the Japanese distaste for Asian people . . . is well known."[34] For some countries—notably China, Korea, Indonesia, and the Philippines—memories of Japanese behavior both before and during World War II remain vivid. They are understandably annoyed when Japanese textbooks downplay Japan's wartime and prewar aggression. Finally, Japan's sizable investments in energy and raw materials in Asian countries arouse suspicion of neo-colonialism. A loose racial affiliation reinforces Japan's identity as an Asian nation vis-à-vis the rest of the world, but it fails to overcome intra-Asian racial prejudices.

At the same time, Japan does not feel entirely at home in the West either. Some Japanese leaders have felt edgy, ambivalent, and self-conscious about joining the "white man's club" as one of the world's major industrial democracies. Other members of the "club" have sometimes ignored these sensitivities. At the Tokyo economic summit in 1979, for example, the United States and its principal European allies organized a key meeting from which several important countries, including Japan, were excluded. For Japan, the host country, the situation was particularly galling. "We felt isolated," said one Foreign Ministry official. His listener was asked to imagine what would have happened if the meeting were held in Paris and the French were excluded.

Japanese sensitivity to racism should not be overlooked. Extremely race-conscious and mindful of the history of discrimination, Japanese are quick to see racism in others. Actually, as argued elsewhere in this book, differences in group behavior and in styles of leadership and communication may be the real problems. The reactions of Westerners may have more to do with feeling ill at ease with the outward behavior of the Japanese than with their race.

Japanese are also sensitive to real or perceived signs of Western condescension. There is a certain psychological price to pay when one is defined in negative terms: Japan is sometimes described as "non-Western." Although many Japanese dislike being grouped with other races, they might appreciate the remark of one Indian intellectual: "To me there are only two races in the world: colored and colorless."

Similarly, many Japanese still react emotionally when Westerners use the term "economic animal" to describe Japanese behavior abroad and refer to Japan's cramped housing as "rabbit hutches." Many agree that these slurs contain at least a germ of truth, but they resent them anyway, not only because these terms compare the Japanese people to animals, but also because of their callous tone. A Japanese professor was provoked into saying that "economic animals" may contribute a whole lot more to global development than "political animals."[35] No doubt many residents of Washington would agree with this statement.

Finally, Japan's defeat in World War II and the subsequent American Occupation left in their wake ambivalence, a love/hate relationship, and feelings of dependency intermingled with an inferiority/superiority complex—all of which color the attitude of Japan's older generation toward America. In the context of the current trade dispute, this legacy sometimes breeds a "victim mentality," indignation, jealousy, extreme sensitivity to perceived pressure, and a sense that the United States should indulge Japanese whims and weaknesses in the spirit of an older brother and protector.[36] If values and social change are thrust upon a society, and if the yardstick of "modernization" and "technology" is external, then the natural human reaction, sooner or later, is bound to be a little defensive.

These attitudes are reinforced by a tendency in some circles to question whether America's commitment to Japan is as firm as its commitment to Western Europe. Citing race and culture, many Japanese are quick to believe that the "common heritage" which Americans and Europeans are said to share binds the Atlantic alliance more closely than its Pacific counterpart. They suspect that in a crisis Japan will have to "go it alone." Accordingly, they favor policies to promote self-sufficiency and tend to resist market-opening measures that could create more dependency on foreign sources.

Although America's close ties with Western Europe retain their long-standing importance, its "common heritage" with Europe is less of a reality nowadays. Recent U.S. presidential elections have swept into power groups from California and the South that have no special ties to Europe. High levels of immigration from Spanish-speaking countries and from Asia—800,000 from Southeast Asia alone in the last decade—have further altered the demographic map of the United States. The so-called

Eastern Establishment retains a special affection for Europe, but its influence has waned considerably.

Moreover, because Americans pay relatively little attention to history, the perceived absence of a "common heritage" with Japan may carry less weight than the perception of "common interest" or a "common destiny." It is true that West Europeans and Americans share the legacy of Greece and Rome and the subsequent flowering of individualism and reasoned debate. But precisely because these values are so deep-rooted, they are taken for granted. They certainly did nothing to moderate the bitter "chicken wars" and other trade disputes of the past.

In emphasizing the lack of a common heritage with the United States, some Japanese may be reflecting their own preoccupation with Japan's uniqueness and overlooking common features of American and Japanese life. Both societies appear to be more egalitarian and less class-conscious compared with Europe. Both are flexible, energetic, adaptable, and eager to learn. The differences that separate them may lie not in race and history, but in the definition of national interest, exacerbated by differences in language, social behavior, styles of leadership and communication, and outdated self-images.[37]

Building a Better Future

If Japan's planners can overcome their misgivings about the rest of the world, a rich opportunity awaits them. Drawing on Japan's assets and using them more imaginatively, they can build on the substantial achievements made to date.

Peacekeeping is one aspect of security to which Tokyo has made and continues to make valuable contributions. In 1980, Tokyo attempted to mediate the conflict between Iran and Iraq. In 1984, it hinted at its willingness to let Japanese civilians participate in the never-realized United Nations peacekeeping operations in Namibia—the first time in postwar history that Japanese personnel would have participated in a peacekeeping mission. Japan also has an active interest and considerable technical expertise in restricting the spread of nuclear weapons, and has already offered to share with other countries its technology for monitoring underground nuclear tests.

On several occasions, Japan has cooperated with U.S.-led economic sanctions against various countries, even though sanctions are unpopular and considered ineffective. Despite its dependence on energy imports, it has even supported sanctions curtailing energy projects—in part because the government has steadily diversified its energy security policy to avoid undue dependence on the Soviet Union.

Finally, to upgrade its defense efforts, Japan is stepping up its early-warning capability by means of over-the-horizon radar, other ground-based and airborne radar, advanced photography, and infrared sensing and imaging. It has improved control and communications within the Self-Defense Forces as well as in joint operations with American forces. Also under way, as noted earlier, are programs to improve antisubmarine warfare capability, air defense, sea-lane defense, and intelligence-sharing with the United States. One opportunity for improving U.S.-Japan relations is to make these contributions more widely known to the "Japan-bashers" without offending Japanese political sensitivities or arousing the fears of Japan's Asian neighbors.

What still seems to be missing in Japanese foreign policy is some definition of what that policy stands for. Japan has become too rich, too grown-up as it were, to get away with narrow economic self-interest. In addition to assuming more responsibility for strengthening the international economic system, Japanese leaders need to devise less reactive, more imaginative noneconomic initiatives. To be successful, such initiatives must draw on politically "safe" symbols and values respected by the population at large. The most promising among them is technology.

Japan is noted for its enthusiasm for technology. Support for traditional values and criticisms of modern society rarely challenge the idea of Japan as a future "information society," wired together by high-technology sinews. The idea of being the world's leader in technology seems to be reassuring to most Japanese. Technology strikes them as universal, politically neutral, and far less visible than the manufactured exports for which they are currently criticized. It is also regarded as humane—a positive contribution to global welfare. At home, technology has proven to be fully compatible with preferred social behavior. Abroad, it can make Japan a leader in the power game without threatening anyone else. To put it another way, Japan can stand for something without having to take sides in global conflicts.

Japan's other outstanding asset is people. Assuming that more Japanese could volunteer for aid- and security-related activities without having their careers derailed, they could apply their technology to global welfare and security in many imaginative ways. Such contributions might include special assistance to the elderly, effective public health programs,

simple and reliable communications systems, measures to cope with severe environmental pollution, selective industrial planning, enhanced
energy efficiency, and education. In the domain of security and defense,
they might contribute abroad to arms control, conflict mediation and
peacekeeping, coastal and border surveillance, and intelligence operations, and, at home, to enhanced readiness and sustainability of defense
operations, combined with improved command and control. These initiatives, launched under the rubric of technology, would skirt many taboos
and bring into play Japan's finest assets.

Like the proverbial tanker changing course, Japan's shift to a more active role in the world is slow and ponderous. While Yasuhiro Nakasone
deserves credit for turning the helm, the shift has been under way since
the mid-1970s. Partly because the shift has been slow, low-key, and without the clear-cut policy pronouncements of which Americans are so fond,
Japan has received little credit for the substantial contributions it is now
making to global security. But the trend is unmistakable; Japanese foreign
policy has become more active, constructive, visible, and autonomous—a
significant departure from its past behavior, which *The Economist* described as "a timorous beastie, indecisive about what to say and loath to
speak lest it might annoy."[38]

The strength of the U.S.-Japan alliance in the post-Nakasone era will
depend in part on whether Japan continues to pursue this more active
course. The next task for Japanese foreign policy planners is to develop
the resources, instruments, and vision to support it. Americans can help
by handling with skill and sensitivity the ongoing round of market-opening measures, thus contributing to a more open, confident, and internationalist Japan. But if market-opening measures are perceived only as
an expression of "Japan-bashing," they will have just the opposite effect.

For Japan and the United States to achieve their common foreign-policy
and security goals, they must overcome the "we versus they" mentality
and carefully manage the alliance, both now and in the future. To pool
and maximize their resources to this end requires a sense of confidence
and broad-mindedness in Japan, credible and consistent leadership from
Washington, and vision and courage in both countries.

Conclusion

"We *and* They": Toward a Coalition Strategy

I n relation to each other, Japan has gotten richer and the United States has gotten poorer. This transition has occurred so suddenly that neither country has been able to adjust to its domestic and international implications. The most visible and disturbing signs of tensions associated with the shift show up in the field of trade, where a bitter debate about "fairness" is reinforcing a "we versus they" mentality, fanning arrogance and resentment in Japan and protectionist sentiments in the United States.

If current economic trends and tensions are allowed to continue unchecked, they can seriously erode the impressive record that the U.S.-Japan alliance has achieved to date. The two economies are likely to remain close, if only because neither partner can disengage very easily from the other. But the alliance will fall far short of its potential, and over time it could begin to unravel.

The fundamental challenge for both countries is to alter long-standing patterns of behavior to correspond more closely to today's economic realities. To meet this challenge, leaders in both the government and the private sector need to overcome outdated perceptions and self-images of wealth and poverty and to redefine the goals and decisions associated with them.

Japan can no longer be considered a poor country whose domestic sacrifices and relentlessly export-oriented policies can be justified in the name of catching up with the West. It may still lack land and natural resources, but it is rich in people and technology—assets well-suited to the twenty-first century. The United States can count on these same assets, as well as on its vast territory, abundant natural resources, and huge internal market. The United States, however, is hobbled by unprecedented trade and budget deficits and threatened with the disappearance (or partial takeover by Japanese firms) of several key manufacturing sectors. By the 1990s, its external debt may well exceed $1 trillion, much of which will be owed to Japanese creditors.

These trends are clearly unhealthy for the alliance, not to mention the world. Yet changing the economic priorities of not one but two complex societies is a long-term proposition. Even if both governments undertake the necessary macroeconomic adjustments, the alliance faces rough sailing until such reforms have had time to bear fruit.

To survive this transition, both sides must endeavor to manage the real conflicts of interest, exorcise the imaginary ones, and abandon "bashing" and brooding in favor of more constructive forms of pressure and persuasion. Success will require conscious teamwork between groups in both societies who support the goals of the alliance and who stand to gain the most from an open trade and investment climate. In short, it is time for a coalition strategy.

The evidence of the 1980s suggests that U.S. leadership of the Western alliance depends to a large extent on a reasonably healthy U.S. economy. Making room at the top—or learning to be good losers—may not be enough. America's commitment to come to the aid of its allies in the event of war—a pledge that forms the bedrock of the Western alliance—is only credible to the extent that Americans face the world in a positive and confident mood. The unchecked erosion of the U.S. economy could sour that mood, causing Americans to retreat into isolationism or at least unilateralism. This prospect worries all of America's allies, but especially Japan, which has placed so many of its eggs in the American basket.

America's leadership depends not only on a healthy economy in general, but also on a reasonably competitive industrial base. This is not to say that antiquated smokestack industries must be preserved at their current level, or indeed at all. Imported components and joint ventures with foreign firms can improve American competitiveness. Essential goods—even for the defense sector—can be purchased from abroad and stockpiled. Yet in the interest of national security broadly defined, a strong manufacturing base on one's own territory obviously counts.

To cite the most obvious link, a healthy manufacturing sector sustains the military power on which U.S. leadership of the Western alliance partly rests. This is not a plea for Fortress America. Simply put, manufacturing creates productive national wealth and prestige in a way that most service industries do not. Advanced know-how does not flourish in thin air; it is hard to imagine a vigorous research and development capability, for example, without a manufacturing sector in which to apply it.

Moreover, manufacturing is a kind of symbol of national strength and viability. To banish the image of a "helpless giant" in historical decline, Americans must show the world that they are coping successfully with their industrial problems. Whether or not these propositions are economically rational is beyond the scope of this book, but they make political sense. To the extent that the United States regains its economic health, it will earn Japan's respect, a key ingredient of the U.S.-Japan alliance.

Some Japanese officials have privately suggested that the United States should produce its own "Maekawa report"—a blueprint for constructive adjustment to new economic realities. Actually, a number of such reports already exist. For the most part their message is the same: the United States must put its macroeconomic house in order. What Americans need is not another report but a massive shock—a Sputnik-type shock—to spur them into doing something about their trade and budget deficits.

The Japanese are not entirely unjustified when they say that "Japan-bashers" are "unfair" to blame others for America's homegrown industrial ills. Americans need to understand that their overall complacency about the economy, their "not invented here" mentality, and their expectations of remaining "number one" have become obsolete and even dangerous. This is a "national security" problem if ever there was one.

Washington's recent surge of interest in the international competitiveness of American industry is encouraging. Still, "competitiveness" joins a long list of slogans whose virtues are self-evident but whose contents are hard to define. Whether Americans will make the hard choices needed to reinvigorate the macroeconomy supporting enhanced competitiveness remains to be seen.

To be sure, the United States has greatly reduced its rate of inflation, created jobs in the service sector, achieved wage stability, and improved quality and productivity. The stock market is booming and the housing sector is fairly strong. But both the budget deficit and the current-account deficit continue to loom large, and personal savings remain low.

As long as priorities at the highest level of the executive branch remain political-military rather than industrial-economic, it is hard to see how America can reform itself. Congress cannot do the job by itself. Leaders in both branches of the government must develop and articulate consistent, long-term, bipartisan policy initiatives to restore and enhance the basic health of the national economy. Their most urgent task is to reduce the budget deficit by carrying out spending cuts and/or tax increases. In the long term, they must concentrate on getting the basics right: education, research and development, a vigorous capital market, an open trade and investment climate, a higher rate of savings, and a more balanced mix of fiscal and monetary policies.

For their part, U.S. business executives must become better informed about other countries, think in terms of a single global market, actively seek information about foreign competitors and their technology, learn more foreign languages, and make the long-term investments necessary to survive and prosper in the global marketplace. When it comes to Japan, they need to do their homework—brushing up not only on technology and business, but also on the rudiments of Japanese history, culture, patterns of behavior, and styles of communication. Perhaps most important, business leaders can help America shed its complacency and lingering "number one" mentality, diminish its "helpless giant" complex and sense of vulnerability, and boost awareness of the need to export and to invest in high-technology research.

Americans have not lost their ability to overcome problems and provide positive leadership. Their typical strengths include genuine optimism, a sincere desire to change the world for the better, a commitment to fairness in its universal sense, willingness to work, and a kind of good-humored pragmatism. When Americans blend these strengths with sophistication and open-mindedness, they still have much to offer the world in general, and to the U.S.-Japan alliance in particular. Americans are not jealous or insecure by nature; the people who invented "Yankee ingenuity" cannot fail to appreciate the human talent and know-how that the Japanese bring to the partnership—provided these are applied to challenges that transcend narrowly defined economic goals. Sooner or later, Western Europe, too, will transcend its preoccupation with trade and recognize its commonalities with Japan. But for now, the United States is in the best position to draw Japan out of its residual insularity into the international community.

On the whole, Americans must save more, invest more, study harder, produce better goods, and develop a new understanding of why it is necessary to do these painful things. In a nutshell, Americans will have to change the ways in which they learn and think about the world and their place in it. This is a challenge at least as formidable as the one Japan faces.

Japan needs to adjust as well—not merely for the sake of averting protectionist trade legislation in the United States, but to fit in better with the rest of global society.

Except for those problematic Americans, Japan has few real friends abroad. Its foreign aid is still perceived to be skimpy and tied to exports. Its business behavior overseas is perceived to be self-centered at best and predatory at worst. Seen at their best, Japanese companies make high-quality products, create jobs, and invest abroad, but they take as much and give as little as possible. Seen at their worst, Japanese companies consciously and ruthlessly weaken their competitors and then, with increasing frequency, try to acquire them.

As long as these perceptions—justified or otherwise—persist, Japan runs the risk of being singled out for retaliation whenever severe economic dislocations arise. It cannot escape this threat entirely; it cannot shirk the responsibility that inevitably accompanies wealth. Because it is an economic superpower, Japan will be blamed for a wide range of problems, whether or not it has anything to do with them.

Besides retaliation, Japan faces the risk of being beaten at its own game. Inspired by Japan's success, a number of countries—notably South Korea—are practicing what amounts to state-guided, export-oriented free enterprise. Given the higher yen, it is not clear that Japanese companies can continue to maintain their lead in a world of little Japans. Paradoxically, by winning too much and too often, Japan could lose out in the long run.

To overcome its narrow economic nationalism and fulfill its international potential, Japan needs a more positive sense of purpose, a goal more benign and universal than market access or secure supplies. In short, it is time for the Japanese to abandon their "small-nation" mentality, to declare victory, and begin to enjoy its fruits.

At home, the Japanese need to adjust their savings and consumption habits—not to American standards, which are arguably wasteful, but to something closer to world standards. The people who labor so long and so diligently are also consumers paying extremely high prices. In this sense, Japan's biggest unfulfilled responsibility is to itself: to institute its own definition of "fairness" in its own society.

Some might ask: With "problems" like these, who needs solutions? Yet much of the large and painful price to pay still lies ahead. Japan will probably have to adjust to a higher yen, introduce more flexible employment patterns, adopt fiscal and financial measures to stimulate domestic consumption, streamline its costly distribution system, accept a higher degree of market penetration by foreign firms, reduce government regulation, import more from developing countries, further shrink the inefficient agricultural sector, and—in the Tokyo area at least—devise bold measures to cope with exorbitant land prices and the housing problems associated with them.

Tokyo is already making significant contributions to advance common U.S.-Japan goals in foreign aid and defense. In general, however, its leadership abroad is still not commensurate with its new wealth. Tokyo must overcome its fear of flying in diplomacy—the concern that a more active and visible Japanese role overseas will somehow let loose uncontrollable and dangerous forces.

Using its two greatest resources, technology and people, Japan can shape a constructive foreign-policy identity that does not revolve around "Nihonism" or a pan-Asian mystique, or slavish imitation of Westerners, or beggar-thy-neighbor economic nationalism, or major rearmament—none of which is very sensible anyway.

Existing patterns of U.S.-Japan cooperation suggest many ways in which the combined resources of the two countries could contribute to solving today's problems. The health of the world's two largest markets can contribute to global economic growth, thus easing the Third World debt crisis. Basic agreement between the world's two biggest trading nations can lay the foundations for reforming the current trading system. A solid, sensible defense posture in the western Pacific can safeguard political stability and democracy in Asia by reducing the sense of external threat. Coordinated efforts to contain Soviet power can promote mutually acceptable arms control agreements.

Japan, a country that has rebuilt itself from the ashes in less than a generation, can surely devise imaginative ways to aid the Third World. Other countries can tap special Japanese strengths and values and benefit from Japan's experience in broad areas of development planning, such as industrial policy, energy, environmental protection, communications, health, population planning, education, agriculture and fisheries, and disaster relief.

Such initiatives cannot buy Japan's way out of current trade friction, but in the long run they can contribute to the kind of stable and prosperous world on which Japan's basic security depends. Such initiatives require an international vision and a certain cross-cultural perspective, both of which have hitherto been noticeably missing in Japan. Ultimately, the

Japanese cult of uniqueness will have to yield to a greater sense of responsibility and concern for human needs around the world.

The more active Tokyo becomes in the international community, the less direct influence Washington is likely to have over Japanese foreign policy. But this is a small and politically safe risk to take. To the extent that both sides seek to resolve their differences in a constructive spirit, Japan's goals will coincide or overlap with those of the United States, for it is in the framework of the alliance that Japan has achieved unparalleled prosperity and stability.

These recommendations still leave the alliance dangling and dangerously exposed for at least another decade. In the interim, how should America and Japan handle their conflicts?

A key problem in U.S.-Japan relations is time. American and Japanese leaders appear to have different ideas about how long adjustment or reform can reasonably be expected to take. Each side tends to give itself more time for adjustment than it is willing to allow the other. For example, when it comes to opening up a hitherto closed sector of the Japanese market, a period of five years might seem long to an American but short to a Japanese. Conversely, many Japanese do not understand why it is taking Washington so long to come to grips with a budget deficit of near-crisis proportions.

In the current climate, "Japan-bashing"—in the sense of undifferentiated hostility expressed in public—is particularly counterproductive. This assertion does not meet with universal agreement in America. The notion that it takes "bashing" and threats of protectionism to change Japanese behavior is one of the most unfortunate consequences of the Japanese style of decision making. Americans may get away with "bashing" in the short run because Japan has no choice but to depend on the United States. But such behavior hardly suits a stable, democratic alliance. More to the point, bashing only makes things worse. It breeds resentment and defensiveness in Japan, and forces Japanese leaders to placate the least efficient sectors of the society. By the same token, it undercuts those elements in Japanese society that seek to reform the system from within, and plays into the hands of their opponents. If bashed too often, the Japanese will indeed end up behaving like "them." Even the most progressive forces in Japan will have no incentive to do otherwise. The United States has a strong stake in avoiding this outcome.

Finally, it can be argued that Americans are in no position to bash Japan. America's own budgetary situation is too ludicrous, and its macroeconomic distortions are all too apparent. Even the U.S. record on aid and trade falls short of Washington's stated objectives. About the only useful function of "bashing" is that when Congress does it, the executive branch looks reasonable by contrast. When others do it, one cannot even say that much. Fortunately, "Japan-bashing" appears to be a periodic but short-lived raindance, a recurrent rash of self-justification, a "filler" sandwiched between tax bills and budget debates.

To do nothing is not a solution either, at least not in Washington. Moreover, many groups in Japan continue to rely on outside pressure to accomplish their own goals. The issue is how to apply pressure constructively.

"Bashing" versus Constructive Pressure

American leaders need to develop credible and consistent goals, and to pursue them patiently. This calls for a change of pace. For in their characteristic haste to "do something," Americans tend to lurch periodically into grand gestures and subsequent retreats. Too often, a new administration will adopt hasty, ill-researched, inconsistent positions that then have to be reversed.

In pursuing these goals, Americans would do well to work closely with those in Japan who are most receptive to a coalition strategy—namely, those with a strong stake in democracy, pluralism, stability, and constructive adaptation to the international environment. Countries will cooperate only if like-minded people join forces across national borders.

Warm personal ties—such as those between Prime Minister Nakasone and President Reagan, and between prominent members of the Japanese Diet and the U.S. Congress—are a useful first step. In Japan, professional success depends heavily on personal trust. The conversations most likely to foster trust are held after hours, one-on-one, and preferably over drinks. Discussions in a relaxed atmosphere, away from the pressures and rituals of group behavior, can be quite frank and specific, producing tangible agreements that seemed remote during formal group meetings.

Institutional ties between Japanese ministries and U.S. Government departments also serve to build coalitions that cut across national boundaries. As they say in Washington, "Where you stand depends on where you sit." An official's perspective on an issue tends to reflect the position that he or she represents. Experts in the Japanese Finance Ministry and the U.S. Treasury Department tend to understand each other very well, and frequently agree on what needs to be done. So do officials in the

Foreign Affairs Ministry and their counterparts in the U.S. State Department. Nevertheless, at the point where real interests diverge—for example, when U.S. agricultural exports encounter quotas in Japan—trans-Pacific bureaucratic partnership may not prevail. In such cases, broadening the institutional dialogue may make it easier to achieve a compromise—if only because no single ministry or department wants to be seen as "soft" on the other in today's environment.

The importance of coalitions between the private sector in Japan and in America cannot be overemphasized. Major companies and banks in Japan already play a role in foreign policy, whether they like it or not. Nowadays new actors are climbing on stage. If up-and-coming Japanese companies are convinced that a certain trade barrier or regulation is not in their interest, they will make their objections heard. U.S. companies whose interests coincide with theirs will also be heard, provided they have planned their political moves correctly. Accordingly, firm-to-firm arrangements could include, where appropriate, an unwritten political component. Even industry associations in the two countries might find it in their interest to develop coordinated approaches to their respective governments.

Those who wish to take advantage of Japan's more pluralistic society to pursue a coalition strategy should follow the rules of political common sense. Generally speaking, the foreigner should not appear to interfere in purely domestic decisions, only in decisions that have some demonstrable effect on outsiders. Nowadays that criterion should not be difficult to meet. One can always make the case, for example, that policies which effectively subsidize inefficient sectors of the Japanese economy soak up resources that could be used for economic expansion, a corresponding increase in imports, or even foreign aid.

Similarly, a coalition strategy is more likely to succeed if its goal is not hopelessly beyond reach. The stated aims need some support from domestic groups, preferably from new or up-and-coming business interests—for example, supermarket entrepreneurs seeking to bypass Japan's byzantine distribution system. Even groups with hitherto marginal influence on Japan's foreign-policy process—consumers, for instance—may come to exert more influence. Foreign pressure is more likely to succeed to the extent that it dovetails with the efforts of those who have the most to gain from deregulation and internationalization.

Americans should make the important distinction between the substance and the pace of change. With some important exceptions, Tokyo is moving—albeit slowly—in the right direction. Thus, Americans should acknowledge progress made to date while siding with those within Japan who are similarly impatient.

Criticizing Japan in public is often counterproductive—especially at the outset of a negotiation, when quiet efforts to promote change have not been fully exhausted. Furthermore, public criticism not only is discourteous—especially in Japan—but also stirs up national pride. Occasionally, however, a timely comment in public can set off many bells in Japan; if it is on target, it can be used to advantage by those who are pressing for change from within.

In the context of a coalition strategy, public criticism is more likely to achieve results if it presses for reforms that would benefit the Japanese. Criticism that takes the form of a statement of fact will meet with a more receptive audience than a critical judgment. Public criticism couched in vague but upbeat language will be more effective than heavily negative language. Stating the criticism in positive terms—"Here is what Japan could do"—will normally drive the point home. The precise means of implementing a suggested reform are best left undefined, so as not to humiliate or corner Japanese businessmen, government officials, or others with a political constituency. Specific complaints or suggestions are best advanced in private.

It helps, too, if public criticism emphasizes that what is being sought is identical to or compatible with Japan's own policy goals. Appropriate themes could be drawn from the policy statements of official or quasi-official advisory bodies—e.g., the current defense program outline or the Maekawa Commission report. To do otherwise would make it seem that the Japanese are bowing to U.S. pressure—a politically damaging if not fatal blow to those who seek change from within.

Japanese leaders, especially businessmen, can help to avert "bashing" by doing their share of managing the tensions of the next decade. At home, they can press for a more liberal trade and investment climate. Abroad, they can curb closed-group behavior and refrain from the kind of economic nationalism that perpetuates the "Japan, Inc." stereotype. They can contribute a larger share of their substantial resources, both capital and technology, to trade reform and global development, on which their own fortunes depend heavily.

Their task in America requires political sensitivity and communication. Before announcing visible and potentially controversial transactions, such as the acquisition of a U.S. company with defense contracts or a major real estate purchase, Japanese businessmen would do well to consult closely with Americans in both the private and public sector. The need to do so is especially pressing in sectors that have acquired special political significance—e.g., semiconductors, supercomputers, telecommunications, and, of course, steel and automobiles.

In making decisions concerning investments in the United States, Japanese businessmen and government officials will frequently find it appropriate and helpful to explain their case directly to American counterparts. Such contacts should not be confined to the upper ranks of Congress and the executive branch. Japanese representatives would be well-advised to approach these institutions at the level of office director or staff member, with a view to avoiding surprises and building an acceptable consensus—in the same way that they would in Tokyo. That a number of major Japanese companies appear to have upgraded their representation in Washington to a level more capable of functioning in this manner is a small but positive sign.

In dealing with Washington, Japanese businessmen should not seek to "buy influence," for influence is a short-lived and sometimes illusory commodity in a decentralized political system. Even to attempt to do so gives everyone—especially foreigners—a bad name when the effort becomes public, as it frequently does. Besides, Japanese leaders no longer need others to open doors for them. Their own stature and importance speak for themselves.

Building a consensus in America will not be as easy as it would be in Tokyo, however. Difficulties with speaking English, transcending closed-group behavior, and mingling freely with foreigners put Japanese businessmen at a disadvantage. So does the relatively passive, faceless, "wet," indirect, and reserved style of leadership and communication that Japanese adopt in public. Adjusting to conditions and styles of behavior in other countries is an urgent task. As matters stand, the contrast between Japanese mannerisms and Japan's economic aggressiveness perpetuates the stereotype of the Japanese as "inscrutable" at best and hypocritical and even deceitful at worst.

Changes in long-standing cultural patterns cannot be dictated by outsiders, but Japanese groups—especially companies—can be nudged from within to adapt to a greater degree than they already have to contemporary international society. While no outsider can tell the Japanese to change their style of leadership and communication at home, Japanese leaders—and especially businessmen—can encourage each other to communicate more directly and effectively with foreigners without fear of hurting their career.

Harmonious relations between any two countries are not a goal in themselves; they must reflect some fundamental complementarity of interest and human concern. Such complementarity is strong in the case of Japan and the United States. At home, both confront the dilemmas of modern industrial society and the challenges of democracy. Abroad, both face similar dangers and opportunities. American and Japanese leaders should be devoting more attention to adjusting their differences and building on their many strengths and shared interests than to the bilateral trade balance.

To put the same point in another way, the United States and Japan can contribute to each other and to the world an extraordinary amount of talent and resources—provided that short-term trade disputes do not lead them to the divorce court in the meantime. They share an overwhelming need to move from bashing and brooding to enhanced cooperation, from "we *versus* they" to "we *and* they."

For the rest of this century and beyond, divorce between the United States and Japan is economically impossible, militarily impractical, and politically unthinkable. Both sides must simply try harder. Whoever wrote the Christian marriage ceremony knew that "for richer, for poorer" is a profoundly meaningful vow.

Notes

Chapter One

1. An example of "bashing" drawn from the Congressional debate in 1985 is then Senate Majority Leader Robert Dole's acid remark, "Japan's attitude continues to be one of selfishness and myopia." Also in 1985, Senate Finance Committee Chairman Robert Packwood snapped, "Frankly, I am not interested in the explanation for Japan's endemic resistance to imports." Senator John Danforth (R-Missouri) has referred to the Japanese as "leeches."

2. "G-5" is negotiating shorthand for the Group of Five: the United States, Japan, Great Britain, France, and West Germany. With the addition of Canada and Italy, the "G-5" becomes the "G-7."

3. James C. Abegglen, "Japan and the United States: Too Close A Relationship?" *Tokyo Business Today* (February 1986), p. 6. Abegglen suggests that Japan should diversify its economic presence abroad, perhaps by expanding business with the Soviet Union.

4. In a famous episode in Japanese history, forty-seven samurai waited for two years to avenge their fallen lord; once justice was achieved, they committed suicide.

5. See, for example, Theodore H. White, "The Danger From Japan," *The New York Times Magazine*, July 28, 1985, in which the late journalist described Japan as a merciless war machine—now economic in form rather than military—dedicated to vengeance against Americans.

6. See Albert Axebank, "The Great Japan-U.S. Compromise," *Journal of Commerce*, July 18, 1986. According to Axebank, a high-level American trade mission to Tokyo complained about an "unacceptable" trade deficit of $4 billion in 1971. After drawing attention to anticipated inroads in the U.S. market for automobiles, aircraft, steel, and computers, the Americans reportedly went away satisfied that the Japanese would exercise "restraint."

7. *Global Competition: The New Reality*, Report of the President's Commission on Industrial Competitiveness, 2 vols. (Washington, D.C.: GPO, 1985), vol. 1, p. 1.

8. U.S. House of Representatives, Committee on Ways and Means, Subcommittee on Trade, *United States Japan Trade Report* (Washington, D.C.: GPO, 1980), p. 5.

9. Hajime Karatsu, "The Deindustrialization of America," *KKC Brief* no. 31 (October 1985). See also Kenjiro Hayashi, "Passing the Torch of World Leadership," *Chuo Koron* (October 1985); reprinted in *Japan Echo*, vol. 12, no. 4 (1985), p. 12.

10. Economic Planning Agency, *Japan in the Year 2000* (Tokyo: Japan Times, Ltd., 1983), p. 100.

11. James C. Thomson, Jr. et al., *Sentimental Imperialists: The American Experience in East Asia* (New York: Harper & Row, 1981), p. 160.

12. For a sample of contemporary right-wing opinions, see Ian Buruma, "A New Japanese Nationalism," *The New York Times Magazine*, April 12, 1987.

13. *Global Competition*, op. cit., p. 9.

14. *Challenges and Opportunities in United States-Japan Relations* (Washington, D.C.: United States-Japan Advisory Commission, 1984), p. v.

15. *Business Week*, July 14, 1986, p. 46.

16. Defense Science Board Task Force, *Industry-to-Industry International Armaments Cooperation: Japan* (Washington, D.C.: Office of the Under Secretary of Defense for Research and Engineering, 1984), p. 51.

17. See C. Fred Bergsten, "America's Unilateralism," in *Conditions for Partnership in International Economic Management* (New York: The Trilateral Commission, 1986), pp. 3–14.

18. See "The Trade Partnership Act of 1985," Statement by the House Republican Leadership, September 26, 1985.

19. *The Daily Yomiuri*, December 16, 1985, p. 2.

20. *National Journal*, no. 45, November 8, 1986.

21. William Schneider, "The New Politics," Unpublished paper prepared for the seventh Shimoda Conference, Oiso, Japan, April 19–21, 1987.

22. *The New York Times*, April 21, 1986.

23. Yukio Matsuyama, *A Japanese Journalist Looks at U.S.-Japan Relations* (Boulder, Colo.: Westview Press, 1984).

24. C. Michael Aho and Jonathan David Aronson, *Trade Talks: America Better Listen* (New York: Council on Foreign Relations, 1985), p. 25.

25. See the discussion of fair trade in Carl Green, "The New Protectionism," *Northwestern Journal of International Law and Business*, vol. 3, no. 1 (Spring 1981), p. 11.

26. Catherine Kelleher, "America Looks at Europe," in Lawrence Freedman, ed., *The Troubled Alliance* (London: Heineman), p. 57.

27. For a sophisticated and well-researched analysis of the Japanese Government's role in a key sector of the economy, see Richard Samuels, *The Business of the Japanese State: Energy Markets in Comparative and Historical Perspective* (Ithaca: Cornell University Press, forthcoming).

28. Unpublished study prepared by Harry Lamar for the Coalition for International Trade Equity, Washington, D.C., 1985.

29. For this list of images, I am grateful to Paul H. Kreisberg, former Director of Studies, Council on Foreign Relations.

30. See, for example, the dialogue between Fuji Kamiya and Kenichi Ito in *Shokon* (October 1985); reprinted in *Japan Echo*, vol. 12, no. 4 (Winter 1985), pp. 21–26.

31. *Sankei Shimbun*, January 17, 1986; Translation Service Center (TSC) no. 678.

32. Address to the Japan Society, July 25, 1985.

33. *Japan Times*, November 9, 1985.

34. Thomson et al., op. cit., p. 8.

35. Hisashi Owada, "U.S.-Japan Economic Interaction in an Interdependent World," Paper presented to the colloquium "Legal Problems of U.S.-Japan Economic Relations," Georgetown University Law School, April 1981.

Chapter Two

1. See, for example, Kaoru Kobayashi, *Japan: The Most Misunderstood Country* (Tokyo: Japan Times, Ltd., 1984), p. 19.

2. George B. Sansom, *The Western World and Japan* (New York: Alfred A. Knopf, 1951), pp. 278–79; see also Yukichi Fukuzawa, *The Autobiography of Yukichi Fukuzawa* (New York: Columbia University Press, 1960), p. 104f.

3. Jiro Osaragi, *The Homecoming* (Tokyo: Charles E. Tuttle Co., 1955), p. 136.

4. In 1950, engineers at Nippon Kokan—Japan's third largest steel company at the time—took note of an article in the German journal *Stahl und Eisen* describing pilot plant experiments in Switzerland featuring a new basic oxygen furnace technique. Although the Japanese steel industry had painfully rebuilt itself after the war using the then prevalent open-hearth method, Japanese companies led the transition to the new technology. See Leonard H. Lynn, *How Japan Innovates: A Comparison with the U.S. in the Case of Oxygen Steelmaking* (Boulder, Colo.: Westview Press, 1982), p. 71ff.

5. Thomas P. Rohlen, *Japan's High Schools* (Berkeley: University of California Press, 1983), p. 251.

6. Benjamin Duke, *The Japanese School* (New York: Praeger Publishers, 1986), p. 99.

7. Ministry of Housing, *Housing in Japan* (Tokyo: Japan Housing Association, n.d.), p. 11.

8. Management and Coordination Agency, "Survey on Consumption in Japan" (December 1985), S-85-10, Foreign Press Center, February 1986; see also Prime Minister's Office, "Public Opinion Survey on Society and State" (April 1986), S-86-3, Foreign Press Center, August 1986.

9. See, for example, the data published in Economic Planning Agency, *Annual Report on the National Life for Fiscal 1985* (Tokyo, 1985).

10. Central Commission for Promotion of Savings, "1985 Survey on Savings" (October 1985), S-85-7, Foreign Press Center, November 1985.

11. Prime Minister's Office, "Annual Report on the Family Income and Expenditure Survey," Foreign Press Center, 1983.

12. Prime Minister's Office, "Public Opinion Survey on [the] Future Image of Japan" (February 1984), S-84-3, Foreign Press Center, May 1984.

13. See Nobutoshi Akao, ed., *Japan's Economic Security* (London: Royal Institute of International Affairs, 1983); see also Natural Resources and Energy Agency, *Energy in Japan: Facts and Figures* (Tokyo: Ministry of International Trade and Industry, 1986).

14. In a speech on "The Internationalization of the Yen," New York City, June 4, 1986, Vice Minister of Finance Toyoo Gyohten, a respected architect of Japan's capital-market liberalization, warned that if global interdependence goes beyond some optimum degree, "there is a danger that adverse side effects may well exceed the benefits." Others have expressed concern that the pace of global interdependence may be too rapid to be sustained by the political climate supporting free trade. See Lester C. Thurow, "America, Europe and Japan: A Time to Dismantle the World Economy," *The Economist*, November 9, 1985, p. 21; and C. Michael Aho and Thomas O. Bayard, "The 1980s: Twilight of the Open Trading System?" *The World Economy*, vol. 5, no. 4 (December 1982), pp. 379–406.

15. Ministry of Health and Welfare, "1985 Population Vital Statistics" (December 1985), S-86-1, Foreign Press Center, February 1986.

16. Ministry of Health and Welfare, *Health and Welfare Services in Japan* (Tokyo, 1986).

17. See Economic Planning Agency, *Annual Report on the National Life for Fiscal 1984* (Tokyo, 1984).

18. Masahiko Ishikuza, "Japan Needs A Cultural Revolution," *Japan Economic Journal*, May 10, 1986.

19. *The Economist*, June 21, 1986.

20. Quoted in *Business Week*, May 12, 1986, p. 47.

21. See, for example, Hayashi, op. cit.

22. According to MITI's interpretation of data collected between 1975 and 1980, Japan's income elasticity of imports was 0.352, while America's was 1.135. It is interesting to note that the two countries' *export* elasticity of income was about the same, 0.732 for Japan and 0.720 for America. See *Japan Economic Almanac, 1985* (Tokyo: Nihon Keizai Shimbun, Inc., 1985), p. 27.

23. See Daniel E. Nolle and Charles Pigott, "The Changing Commodity Composition of U.S. Imports from Japan," *Federal Reserve Bank of New York Quarterly Review*, vol. 11, no. 1 (Spring 1986).

24. See the discussion in Chalmers Johnson, *MITI and the Japanese Miracle* (Stanford: Stanford University Press, 1982), pp. 246–47.

25. Harald B. Malmgren, "Technological Challenges to National Economic Policies of the West," *Washington Quarterly*, vol. 10, no. 2 (Spring 1987), pp. 21–23.

26. Karatsu, op. cit.

27. The most forceful argument to this effect can be found in Robert Z. Lawrence, *Can America Compete?* (Washington, D.C.: The Brookings Institution, 1984). A cogent case against "industrial policy" and in favor of "getting the fundamentals" right—education, investment, and sound economic policies in general—appears in George C. Eads and Richard R. Nelson, "Japanese High Technology Policy: What Lessons for the United States?" in Hugh Patrick, ed., *Japan's High-Technology Industries* (Seattle: University of Washington Press, 1986), pp. 243–69.

28. *Global Competition*, op. cit., p. 7.

29. The Business Roundtable, *Strategy for A Vital U.S. Economy* (New York, May 1984), p. 5.

30. Policy statement by the Defense Policy Advisory Committee on Trade, November 26, 1986.

31. Lee A. Iacocca, *Iacocca: An Autobiography* (New York: Bantam Books, 1986), p. 348.

32. See I. M. Destler, *American Trade Politics: System Under Stress* (Washington, D.C.: Institute for International Economics, 1986), p. 167. As Destler has argued convincingly in this study, trade policy is simply not an effective instrument for addressing problems that are really macroeconomic in nature. This is especially true of the trade between America and Japan, two economies that have become so closely intertwined.

33. The survey, conducted by *Nihon Keizai Shimbun*, is cited in James C. Abegglen and George Stalk, Jr., *Kaisha: The Japanese Corporation* (New York: Basic Books, 1985). As one way of comparing leading U.S. and Japanese companies, Abegglen and Stalk measured pretax appreciation plus cumulative dividends expressed as a percentage gain over the original price of an average share. They conclude that Japanese stockholders did better than their U.S. counterparts.

34. See the discussion in ibid., Chap. 7.

35. *National Accounts of OECD Countries* (Paris: Organization for Economic Cooperation and Development, 1983).

36. For a sample of the discussion on how to measure savings, see Kazuhiko Nagato, "Savings: Japan vs. US," *Journal of Japanese Trade and Industry*, vol. 5, no. 5 (Sept.-Oct. 1986); and Michael J. Boskin and John M. Roberts, "A Closer Look at Savings Rates in the United States and Japan," Working Paper no. 9 (Washington, D.C.: American Enterprise Institute, June 1986).

37. See Gary C. Hufbauer, Diane T. Berliner, and Kimberly Ann Elliott, *Trade Protection in the United States: Thirty-One Case Studies* (Washington, D.C.: Institute for International Economics, 1985).

38. House Armed Services Committee, "The Ailing Defense Industrial Base," Print no. 29, Washington, D.C., 1980.

39. U.S. General Accounting Office, "Overview of the Status of the Defense Industrial Base and DoD's Industrial Preparedness Planning," NSIAD-85-69, Washington, D.C., May 23, 1985.

40. Defense Science Board Task Force, *Defense Semiconductor Dependency* (Washington, D.C.: Office of the Under Secretary of Defense for Research and Engineering, 1987).

41. The Office of the Under Secretary of Defense for Research and Engineering has launched an ambitious study aimed at identifying the ills of the industrial base and enhancing the Pentagon's ability to address them in an interagency context.

42. Robert Lawrence Kuhn, ed., *Commercializing Defense-Related Technology* (New York: Praeger Publishers, 1984), p. vi.

Chapter Three

1. "G-5 Communiqué" (Plaza Agreement) of September 5, 1985.

2. Address of Masaru Yoshitomi, Deputy Director General of the Economic Research Institute, Economic Planning Agency, to a conference organized by the Institute for International Economics, Washington, D.C., September 21–23, 1984.

3. Martin Feldstein, "American Economic Policy and the World Economy," *Foreign Affairs*, vol. 63, no. 5 (Summer 1985), p. 1001.

4. Address by Manuel H. Johnson, "The Yen-Dollar Relationship," New York City, June 4, 1986.

5. See "Report of the Advisory Group on Economic Structural Adjustment for International Harmony," Tokyo, April 7, 1986.

6. Keizei Koho Center, *KKC Brief* no. 37 (November 1986), p. 4.

7. Industrial Structure Council, *An Outlook for Japan's Industrial Society Towards the 21st Century* (Tokyo: Ministry of International Trade and Industry, May 26, 1986), pp. 7–9.

8. Vincent Reinhart, "Macroeconomic Influences on the U.S.-Japan Trade Imbalance," *Federal Reserve Bank of New York Quarterly Review*, vol. 11, no. 1 (Spring 1986); reprinted in *JEI Report*, no. 25A (July 11, 1986).

9. Gary Fowler, as quoted in *The New York Times*, August 9, 1986. See also Cecil E. Sears, *Japanese Real Estate Investment in the United States*, Summary of a conference held at the Japan Society, New York City, October 2, 1986. Since 1985, the Japanese Government no longer requires Japanese companies to report overseas real estate purchases.

10. Data derived from an unpublished survey conducted by the Japan External Trade Organization (JETRO) in 1985.

11. Speech by JETRO official Mitsuaki Sato, September 9, 1985.

12. Elias Buchwald, "Under Western Eyes," *Speaking of Japan*, vol. 7, no. 65 (May 1986).

13. Charles J. Stewart, Jr., "Comparing Japanese and U.S. Technology Transfer to Less-Developed Countries," *Journal of Northeast Asian Studies*, vol. 4, no. 1 (Spring 1985).

14. Summary statement of the Second U.S.-Japan Conference on High Technology and the International Environment, Kyoto, Japan, November 1986.

15. Survey conducted by Management and Coordination Agency, cited in *The Japan Times Weekly*, January 10, 1987, p. 2.

16. Selling their R&D to others, as practiced by some cash-strapped American companies, or altering R&D outlays in response to current profits seemed inconceivable to Japanese corporate R&D executives interviewed by the author in 1984.

17. Address by Kazutoshi Kuwahara to the American Chamber of Commerce (Japan), Tokyo, September 12, 1984.

18. For a small sample of this debate, see "Faces of High-Tech Society," *Japan Echo*, vol. 13, no. 2 (Summer 1986).

19. Martha Caldwell Harris, "Japan's Technology Trade," Unpublished paper prepared for the U.S. Office of Technology Assessment, 1985.

Chapter Four

1. For a fuller discussion, see Michael R. Czinkota and Jon Woronoff, *Japan's Market: The Distribution System* (New York: Praeger Publishers, 1986), p. 22.

2. Daun Bhasanvanich, "An American in Tokyo: Jumping to the Japanese Beat," *IEEE Spectrum* (September 1985).

3. Remarks quoted in *Nihon Keizai Shimbun*, October 10, 1985; reprinted in *Economic Eye* (December 1985), p. 8.

4. Chie Nakane, *Japanese Society* (Tokyo: Charles E. Tuttle Co., 1970), Introduction.

5. Robert N. Bellah, *Tokugawa Religion* [1957] (New York: The Free Press, 1985), p. 37.

6. Ruth Benedict, *The Chrysanthemum and the Sword* [1946] (Tokyo: Charles E. Tuttle Co., 1985).

7. Kazuo Kawai's explanation of Japan's ready adaptability to the American Occupation draws heavily on this theme; see his *Japan's American Interlude* [1960] (Chicago: University of Chicago Press, Midway Reprint, 1979).

8. Henry Wheeler Shaw ("Josh Billings"), 1818–1885; in *Bartlett's Familiar Quotations* (Boston: Little, Brown & Co., 1955), p. 595a.

9. Takeo Doi, *The Anatomy of Dependence* (New York: Kodansha International, Ltd., 1973).

10. See Lafcadio Hearn, *Japan: An Interpretation* (Tokyo: Charles E. Tuttle Co., 1962), pp. 403–05. Hearn, an American writer and teacher who settled in Japan in 1890, found that contractors and gardeners in effect came with the house.

11. This observation by Shichihei Yamamoto, author of *Nihon Shihonshugi no Seishin* (The Spirit of Japanese Capitalism), is cited in Jared Taylor, *Shadows of the Rising Sun* (New York: William Morrow & Co., 1983), p. 72.

12. Survey cited in a speech by Yukio Matsuyama to the Japan-Australia Society, March 1981.

13. See, for example, Robert M. Adams, "Jane Austen in Japan," *The New York Review of Books*, vol. 33, no. 2 (February 13, 1986), pp. 26–27.

14. Hiroshi Wagatsuma, "Internationalization of the Japanese: The Group Model Reconsidered," in Hiroshi Mannari and Harumi Befu, eds., *The Challenge of Japan's Internationalization* (Tokyo: Kodansha International, Ltd., 1983), p. 304.

15. Bellah, op. cit., pp. 37–39; and Doi, *Anatomy of Dependence*, op. cit.

16. Yukiro Watanabe, "The Role of Academic Background in Japanese Society," *The Wheel Extended*, vol. 14, no. 1 (1984), p. 93. Watanabe is a professor of education at Aichi University.

17. Kusaka Kimindo, "What is the Japanese Middle Class?" *Japan Echo*, vol. 12, no. 3 (Autumn 1985), p. 41.

18. Unpublished survey by the Japan Export Trade Organization (JETRO), September 1985.

19. Clinton Rossiter, *The First American Revolution* (New York: Harvest Books, 1956), pp. 31–32.

20. Oscar Handlin, *The Uprooted* (New York: Grosset & Dunlap), pp. 303–05.

21. See the interview with Yukio Okawara, former Japanese Ambassador to the United States, in *Journal of Japanese Trade and Industry*, vol. 4, no. 5 (Sept.-Oct. 1985).

22. Address cited in Chap. 1, note 32.

23. Harumi Befu, "The Social and Cultural Background of Child Development in Japan and the United States," in Harold Stevenson, Hiroshi Azuma, and Kenji Hakuta, eds., *Child Development and Education in Japan* (New York: W. H. Freeman & Co., 1986), p. 22.

24. Provisional Council on Educational Reform, *First Report on Educational Reform* (Tokyo, 1985), p. 27. A study group led by Professor Sumiko Iwao of Keio University concluded that the growing emphasis on individual lifestyles has brought forth a younger generation whose attention is focused on the pursuit of here-and-now physical and spiritual comforts. See "Changing Values and Economic Behavior," in *Look Japan*, vol. 31, no. 351 (June 10, 1985), p. 10.

25. For comments on this experiment, see Wagatsuma, op. cit., pp. 304–05.

26. See Ichiro Hori, *Folk Religion in Japan* (Chicago: University of Chicago Press, Midway Reprint 1983), p. 84.

27. *The Japan Times Weekly*, August 23, 1986, p. 12.
28. "Where Foreigners are Hardly Human," *Manchester Guardian Weekly*, December 29, 1985.
29. See Taylor, op. cit., Chap. 1.
30. *The Japan Times Weekly*, December 6, 1986.

Chapter Five

1. See Wagatsuma, op. cit. See also Ross E. Mouer and Yoshio Sugimoto, "Internationalization as an Ideology in Japanese Society," in Mannari and Befu, eds., op. cit.
2. Pollster George Gallup once told an interviewer that inaction hurts a president more than anything else, adding that, "A President can take some action, even a wrong one, and not lose his popularity." Quoted in Murray Edelman, *The Symbolic Uses of Politics* (Chicago: University of Illinois Press, 1973), p. 78.
3. Thomson et al., op. cit., p. 15.
4. Wm. Theodore de Bary, *Sources of Japanese Tradition* (New York: Columbia University Press, 1964), pp. 48–51.
5. Americans found it hard to believe that the Japanese launched a major war with no clear view of their objective and no idea of how it would end, but the conscious and active leadership that they were looking for just wasn't there. See, for example: Ronald H. Spector, *Eagle Against the Sun* (New York: Vintage Books, 1985); Akira Iriye, *Power and Culture* (Cambridge, Mass.: Harvard University Press, 1981); Hiroyuki Agawa, *The Reluctant Admiral: Yamamoto and the Imperial Navy*, trans. John Bester (New York: Kodansha International, Ltd., 1974); and Joseph C. Grew, *Ten Years in Japan* (New York: Simon and Schuster, 1944). Grew served as U.S. Ambassador to Japan in the decade that ended with Pearl Harbor.
6. See, for example, Matsuyama, op. cit., p. 20.
7. Lady Murasaki's *Tale of Genji* and Sei Shonagon's *Pillow Book* are two of the most famous examples of Heian period literature.
8. Quoted in Benedict, op. cit., p. 216.
9. Masao Kunihiro, "U.S.-Japan Communications," in Henry Rosovsky, ed., *Discord in the Pacific* (Washington, D.C.: Columbia Books, Inc., 1972), p. 162.
10. When the renowned Admiral Yamamoto became Commander in Chief of the Combined Fleet in 1939, his expression was described by an admiring Japanese press as "solemn with emotion and resolve." See Agawa, op. cit., p. 6.
11. Mark Zimmerman, "Getting on the Japanese Wave Length," *Across the Board*, vol. 22, no. 4 (April 1985), p. 30.
12. Dean C. Barnlund, "The Public Self and the Private Self in Japan and the United States," in John C. Condon and Mitsuko Saito, eds., *Intercultural Encounters with Japan* (Tokyo: Simul Press, 1974), pp. 72–76.

13. See Ivan Morris, *The World of the Shining Prince* (New York: Alfred A. Knopf, 1964).

14. For excerpts from Motoori Norinaga's essay on *The Tale of Genji*, see de Bary, ed., op. cit.

15. Donald Keene, *Some Japanese Portraits* (Tokyo: Kodansha International Ltd., 1983), pp. 188–89.

16. Masao Maruyama, "Japanese Thought," reprinted in Irwin Scheiner, ed., *Modern Japan: An Interpretive Anthology* (New York: Macmillan Publishing Co., 1974), p. 208.

17. Hearn, op. cit., pp. 352–53.

18. Isaiah Ben-Dasan (pseud.), *The Japanese and the Jews* (New York: Asahi/Weatherhill, 1984), pp. 91–93. The author is actually a Japanese journalist.

19. George B. Sansom, *Japan: A Short Cultural History* (New York: Charles E. Tuttle Co., 1973), pp. 244–45, 421.

20. D.T. Suzuki, *An Introduction to Zen Buddhism* (New York: Causeway Books, 1974), pp. 64, 88.

21. See Kawai, op. cit., p. 4f.

22. Rossiter, op. cit., p. 217.

23. Ibid., pp. 219–20.

24. Condon and Saito, eds., op. cit., p. 13.

25. Ishikawajima-Harima Industries, Ltd, *Japanese Language Know-How* (Tokyo: Gakuseisha, 1985), p. 40.

26. A related duality is *omote-ura*, which translates roughly as "outward- and inward-facing surfaces" or "front and back." See Takeo Doi, *The Anatomy of Self* (Tokyo: Kodansha International, Ltd., 1986). As Doi puts it, *omote* and *ura* are "mutually constitutive pairs"; one cannot exist without the other. It is simply not proper to reveal the inside when what is called for is displaying the surface.

27. See Keiko Ueda, "Sixteen Ways to Avoid Saying 'No' in Japan," in Condon and Saito, eds., op. cit., pp. 185–92.

28. St. Clair McKelway, "An Affix for Birds," in E. B. White and Katharine S. White, eds., *A Subtreasury of American Humor* (New York: Coward-McCann, Inc., 1941), p. 156.

29. Thomas Pepper et al., "Alternative Futures in U.S.-Japanese Relations," p. 25, Unpublished paper prepared for the U.S.-Japan Advisory Commission, September 1984.

30. The Pacific War Research Society, *Japan's Longest Day* (Tokyo: Kodansha International Ltd., 1980), p. 17.

31. Cited in Rohlen, op. cit., p. l00.

32. Cited in Momoko Nisugi, "Images of Spoken Japanese and Spoken English," in Condon and Saito, eds., op. cit., p. 204.

33. Jane Condon, *A Half-Step Behind* (New York: Dodd, Mead & Co., 1985), p. 189.

34. Sansom, *Japan: A Short Cultural History*, p. 255.

35. Richard Samuels and Samuel Coleman, "Applied Japanese Studies for Science and Engineering at American Universities," MIT, 1985. See also the interview with J. David Edwards, Executive Director of the Joint National Committee for Languages, in *The New York Times*, December 29, 1985.

36. Unpublished survey cited in "Japanese Studies in American Universities and Corporate Need for International Expertise," Background paper prepared for the Twenty-second Japan-U.S. Business Conference, Honolulu, July 1985, p. 7.

37. See "Negotiating with the Americans," *Contract Management* (March 1983), p. 6. In this perceptive "briefing paper," allegedly translated from the Japanese but actually written by an anonymous American, the author says, "Sometimes U.S. representatives seem to make mistakes or to be ignorant of commonly known facts."

38. Mark Zimmerman, *How to Do Business With the Japanese* (New York: Random House, 1985), pp. 4–5.

39. Loet A. Velmans, "A Deep Misunderstanding: The U.S. Communication Gap with Japan," *Speaking of Japan*, vol. 7, no. 67 (July 1986), p. 19.

40. See Richard Hofstadter, *The Anti-Intellectual Tradition in American Life* (New York: Alfred A. Knopf, l962).

41. Alexis de Tocqueville, *Democracy in America* (New York: Doubleday Anchor Books, 1969), pp. 55–56.

42. Handlin, op. cit., p. 265.

43. The argument that ignorance of history itself leads to a military-oriented response to a crisis is set forth in William Pfaff, "American Leaders Ought to Read History," *International Herald Tribune*, December 4, l986.

Chapter Six

1. See Economic Planning Agency, *Japan in the Year 2000*, op. cit. The "information society" means an information-intensive society in which high-technology communications and services play a leading role.

2. Japanese Government statistics cited in *JEI Report*, no. 27A (July 22, 1983).

3. "Changing Values and Economic Behavior," *Look Japan,* vol. 31, no. 351 (June 10, 1985), p. 10.

4. *The Women of Japan* (Tokyo: Prime Minister's Office, 1984), pp. 26–27.

5. Sawako Ariyoshi's *Kokotsu no Hito* (The Twilight Years), a painfully realistic novel describing the ambivalent feelings of a working woman coping with her senile father-in-law, has sold more than two million copies in Japan since its publication in the 1960s.

6. Younger, less traditional women of the baby boom generation are likely to put more pressure on the government to provide alternatives to stay-at-home care for their aging parents; see Fumio Kanari, "Japanese Baby Boom Generation and the Aging Society," *The Wheel Extended*, vol. 15, no. 3 (1985).

7. *The New York Times*, January 17, 1986, p. A-11.

8. *Japan 1987: An International Comparison* (Tokyo: Keizei Koho Center, 1987), p. 92.

9. Report of the Study Group to the Ministry of Health and Welfare, cited in *The Japan Times Weekly*, January 4, 1986, p. 3.

10. Seizaburo Sato, "Social Change in Japan and its Impact on U.S.-Japan Relations," in Alan D. Romberg, ed., *The United States and Japan: Changing Societies in a Changing Relationship* (New York: Council on Foreign Relations, 1987), p. 45.

11. A common complaint is that unionized job classifications are unduly specialized. A senior member of the Nomura Research Institute calls such classifications "outrageous . . . reminiscent of the Indian caste system." See Masanori Moritani, *Japanese Technology: Getting the Best for the Least* (Tokyo: Simul Press, 1982), p. 96.

12. Takeshi Inagami, "The Japanese Will to Work," *The Wheel Extended*, vol. 14, no. 1 (1984).

13. *The Japan Times Weekly*, January 4, 1986, p. 10.

14. See Herbert Passin, "Changing Values: Work and Growth in Japan," *Asian Survey*, no. 10 (October 1975).

15. Frank Gibney, *Japan: The Fragile Superpower*, rev. ed. (New York: Meridian Books, 1980), p. 356.

16. Prime Minister's Office, "Public Opinion Survey on Leisure and Travel" (April 1986), S-86-2, Foreign Press Center, 1986.

17. Cited in "Cracks in the Japanese Work Ethic," *Fortune* (May 14, 1984), p. 162.

18. *The Japan Times Weekly*, December 21, 1985, p. 10.

19. *Japan Economic Journal*, January 18, 1986, p. 1.

20. Conversation with Dr. Suehiko Matsuda, Managing Director, Fujitsu System Integration Laboratories, Ltd., November 1985.

21. Max Hastings, "Reagan's America," *Sunday Times of London*, November 3, 1985, p. 18.

22. See especially Merry White, *The Japanese Educational Challenge: A Commitment to Children* (New York: The Free Press, 1987).

23. See U.S. Department of Education, *Japanese Education Today* (Washington, D.C.: GPO, 1987), p. vii.

24. The advantages enjoyed by Japanese companies in recruiting well-educated workers are illustrated in Duke, op. cit.

25. Rohlen, op. cit.

26. See Provisional Council on Educational Reform, op. cit., pp. 18–22; and National Council on Educational Reform, *Summary of Second Report on Educational Reform* (Tokyo, 1986). The Provisional Council became the National Council in 1985.

27. National Commission on Excellence in Education, *A Nation at Risk* (Washington, D.C.: GPO, 1983).

28. See Gerald L. Curtis, *Election Campaigning Japanese Style* (New York: Columbia University Press, 1971), in which the author records first-hand observations of a successful campaign for a seat in the Diet.

29. For an example of the construction industry's arguments against foreign participation in the Kansai International Airport construction projects, see Taichiro Kumagai, "International Bidding Won't Work in Japan," *Shinkan Toyo Keizai* (Bulletin of the Japan-America Society of Washington), November 1986.

30. See Seizaburo Sato and Tetsuhisa Matsuzaki, "The Liberal Democrats' Conciliatory Reign," *Economic Eye*, vol. 1, no. 4 (December 1985).

31. For a more detailed discussion of the evolution of Japanese politics, see the lucid and informative analysis in Gerald L. Curtis, *The Japanese Way of Politics* (New York: Columbia University Press, forthcoming). See also Hans Baerwald, *Political Parties in Japan* (Boston: Allen & Unwin, 1986).

32. Prime Minister's Office, "Public Opinion Survey on the Society and the State," op. cit.

33. For an overview of the two legislative bodies, see Francis R. Valeo and Charles E. Morrison, eds., *The Japanese Diet and The U.S. Congress* (Boulder, Colo.: Westview Press, 1983).

34. Quoted in *The Pacific Rivals*, op. cit., p. 159.

35. Ibid., p. 160.

36. For an excellent case study of the student riots of 1960, which forced President Eisenhower to cancel his visit to Japan, see George Packard, *Protest in Tokyo: The Security Treaty Crisis of 1960* (Princeton: Princeton University Press, 1966).

37. Quoted with permission from a draft version of Curtis, *The Japanese Way of Politics*, op. cit.

Chapter Seven

1. Final Communiqué of the Williamsburg summit conference, May 30, 1983; printed in *The New York Times*, May 31, 1983.

2. See Japan Defense Agency, *Defense of Japan, 1985* (Tokyo: Japan Times Ltd., 1985), and *The Military Balance, 1986–87* (London: Institute of International Strategic Studies, 1986). James Auer of the Department of Defense kindly supplied more recent data.

3. For a thoughtful and well-informed discussion, see *Japan and Europe: Towards Closer Cooperation* (Tokyo: Japan Center for International Exchange, 1984).

4. See, for example, the speech by Foreign Minister Shintaro Abe at the United Nations, New York City, October 23, 1985.

5. Serious economic studies have heavily discounted the "free ride" as a factor contributing to Japan's current prosperity. In no realistically constructed model does the small percentage of GNP spent on defense appear to have bolstered Japan's economic growth by any significant amount. See Daniel I. Okimoto, "The Economics of National Defense," in Daniel I. Okimoto, ed., *Japan's Economy: Coping with Change in the International Environment* (Boulder, Colo.: Westview Press, 1982), p. 249ff.

6. For a summary of the diplomatic exchanges and the pressures behind them, see Tomohisa Sakanaka, "Perception Gap Between Japan and the United States on Defense Cooperation," Unpublished paper, n.d. Begun in earnest in 1983, the sea-lane study was concluded in 1986.

7. "Statement by the Chief Cabinet Secretary on SDI Research Program," Tokyo, September 9, 1986.

8. *Annual Report to the Congress, Fiscal Year 1987* (Washington, D.C.: U.S. Department of Defense, 1986), pp. 66, 276–78; and *Report on Allied Contributions to the Common Defense* (Washington, D.C.: U.S. Department of Defense, 1986), pp. 67–69.

9. See the address cited in note 4, above.

10. Ibid.

11. Edwin O. Reischauer, *My Life Between Japan and America* (New York: Harper & Row, 1986), pp. 346–47.

12. For data on coproduction programs, see Reinhard Drifte, *The Japanese Arms Industry* (Boulder, Colo.: Westview Press, 1986).

13. For the text of the 1983 exchange of notes, see Department of Defense, *Japanese Military Technology: Procedures for Transfer to the United States* (Washington, D.C.: U.S. Department of Defense, 1986), Tab B. See also *Electro-optics Millimeter/Microwave Technology in Japan*, Report of DoD Technology Team (Washington, D.C.: U.S. Department of Defense, 1985), and Defense Science Board Task Force, *Industry-to-Industry International Armaments Cooperation: Japan*, op. cit.

14. *Japan Times*, April 6, 1986, p. 4.

15. Japan Defense Agency, *Defense of Japan, 1983* (Tokyo: Japan Times, Ltd., 1983), p. 3.

16. *JEI Report*, no. 43A (November 9, 1984), pp. 2, 5.

17. Research Institute for Peace and Security, *Asian Security 1984* (Tokyo: Nikkei Business Publishing Co., Ltd., 1984), p. 202.

18. For a concise description of the Okinawa debate, see Richard Sneider, *U.S.-Japanese Security Relations: A Historical Perspective* (New York: East Asian Institute, Columbia University), 1982.

19. For a discussion of the role of banks in Japanese foreign policy, see J. Andrew Spindler, *The Politics of International Credit* (Washington, D.C.: The Brookings Institution, 1985).

20. *Japan 1987: An International Comparison*, op. cit., p. 55; *Japan's Official Development Assistance: 1985 Annual Report* (Tokyo: Association for Promotion of International Cooperation, 1986), p. 3. See also the address by Trade Minister Hajime Tamura to the Japan National Press Club, May 29, 1987, MITI Document NR-342 (87-12), June 1987, p. 11.

21. See Saburo Okita, "Forces of Global Economic Change," Unpublished paper prepared for the CSIS Quadrangular Forum, Center for Strategic and International Studies, Washington, D.C., April 1987.

22. *The New York Times*, April 10, 1986.

23. *Japan's Official Development Assistance: 1985*, op. cit., p. 27.

24. See "Report of the Comprehensive National Security Study Group," summarized in Robert W. Barnett, *Beyond War: Japan's Concept of Comprehensive National Security* (Washington, D.C.: Pergamon-Brassey's, 1984), pp. 1–6.

25. *Japan's Official Development Assistance: 1985*, op. cit., p. 2.

26. See his address, "The Global Security Initiative," to the Keidanren, Tokyo, February 18, 1986, p. 14ff.

27. *Japan's Official Development Assistance: 1985*, op. cit., p. 4.

28. *Japanese Philanthropy and International Cooperation* (Tokyo: Japan Center for International Exchange, 1985).

29. For a discussion of this debate, see Kenneth B. Pyle, "The Future of Japanese Nationality: An Essay in Contemporary History," *Journal of Japanese Studies*, vol. 8, no. 2 (1982), pp. 225–63. Pyle's categories (p. 242) are: progressive, liberal-realist, mercantilist, and new nationalist.

30. See Barnett, op. cit., pp. 1–6.

31. See Shumpei Kumon, *The Evolving International System and Its Ramifications for Japan* (Tokyo: Japan Institute of International Affairs, 1986). Kumon, a professor at Tokyo University, points out that the "power game" and the "wealth game" are evolving into the "knowledge game," which Japan is in a good position to play.

32. As early as 1908, the Japanese Government sought to forestall exclusionary legislation by "voluntarily" restricting the number of U.S.-bound Japanese emigrants. The parallel with trade is worth pondering: today's Japanese wonder whether "voluntary restraint agreements" will succeed in fending off full-scale protectionism.

33. Ministry of Foreign Affairs, *Waga Gaiko no Kinkyo*, vol. 1 (1957), pp. 7–10; cited in Akio Watanabe, "The United States, Japan, and the Asia/Pacific: A Japanese Perspective," Unpublished paper prepared for the colloquium "Japan and the United States in a Changing World Setting," Center for Strategic and International Studies, Washington, D.C., March 26–27, 1985, p. 4.

34. *Japan Economic Journal*, January 18, 1986, p. 6.

35. Hideo Kanemitsu, "Changes in the International Economic Environment," in Okimoto, ed., op. cit., p. 20.

36. These attitudes are described more fully in Kazuo Ogura, *Trade Conflict: A View from Japan* (Washington, D.C.: Japan Economic Institute, 1982), pp. 22–23.

37. America's "common heritage" with Europe and its effect on U.S.-Japan relations is explored in an unpublished paper by Koji Watanabe, "Japan in U.S. Foreign Policy Perspective: Interview with Professors by an Inscrutable Oriental," 1974, p. 11. Watanabe, a senior Foreign Ministry official, based his study on interviews conducted at Harvard University.

38. *The Economist*, December 7, 1985, p. 4.

For Further Reading

Bibliographies

For readers wishing to learn more about Japan, a good starting point is the anno-
tated bibliography *What Shall I Read on Japan: An Introductory Guide*, published
in 1984 by the Japan Society, Inc. (333 East 47th Street, New York, N.Y. 10017). For
reports and publications on U.S.-Japan economic issues, an excellent source of
titles is *The U.S.-Japan Economic Agenda*, published by the Carnegie Council on
Ethics and International Affairs (170 East 64th Street, New York, N.Y. 10021).
Japan for Westerners, edited by Cris Popenoe and published by Yes! Inc. (1035
31st Street, N.W., Washington, D.C. 20007) is especially helpful in locating books
on religion, literature, and art.

The Japanese Government publishes a large number of books, reports, and
pamphlets in English. A catalog called *List of Publications: Governmental and
Similars* is available from the Government Publications Service Center (2-1,
Kasumigaseki 1-chome, Chiyoda-ku, Tokyo 100, Japan) or OCS America, Inc.
(National Press Building, Room 1186, Washington, D.C. 20045). A visit to either
one of the two Japanese Government bookstores in Tokyo—one near the Foreign
Ministry in Kasumigaseki, the other near the Japan Development Bank in
Otemachi—is well worth the time and effort.

Newspapers and Magazines

English-language newspapers and magazines from Japan are an excellent source
of up-to-date information. For a list, see *Japan Periodicals*, published by the Keizai
Koho Center (6-1, Otemachi 1-chome, Chiyoda-ku, Tokyo 100, Japan). Among
the various publications of the Keizai Koho Center, the slim, fact-filled annual volume *Japan: An International Comparison* is especially valuable.

The Japan Times Weekly offers widespread coverage of political, social, and
cultural topics from a moderate and internationalist perspective. (To subscribe,
contact the Japan Times, Ltd., C.P.O. Box 144, Tokyo 100-91, Japan.) The *Nihon
Keizai Shimbun*, nicknamed "the *Wall Street Journal* of Japan," publishes a
weekly English-language version called *Japan Economic Journal*, available by
subscription from OCS America, Inc. (JEJ Subscription Department, P.O. Box
1654, Long Island City, N.Y. 11101.)

Among the many useful magazines are *Look Japan* (published monthly by Look Japan, Ltd., 2-2 Kanda-Ogawamachi, Chiyoda-ku, Tokyo 101, Japan) and *Journal of Japanese Trade and Industry* (published bimonthly by Japan Economic Foundation, 11th Floor, Fukokum Seimei Building, 2-2 Uchisaiwai-cho 2-chome, Chiyoda-ku, Tokyo 100, Japan). The Japan Economic Institute (1000 Connecticut Avenue, N.W., Washington, D.C. 20036) issues accurate and concise reports on various subjects on a weekly and monthly basis.

Articles on Japan appearing in major newspapers and wire services are compiled and reproduced weekly by the Associated Japan-America Societies of the United States, Inc. (333 East 47th Street, New York, N.Y. 10017).

For further assistance, try the Japan Information Center (Consulate General of Japan, 299 Park Avenue, 19th Floor, New York, N.Y. 10171). For information on business and trade, contact the Japan External Trade Organization (JETRO, 1221 Avenue of the Americas, 44th Floor, New York, N.Y. 10020).

Books

Among the many books on U.S.-Japan relations, a number are particularly clear, sensible, and short: *Challenges and Opportunities in U.S.-Japan Relations*, a report of the United States-Japan Advisory Commission, Washington, D.C., 1984; *The Japanese American Alliance: A Framework for the Future*, a report of the United Nations Association of the United States of America and the Asia Pacific Association of Japan, New York, 1983; and *The United States and Japan in 1986— Can the Partnership Work?*, School of Advanced International Studies, Johns Hopkins University, Washington, D.C., 1986. For a friendly but critical view of American behavior by a leading Japanese newspaperman, see Yukio Matsuyama, *A Japanese Journalist Looks at U.S.-Japan Relations* (Boulder, Colo.: Westview Press, 1984).

Recommended books about Japan of a general, introductory nature include: Edwin O. Reischauer's clearly written and still timely *The Japanese*, rev. ed. (Cambridge, Mass.: Belknap Press, 1981); Frank Gibney's insightful *Japan: The Fragile Superpower*, rev. ed. (New York: Meridian Books, 1980); and Robert Christopher's *The Japanese Mind* (New York: Linden Press, 1983), which addresses a number of interesting themes.

A clear and readable collection of primary-source material from Japanese history appears in *Sources of Japanese Tradition*, edited and introduced by Wm. Theodore deBary (New York: Columbia University Press, 1958.)

Selected viewpoints and influences from the past are compiled in *Modern Japan: An Interpretive Anthology*, edited by Irwin Scheiner (New York: Macmillan Publishing Co., 1974). For a look at Japan's future, see the well-researched study by Japan's Economic Planning Agency, *Japan in the Year 2000* (Tokyo: Japan Times Ltd., 1983).

Two particularly readable and interesting books offering an explanation of Japanese behavior in psychological or sociological terms are Takeo Doi's *The Anatomy of Dependence*, which stresses the Japanese search for indulgent love or *amae* (New York: Kodansha International, Ltd., 1973) and Chie Nakane's

Japanese Society, which focuses on patterns of hierarchy and group behavior (Tokyo: Charles E. Tuttle Co., 1970).

For a cultural approach to U.S.-Japan relations, see John C. Condon and Mitsuko Saito, eds., *Cultural Encounters with Japan* (Tokyo: Simul Press, 1974). Various aspects of "internationalization" are examined in a collection of articles edited by Hiroshi Mannari and Harumi Befu, *The Challenge of Japan's Internationalization: Organization and Culture* (Tokyo: Kwansei Gakuin University and Kodansha International, Ltd., 1983). A book that deliberately highlights the "dark" side of Japanese society, such as its tendencies toward intolerance and discrimination, is Jared Taylor's *Shadows of the Rising Sun* (New York: William Morrow & Co., 1983).

Books and articles on Japanese business behavior, the Japanese economy, and U.S.-Japan trade could fill an entire bookstore. An outstanding summary volume is *Understanding the Industrial Policies and Practices of Japan and the United States: A Business Perspective* (Tokyo and Washington, D.C.: The Japan-U.S. Businessmen's Conference, July 1984). An upbeat, informative analysis containing much useful information is *Japan: Business Obstacles and Opportunities* (New York: McKinsey & Co., Inc., 1983). *Kaisha, The Japanese Corporation,* by James C. Abegglen and George Stalk, Jr. (New York: Basic Books, 1985), strips away much nonsense about the behavior of Japanese companies and substitutes extensive knowledge and common sense. Yoshihara Kunio's *Sogo Shosha: The Vanguard of the Japanese Economy* (Oxford: Oxford University Press, 1982) contains a wealth of information about Japan's huge trading companies. Among the best of the practical, "how-to-do-it" guides is Mark Zimmerman's *How to Do Business with the Japanese* (New York: Random House, 1985). The late Mr. Zimmerman, a U.S. corporate executive with years of experience in Japan, stressed that developing close personal relations is the key to success in business.

For a good overview of the Japanese economy, see *America Versus Japan,* edited by Thomas K. McGraw (Boston: Harvard Business School Press, 1986), which offers chapters on agriculture, energy, environmental regulation, and a host of other relevant topics. Also recommended is *Japan's Economy: Coping with Change in the International Environment,* edited by Daniel I. Okimoto (Boulder, Colo.: Westview Press, 1982), especially Okimoto's analysis of the relationship between Japan's economic growth and its low level of military spending. For a more specialized discussion of exchange rates, macroeconomic policies, and financial market innovations, see *Japan and the United States Today,* edited by Hugh T. Patrick and Ryuichiro Tachi (Montpelier, Vt.: Capital City Press, 1986).

The United States-Japan Economic Problem, by C. Fred Bergsten and William R. Cline (Washington, D.C.: Institute for International Economics, 1985) examines the macroeconomic causes of current U.S.-Japan trade frictions. A similar story, presented as a series of graphs, is set forth in Joseph G. Kvasnicka's "The Dimensions and Significance of U.S.-Japan Trade and Trade Frictions," a study prepared for the Governors Conference on International Trade and Security, Jackson, Mississippi, September 26–27, 1986. Still timely is an excellent case study of the U.S.-Japan textile disputes of the late 1960s, *The Textile Wrangle,* edited by I. M. Destler, Harihiro Fukui, and Hideo Sato (Ithaca: Cornell University Press, 1979).

George Fields, a bilingual advertising consultant based in Tokyo, has written a series of amusing but extremely perceptive case studies showing why Americans often find it difficult to sell in Japan: *From Bonsai to Levis* (New York: Macmillan Publishing Co., 1983). Kazuo Ogura's *Trade Conflict: A View from Japan* (Washington, D.C.: Japan Economic Institute, 1982) offers a short but perceptive analysis of some typically Japanese reactions to U.S. trade pressure.

For a taste of Japan's cultural traditions, the classic book is Lady Murasaki's famous novel, *The Tale of Genji*, now some ten centuries old but still influential. Connoisseurs believe that Arthur Waley's translation (New York: Modern Library, 1960) comes closer to the spirit of the original, but others prefer the more modern translation by Edward Seidensticker (New York: Alfred A. Knopf, 1978). Life at the elegant Heian court is well described in Ivan Morris, *The World of the Shining Prince* (New York: Alfred A. Knopf, 1964).

On other cultural topics, a rich source is Sir George Sansom's *Japan: A Short Cultural History* (Englewood Cliffs: Prentice-Hall, 1961). Another is Donald Keene's *Appreciations of Japanese Culture* (New York: Kodansha International, Ltd., 1971). Liza Dalby's *Geisha* (New York: Vintage Books, 1983), a popular version of her Ph.D. thesis in cultural anthropology, is a fascinating first-hand account of life as a geisha in Kyoto. At the other extreme, Ian Buruma's bizarre but interesting description of "low culture" in Japan, *Behind the Mask* (New York: Meridian Books, 1984), is not to be missed for its vignettes of gangsters, transvestites, comic book characters, and a host of other colorful figures. John David Morley's *Pictures from the Water Trade* (London: Fontana Paperbacks, 1986) also explores Japan's low life, but Morley's reflections on the Japanese language—and what happens to a foreigner who learns to speak it fluently—are sensitive and highly influential.

Japanese education is the topic of several provocative and informative books. A classic is Herbert Passin's *Society and Education in Japan*, rev. ed. (New York: Kodansha International, Ltd., 1982). Merry White's *The Japanese Educational Challenge* (New York: Free Press, 1987) documents what she calls "a commitment to children" on the part of the entire society. Thomas P. Rohlen's *Japan's High Schools* (Berkeley: University of California Press, 1983) examines daily life in four high schools in Kobe. Benjamin Duke's *The Japanese School* (New York: Praeger, 1986) traces Japan's industrial success to high educational standards, especially in mathematics. *Child Development and Education in Japan*, edited by Harold Stevenson, Hiroshi Azuma, and Kenji Hakuta (New York: W. H. Freeman & Co., 1986), contains excellent articles ranging from a case study on teaching mathematics to definitions of what is a "good" child.

For an overview of Japan's foreign relations, *The Foreign Policy of Modern Japan*, edited by Robert A. Scalapino (Berkeley: University of California Press, 1977), is still timely after a decade. An excellent little volume on defense is Richard Sneider's *U.S.-Japan Security Relations: A Historical Perspective* (New York: East Asian Institute, Columbia University, 1982). Equally short and valuable is Yukio Satoh's *The Evolution of Japanese Security Policy*, Adelphi Paper No. 178 (London: International Institute for Strategic Studies, 1982). The Japanese concept of "comprehensive security" is explored in Robert W. Barnett's *Beyond War: Japan's Concept of Comprehensive National Security* (Washington, D.C.: Pergamon-Brassey's, 1984). The White Papers published annually by the Japan Defense Agency contain a wealth of factual information and some carefully worded policy analysis.

Index